# The War Diary of Hauptmann Helmut Lipfert
## JG 52 on the Russian Front
## 1943-1945

*Also by Werner Girbig*
SIX MONTHS TO OBLIVION

# The War Diary of

## Hauptmann
# Helmut Lipfert

## JG 52 on the Russian Front 1943-1945

Helmut Lipfert/Werner Girbig

*Translated from the German by David Johnston*

**Schiffer Military History**
**Atglen, PA**

Book design by Robert Biondi.


Library of Congress Catalog Number: 92-61775.



Printed in China.
ISBN: 978-0-88740-446-7

This book was originally published under the title,
*Das Tagebuch des Hauptmann Lipfert*,
by Motorbuch Verlag, Stuttgart.



Published by Schiffer Publishing Ltd.
4880 Lower Valley Road
Atglen, PA 19310
Phone: (610) 593-1777
FAX: (610) 593-2002
E-mail: Schifferbk@aol.com
Visit our website at: www.schifferbooks.com
Please write for a free catalog.
This book may be purchased from the publisher.
Try your bookstore first.

# Contents

# CHAPTER I
# The Air War in the East

From the first bomber and fighter sorties against airfields in White Russia during the morning hours of June 22, 1941, to the costly low-level attacks against advancing Russian columns on the roads of Silesia and then at the gates of Berlin in 1945, operations by the German Luftwaffe in the East were determined exclusively by the needs of the Army and were thus of a tactical nature. Moreover the Luftwaffe high command surrendered itself to a terrible fallacy right at the outset of the Eastern Campaign. At the time of the German attack the Soviet Air Force was involved in a modernization process and was for the most part able to field only obsolescent types, which naturally made it inferior to a modern air force. The Luftwaffe did in fact succeed in virtually crippling the Soviet air arm by attacking its front-line airfields. The element of surprise obviously played a significant role in this success.

The Luftwaffe command believed that this terrific blow against the Soviet aviation units had finished the enemy's air force. But the Germans badly underestimated their enemy in the East. There was no question that they possessed air superiority at first, but it was soon obvious that their missions were anything but pleasure flights, and within four weeks of the commencement of the Russian Campaign the Luftwaffe had lost almost 1,300 aircraft.

When Operation "Barbarossa" began there were 59 German fighter *Staffeln* with a total of 720 aircraft facing about 2,000 Soviet fighters.

Fewer than 15% of the Russian machines were the latest types. One aircraft predominated in the sometimes bitter fighting in the air in 1941: the Polikarpov I-16 "Rata." It was a small, squat, extremely maneuverable single-seat fighter, which the Republicans had used with some success against the *Legion Condor* in Spain. The Rata could still be dangerous, as more than a few pilots of JG 3, JG 27 and JG 51 discovered. Its greatest advantage was its ability to turn almost on a dime, which often enabled it to outmaneuver the much faster German fighters.

Once it had recovered from the initial shock, the Soviet Union did its utmost to increase aircraft production and develop new types, especially fighters, which were suited to conditions at the front. The speed with which the Soviets accomplished this is more than impressive. It wasn't long before the German fighter pilots began to sense that the enemy was becoming more of a match for them, and not just in terms of materiel. The quality of their pilots had also undergone a considerable improvement. By the summer of 1943 Soviet Air Force fighter strength was again more than 3,000; the ratio between German and Soviet fighter forces now stood at 1 : 5. This development was able to come about with no German interference, because the Luftwaffe had no strategic bomber fleet which might have knocked out the Russian production centers far beyond the front. The inability of the Luftwaffe to plan strategically must also be measured in the German defeat in the East.

Even today, many consider the air war in the East to have been child's play on account of the high scores of the leading German pilots. They compare it to the difficult battles in the West and the sacrificial operations in the Defense of the Reich. However a mere comparison of facts is not objective enough. Conditions in the skies over the vastness of Russia were far different from those over the Western Front. In no way were the German fighter pilots dealing with a second-rate opponent. By the end of the war a number of Russian pilots, especially some from the elite guards fighter units, could boast significantly higher kill totals than the fighter aces of the western powers. At the top of the list was Major General Ivan Kozhedub, who destroyed a total of 62 German aircraft.

The Luftwaffe suffered its most decisive defeat in the East in the Battle of Stalingrad – the fighter arm alone lost about 120 machines –

and it is significant that only a single "airfield defense *Staffel*" (elements of 4./JG 3 at Pitomnik) was available to cover transport aircraft landing and taking off in the pocket. By mid-1943, or about six months after the tragedy on the Volga, air superiority had long since passed into Soviet hands. At the end of the war the ratio of forces between German and Soviet fighters stood at 1:15. Bolstering the Soviet effort were whole squadrons of fighter aircraft of British and American manufacture which were delivered under the lend-lease program. These aircraft were sent to the front as soon as they arrived in Russia.

Nevertheless the victory totals of some German fighter pilots continued to climb. Totals of 150 or even 200 kills were no longer unusual. As the Russians generally operated en masse, the German fighter pilot in the East had a much better chance of engaging and shooting down enemy aircraft than his opposite number in the West, the Mediterranean or Africa. Another consideration was that, unlike in other theaters, on the Russian Front the fighters flew mostly in small formations, usually in *Rotte* or *Schwarm* strength and sometimes even alone, and were thus much more flexible. The preferred tactic was the so-called "*freie Jagd*," or "free hunting," which was practiced much more in the East than in other theaters. Fighter pilots often flew several combat sorties in a single day, as enemy aircraft could sometimes be found practically everywhere within minutes of taking off.

Whereas it had been the Rata which had made its presence felt in the initial stages of the war, after that and until the end of hostilities it was the Il-2 close-support aircraft, which appeared over the front in large numbers, that dominated. There is scarcely a German fighter pilot who would not speak of this aircraft with respect. The Il-2's armor was almost impervious to standard weapons, and only a hit from below, in the oil cooler, could bring one down.

The number of German fighters which were struck by the wreckage of a downed enemy aircraft and subsequently crashed during combat in the East is surprisingly high. In other cases they collided with stricken aircraft or were rammed by the aircraft they had shot down, and not a few pilots lost their lives in this way. One can see another characteristic of the air war in the East in these facts. On the one hand, pilots of both sides tried to get as close to the enemy as possible and as a result most kills were made from close range, and on the other hand most encounters took place at a relatively low altitude which did not always allow a safe escape by parachute.

The team of Nowotny, Döbele, Rademacher and Schnörrer comprised one of the most successful *Schwärme* in the Luftwaffe. These four fighter pilots, members of I./JG 54, amassed a total of more than 470 kills in the East during 1942/43. *Leutnant* Anton Döbele was killed in Russia on November 11, 1943, while *Major* Nowotny died on November 8, 1944 while flying the Me 262 jet fighter in home defense operations.

Unfortunately Soviet historical writings do not include detailed information on their own materiel losses from which one could make a comparison of successes and losses. The Russians suffered unimaginably high losses, but the same was true for the German fighter arm. In total, the three *Jagdgeschwader* which spent the bulk of their existence in the East – JG 51, JG 52 and JG 54 – lost about 1,000 pilots killed or missing. Added to this is the same number of killed and missing from other units which were deployed on the Eastern Front for various periods of time, such as JG 3, JG 5, JG 27, JG 53 and JG 77.

In the end one thing is certain; like their comrades in the West, the German fighter pilots in the East gave their utmost to the very end.

Werner Girbig

# CHAPTER II
# Initial Experiences

The farewell address by the commander, *Major* Andres, to the future fighter pilots drew to a close. Most of the pilots had already been assigned to the various *Geschwader*. I waited with those who were left. Three of us would have to stay behind as flight instructors. At 26 I was the oldest pilot there. Was I to be held back on account of that? By all means I wanted to see action as a fighter pilot, wanted to prove myself and achieve something! I could have shouted with joy when I received the news: "You, *Leutnant* Lipfert, have been assigned to *Jagdgeschwader* 52. As detachment leader you are to drive to Krakow with the other pilots assigned to the Eastern Front. The forward directing center will inform you of your unit's area of operations!" I had done it! It was several days before my "troop" and I arrived at Krakow. My drive to get to the front was halted abruptly at the airfield. It was made unmistakably clear to me that one should never do anything in a hurry – especially in the aviation element. To be sure there were plenty of aircraft waiting to be ferried to the front, but persistent "qbi" (bad weather) prevented any takeoffs in the following days. Finally it cleared up. My Messerschmitt (Bf 109 G-2) had been ready to go for some time. None of us budding fighter pilots had ever flown a 109 G-2. My heart pounded considerably during two practice takeoffs. Like all the other pilots I had my hands full getting the machine into the air and bringing it down again in one piece. Already it was evident that our training as fighter pilots had been too short and that we were not qualified. As proof of this, only three pilots from my detachment reached the front by the turn of the year 1943. Ten further pilots reached their units by March 1943 after making emergency landings. Four of those who took off never reached their destinations.

I took off from Krakow for Lvov (Lemberg) at 1227 on December 2, 1942, accompanied by *Leutnante* Deinert, Kurz, Obleser and Puls and *Unteroffiziere* Landgraf and Obst.

The general nervousness finally abated when we assembled after takeoff while making a wide circuit of the airport. We then increased speed and set course.

Krakow lay far behind us. I compared my map with the earth below and began, as the pilot says, "to check my course." I lined up my Messerschmitt parallel with the railway line to check my heading with the calculated course. It was roughly the same, so this had to be the railway line to Lvov.

I had been almost the last to take off and caught up with the others just short of Prczemysl. They flew nicely in a line over the city and then out along a railway line. Suspecting nothing I followed, until a casual glance at the compass revealed that we were on the wrong heading. We were supposed to be flying east, but our heading was almost west! I pushed the throttle forward and flew past the others until I was abeam the formation leader, waggling my wings and gesturing toward the rear with my thumb to warn them. Afterward I turned around and headed back toward Prczemysl. The others followed hesitantly.

Soon we were over the city again and it was damned hard to find the right line from the air. Five or six tracks led out of a railhead. I climbed to get a better view, finally found the right railway line and headed away from Prczemysl.

Our destination was supposed to be Lvov. The "old hands" at Krakow were greatly amused when we declared that we only wanted to fly to Lvov and not Proskurov. Their calculations were based on their skill level, not ours. It was 300 kilometers to Lvov, another 225 to Proskurov. A beginner could do it only if he didn't waste a minute and flew a precise heading at the correct altitude. The "red lamp" was already burning as I neared Lvov, meaning I had only ten minutes fuel left. Proskurov was out of the question.

Although it was an unfamiliar airfield the landing came off quite well, even if I was forced to pull up once and go around. I touched down at Lvov at precisely 1355.

Bad weather made it impossible for us to continue on our way immediately and it was three days before we took off again. Our ranks had already been thinned somewhat. Several pilots were forced to stay behind at Lvov with mechanical problems. As the others took too long to get airborne I set course alone for Vinnitsa, our next destination. Only Lt. Kurz followed a short time later.

I took off alone again on December 8 and headed in the direction of Zaphorozhye. I flew by compass only with no landmarks to guide me. I felt a growing sense of uneasiness as I flew along, especially since the ceiling was dropping and darkness was not far off. I was certain of only one thing: sometime or other I had to come to a large river, the Dniepr. There, if the clouds allowed me, I must find Zaphorozhye.

All at once the engine began to roar strangely. Suddenly my aircraft became an unfamiliar monster and fear set in: fear of the unknown. The cloud base dropped. Visibility deteriorated. When the clouds were almost touching the ground, I decided with a heavy heart to turn back. Cautiously I tried to reverse course and in the next instant I was in cloud. A second attempt almost caused me to fly into the ground. So turning back was out of the question. I gave up on another attempt and decided to make a belly landing if things got any worse. But it was not to come to that; before I was really aware of it, I found myself in a valley over the middle of a broad river – the Dniepr!

The next minute I was over a large city. I was still trying to get my bearings when numerous smoke trails began zipping past the wings and fuselage of my Me. To my horror I realized that I was being fired at by anti-aircraft guns. I was debating whether I might be over Russian territory, when I saw a huge dam below me. That could only be Dniepropetrovsk! I had to get out of there! The firing had meanwhile stopped and instead I saw a series of green flares in the mist to my left. I flew toward them and soon saw an airfield below me. After a smooth landing my brave 109 finally rolled to a stop between a fire truck and an ambulance. I learned from the ground crew that I owed my "baptism of fire" to the Rumanian bridge guards.

The next day I reached Zaphorozhye in somewhat better weather and on December 10 arrived at Taganrog on the Black Sea. Uffz. Obst was the second pilot of my detachment to arrive. Unfortunately he was sent to another unit (JG 3) and was later shot down over the Stalingrad pocket.

From Taganrog my flight path took me over Krasnodar to Maikop. I arrived there as darkness was falling. There was no sign of the airfield anywhere. I circled above the city several times, unsure whether I was at my destination. As I was about to fly on toward the east I saw rockets rising from the edge of the city and decided to land.

Those in the JG 52 command post were more than a little astonished at the new pilot who introduced himself with a night landing. Afterward I was taken to the officer's mess, where I reported to *Kommodore* Hrabak. He informed me that I was to join JG 52's II *Gruppe*.

Late on the morning of December 16 I took off for Simovniki as per orders. The town lay about 80 kilometers southwest of Stalingrad in the great steppe near the Manych River. There, with the *Gruppe*'s 6 *Staffel*, I was to gain my first combat experience. On arriving at Simovniki, however, I learned that the previous day the *Gruppe* had transferred to Kotelnikovo, 30 kilometers to the northeast and therefore nearer to Stalingrad. So I took off again and finally reached II./JG 52.

Two days later it appeared my luck had changed. An aircraft came out of the repair shops and understandably none of the pilots wanted to fly it. The aircraft was assigned to none other than 6 *Staffel*. I was naturally very keen to have it and stood by with parachute, oxygen mask, flying helmet, map and emergency kit while the engine was "run up" one last time. The Me wore a yellow "2" on its fuselage. I joyfully took possession of this machine and together with *Unteroffizier* Haas, who had been assigned as my mechanic, immediately began cleaning and polishing my "mill." When I had once more familiarized myself with the map and the front line I was ready to go.

My first mission at the front began at 1145 on December 18, 1942. Naturally I had to fly as wingman, or *Katschmarek*, at first. My assigned element leader was Ofw. Sturm. The two of us took off on a *freie Jagd*[1] sortie, meaning we had no particular mission. If we encountered enemy aircraft we were free to engage them immediately.

[1] *Freie Jagd*, or literally "free hunt." A tactic employed by the German fighter arm, whereby a formation of fighters patrolled a given area searching for enemy aircraft.

As soon as I was airborne I switched on my radio and soon heard the voice of my element leader: "Six two from six one, are you reading me?" I pressed my transmit button and replied as if this was old hat to me: "Six one from six two, *Viktor*, *Viktor*!"[2] Radio communications were alright.

For a beginner it was not so easy to hold a position in the air. I tried to stay 100 meters to the side and about 50 meters behind my element leader. Although I struggled to hold this position it was extremely difficult at first. Once I dropped too far behind and I heard: "Close up!" When I dropped too low I was asked if I had joined the prospectors and when I climbed too high I was asked to descend. Cruising around in front of the leader's "nose" or "on his tail" was especially taboo. It made even the calm Ofw. Sturm wild if I took up one of these positions.

I had absolutely no idea to where we had flown, where we were or how we were supposed to find our way home again. I was so tense that I forgot that a fighter pilot must spend at least two thirds of his time looking behind him as that is where the greatest danger lies.

I was more or less holding position when I heard over the radio: "Ahead and to the left, below us, four enemy fighters! Do you see them? They're about to attack the eight He 111s flying directly beneath us!" As I saw nothing at all I preferred to keep silent. Then Sturm called: "Stay close, we're going to attack!"

I followed the *Oberfeldwebel* when he dropped his Me's wing, and as we dove I saw four aircraft ahead and to the left. At first they were tiny, but then they quickly became larger. Two of the Russians immediately rolled onto their backs and dove away when my element leader opened fire. The other two hauled their machines around and turned toward us. I pulled mightily on the stick and pressed all the triggers, thinking I could hit one of them, but I missed by a mile and fired into the He 111 formation, which I now saw for the first time. As the "Ivans" had meanwhile turned again and were now almost behind me, Sturm called and said that I should climb and take no further part in the air battle.

I climbed steeply and circled while Sturm tangled futilely with the enemy. In the meantime the fighters below me had dropped ever lower. One after another they disappeared to the northeast. Finally the last Russian gave up the turning match and flew away along a rail line at low

[2] *Viktor*. Code word used in radio communications meaning "Roger," or understood.

level. Ofw. Sturm called. I came down to join him and we flew back to our airfield together.

So that had been my first mission; I had even made contact with the enemy. It was a clear demonstration of how far I was from being an element leader and shooting down an enemy aircraft, and an indication of the difficulties which lay ahead of me.

I was back in the air with Ofw. Sturm the next day. This time things went a little better, at least I was able to hold position quite well.

As we cruised along at 3,500 meters Ofw. Sturm brought it to my attention that the railway line along which we were flying was the only point of reference in this whole sector. Far and wide there was nothing else with which to orientate oneself, not a house, a hill, a lake, nothing, only the monotonous sameness of the steppe. The only change in the countryside was caused by the snow, which had melted or blown away in many places, revealing the sandy soil beneath. Sturm ordered radio silence and we flew about 20 kilometers into Russian territory without seeing a single enemy machine.

Suddenly there was a powerful odor in my cockpit. It wasn't gasoline or coolant, it was another smell. At the same time I noticed that the engine was running roughly. At first I paid it little notice, but then I engaged the individual magnetos to check the revolutions. When I did, my machine began to bang and rattle violently. Terrified, I immediately switched back to both magnetos. But the vibrating did not stop. My Me shook so badly that even my gunsight was bounced around. That was too much. I called Sturm and told him what was happening. He suggested that it was probably just ignition trouble, but being a cautious pilot he reversed course. My aircraft was still shaking badly. I sat there with clenched teeth, grasping the stick tightly with both hands. Then I asked for permission to fly home. The *Oberfeldwebel* answered that we were already halfway there and that my machine was now leaving a black smoke trail. "Soon the trail will become darker," I thought, "and then the crate will catch fire." We were still about 15 kilometers inside Russian territory.

I was thinking about what I had to do in the event I was forced to take to my parachute when the first flames licked up between my feet. Following my element leader's instructions, I had stayed at altitude and flew the compass heading he gave me, which took me away from the railway line to the left.

Flames repeatedly shot up by my left leg. At the same time the cockpit began to fill with smoke, forcing me to open the cockpit sliding panel. This sucked out some of the smoke but caused the flames to flare up. I was forced to close the window again. I would gladly have ended this affair by taking to my parachute, but Sturm had just told me that we were still over enemy territory.

Finally, however, the flames were scorching my trouser leg and I could barely stand the smoke in spite of having put on my oxygen mask; I decided to bail out. I ripped off my oxygen mask and prepared to jump. Then I pulled the canopy release lever and pushed on the glass roof. But the canopy would not detach. Now there was only one possibility: descend and make a belly landing.

I descended in a glide, keeping the nose of my mill pointed toward the southwest so as to get as close to our lines as possible. I was flying at more than 500 kph. I was about to lower my landing and radiator flaps in order to lose speed when I saw the railway line in front of me. I had to get across. My aircraft was already quite low, but I just made it over the railway embankment. I could keep my heavily-smoking crate in the air no longer. I tightened my straps, quickly removed the gunsight, so as not to strike my head against it on landing, and set down the "109." It immediately bounced back into the air and I had to force it down onto the ground again. After several more hops it stayed down and slid along a flat, snow-covered plain until it finally came to a halt. In an instant I sat up, released my straps and began pushing against the cockpit roof with all my strength. It gave way immediately and flipped open. Contact with the snow had extinguished the flames on the underside of my machine. I removed the cowling and put out the engine fire with snow. Then I looked around. Where was I? For certain still in Russian territory!

My first thought was to flee. When I was 200 meters away from the crash site I realized that it would be impossible to find a human settlement as I had no idea of my present position. I dared not travel along the railway line, as there would certainly be Russian soldiers there. So I turned back, sat on the wing of my Messerschmitt and waited for what was to come. And it was clear to me that something was going to happen, because it couldn't have gone unnoticed that an aircraft had crash-landed near the railway line.

Soon several figures approached from the railway embankment. Their number grew. They came toward me gesticulating wildly and shouting loudly. The men were wearing brown uniforms and speaking in a foreign tongue. I pulled my pistol from its holster, ready to take a few of them with me, and waited. Several of the soldiers were within 20 meters; they were carrying their rifles slung across their backs. They talked and shouted, but I couldn't understand a word. But there were two figures in the second group wearing field-gray uniforms! Soon I could see that they were two German NCOs.

When they were within shouting distance, I asked: "Am I among the Russians here?" "No, the Rumanians!" was the answer.

It felt as if a great weight had been lifted from my soul. The two NCOs told me that I had come down barely two kilometers behind the front. I resolved in the future never to take to my parachute if I could at all avoid it.

That evening I was driven back to the airfield in a truck and made my report. "You've begun well," observed *Kommandeur* Steinhoff, "Combat on your first mission and within a hair of not coming back on your second. Now go and recover from your ordeal."

It appeared that my flying career at the front had not begun under a particularly lucky star. My first two missions had made me the subject of much comment. Several of my comrades predicted that they wouldn't put up with me for long, and observed that I would only be making a brief guest appearance at the front. I myself had something else in mind, but so had many others before me who nevertheless failed to return from their first combat mission.

My third mission came on Christmas Day 1942. I took off at 0450 with Ofw. Sturm on a weather reconnaissance flight. Our mission was: "Find out how the weather is over the front and in Russian territory." The mission was uneventful, we flew almost as far as Stalingrad. The sun had just come up and we were all alone in the sky. A fantastic sight! But then I remembered that my machine had only one engine and my high spirits sank. I had already had my share of bad experiences with engines.

I carried on in spite of a general feeling of unwellness, fever and chills. I took off without saying a word about my condition, but after we had landed I felt so weak that I could barely get out of my aircraft. Like it or not, I was forced to go into our so-called "*Staffel* mess" – a simple room in a Russian cottage – and go to bed. And this on a holiday! I spent the rest of the day in bed, feverish or shivering, and sucked strenuously on Atebrin, because I at least wanted to take part in the small Christmas celebration being held by the pilots that evening.

There was wine and schnapps, and each pilot was even given a bottle of champagne. As well there were the takeoff and special rations which had been put aside – and the Christmas mail. But in spite of the preserving effect of the alcohol, I had to spend four days in bed before I was better. The *Gruppe* flew little in this time, as there was almost no contact with the enemy.

We soon transferred to Simovniki, the place where I had landed once before. An officer was supposed to lead the ground elements, who were to be moved by truck. As I could not fly on account of my illness I was chosen for the job. It wasn't very pleasant for me on the evening of December 27 to watch one machine after the other take off and disappear in the distance. What was more, the Russians were only three or four kilometers away and their tanks had even broken through in several places. To an infantryman that was no big deal. But to me, a pilot, who had no idea how to act on the ground, it was still the source of several headaches.

I drove out to the dispersal at about two in the morning and experienced my first Russian bombing raid. We heard the whistle of falling bombs; one exploded nearby, followed by a second and then the others at regular intervals. We knew from the old hands that the Russians usually dropped six bombs from this type of aircraft. The fourth had just exploded, and the fifth must strike somewhere in our immediate vicinity. While I was thinking about that I saw our people jumping down from the vehicle one after another. Then the sixth bomb exploded beyond the road. The one before it had been a dud and had bored into the ground beside the truck. We had gotten off lucky once again.

We began our journey toward the southwest as morning dawned. It was high time too, because a firefight appeared to be under way in a village no more than a kilometer and a half away. Guns crashed and bullets whizzed past us. We ducked our heads and drove cross-country at full throttle in the direction of Simovniki. Curious: the retreat began when I came to the front and during my time at the front with the Luftwaffe I participated only in retreats.

On December 30 we transferred from Simovniki to Gigant. The Russians had broken through everywhere, and we were not exactly sure where they were or if the Rumanians still existed at all. We therefore had to employ our fighters in a close-support role. This was a dangerous affair in the Me, which was easily wounded. A single lucky shot from a Russian waving his pistol around in the air, perhaps even without aiming, was enough to do in a "109." And the Russians fired everything that could shoot. They often had good results with their persistent defensive fire. In time they killed my initial joy at flying low behind the front through repeated direct hits.

There was only one assignment during my next nine missions in the period December 30 to January 2: low-level attacks. I quickly developed unsuspected abilities. Once I had tried it, I dove to ten meters or even lower, while Sturm always pulled out at 50 to 100 meters. I was most expert at attacking enemy trucks and could shoot up and set fire to a whole row of them. Often it happened that the vehicles' cargo exploded and I was forced to fly through the fireball. I soon gave up on this after being warned earnestly by my element leader, and realizing myself that it was a dangerous thing to do.

II./JG 52 fell back through Gigant and Sernovoy, near the Manych, to Rostov, exacting a heavy toll from the pursuing Russians.

Throughout most of the war in the southeast it was arranged for the pilots and ground crew to occupy quarters in villages near the airfields. Usually ten to fifteen pilots shared one of these cottages. While each *Staffel*'s "technical personnel" were fed by a field kitchen, the pilots, as the unit's fighting men, were assigned one or two orderlies. It was their job to prepare more or less palatable meals for the pilots.

In spite of the division, pilots here, technical personnel there, there was never any discord. The pilots needed the "technicians," and the latter were proud to played an important role in the success of the pilots. Each member of the technical personnel was assigned to a particular pilot, and every mechanic took pride in seeing to it that "his" aircraft was always combat-ready. Even the best pilot could achieve nothing if the motor did not run properly or his weapons failed.

Every pilot therefore had a very good relationship with his mechanic. The mechanic gave his best and the pilot thanked him with success and by sharing with him some of the things he received more of, especially takeoff and special rations. Each day a pilot received as takeoff rations extra biscuits, an egg and some butter. But for every successfully-completed mission he also received 20 grams of real coffee, half a tin of chocolate and a bag of mixed nuts and raisins or some other such delicacy. Pilots just arrived at the front used these special issues for themselves or sent them home. Once they had been in action for a longer time it was an unwritten law that they share them with the mechanics assigned to them.

Rostov North was a large airfield capable of accommodating every current type of German aircraft. It nevertheless had its difficulties and tricks for a young "buck" like me. Each takeoff and landing was a small breaking test for my nerves. I was always greatly relieved when I got up or down, as the case might be. Since the field sloped slightly to one side I was never able to properly establish my altitude while landing. In addition the snow irritated me terribly. But the worst, however, was the tall factory building situated right in the final approach zone close to the landing field. Once, after just about touching down on the flat roof of the building, I found myself at my wits end about landing. I was so unsure of myself that the *Staffelkapitän*, Hptm. Resch, had to reprimand me frequently. Nevertheless he allowed me to go on flying with him.

There was not much going on in the air at that time. We had scarcely any contact with the enemy. Then came January 30, 1943. I took off at 1225 as Hptm. Resch's wingman. It was my 18th combat mission. We climbed out from Rostov and flew along the Manych. My takeoff had been poor and now I was having difficulty staying in position behind my element leader. Nevertheless I scanned the airspace around us attentively and from an altitude of 4,500 meters spotted the two Russians at the same time as Hptm. Resch. They were below us and to the left and seemed to be enjoying some aerobatics.

My heart almost stopped, both for joy and terror. Resch instructed me to close up. "Stay close!" he ordered. "We're attacking!"

Then he positioned himself and dove on the two Russian aircraft from out of the sun. Just then the enemy aircraft split up. One flew to the left, the other to the right. Resch attacked the right aircraft. I saw tracers snaking across and hits flashing on the Russian. The LaGG-5 exploded before it could take any evasive action. The larger pieces of wreckage plunged to earth like blazing torches.

While I shouted "*Abschuss, Abschuss*!"[3] Resch pulled up and placed himself in the sun again. Meanwhile the Russian who had flown off to the left came right in front of my nose in a gentle turn, probably in the belief that I was his companion.

"I'm attacking!" I shouted to my element leader over the radio, and without waiting for permission or orders immediately placed myself behind the Russian. He must have smelled a rat just before I reached favorable firing range. Just as I was about to open fire he turned away sharply to the left. I hauled on the stick with all my strength, turned tighter and pulled plenty of lead. Then I "let him have it with all barrels." The Russian immediately turned to the right again.

I had now closed to 200 meters and turned as tightly as I could – the stick forces were quite enormous on account of my high rate of closure – and fired in the turn, aiming in front of his nose. Once again he tried to change his heading, but I was right on him and he caught a full burst. I saw hits on his fuselage and pulled up. I was about to dive on him again when the aircraft began to stagger. The LaGG went down in a spin from 3,500 meters. I had apparently hit the pilot.

Circling around and repeatedly shouting "*Abschuss*!", I followed the enemy aircraft down until it crashed and exploded. I wanted to see exactly what happened to him.

Much later I heard the voice of my element leader, telling me for the second or third time to cease my mad shouting and rejoin formation.

After Resch had confirmed my victory I tried to carry out his orders but I was simply too excited and happy to fly. The aircraft seemed to no longer want to respond. I swung about in the sky at low speed like a frightful beginner. Any novice could have shot me down easily. Finally it was all too much for Hptm. Resch. He instructed me to fly back to base at once and refused to answer me no matter how many times I called him. Slowly I regained control over my Bf 109, set course for "Garden Fence"[4] and landed – this time safely – at Rostov North. I forgot to waggle my wings, which was customary when a pilot came home with a kill, but I intended to make up for it on my next mission.

Resch, who had landed before me, had already reported our two kills. As soon as I taxied in the pilots and mechanics of 6 *Staffel* came

[3] *Abschuss*. Kill.

[4] Garden Fence (*Gartenzaun*). Base airfield.

over to congratulate me on my "first." As I climbed out I resolved not to go on leave until I had shot down nine enemy aircraft and thus met the requirements for the award of the Iron Cross, First Class. Naturally I had to let those at home know of my success immediately. It was a great day for me. I was convinced that I was going to become a good pilot if luck stayed with me.

From Rostov North we transferred through Kuteinikovo to Slavyanskaya. This small village had a large airfield from which one could have taken off easily had it not been so muddy. Some dexterity was required to reach the quarters without sinking into the mud of the footpaths. In addition we were visited every night by Russian bombers. I resided in a "room" of a small cottage. As soon as the bombs started falling my quarters personnel came to me trembling and crying, asking to be allowed to remain. They felt safer with me.

Then came February 13, 1943. My flight log shows the following entry for that eventful day: "Running flight number: 28 – Pilot: Lipfert – Type: Bf 109 G + 1 – Date: 13. 2. – Takeoff: 1330 Slavyanskaya – Landing: 1515 at Krasnoarmeyskye. Emergency landing after 105 minutes flight time."

Meanwhile, at Slavyanskaya 6 *Staffel* had received a new *Kapitän*. Hptm. Resch had been transferred to another *Geschwader* and soon afterward failed to return from a sortie. I took off on my second mission from Slavyanskaya with the new Kapitän, Knight's Cross wearer *Oberleutnant* Denk, who had 76 kills. Our assignment: orientation in the airspace over the front and scouting of enemy airfields.

"Six two from six one, are you receiving me?" – "Six one from six two, *Viktor*, *Viktor*!"

Radio communications were in order. We had carried out the radio check while selecting undercarriage and flaps up and placing radiator controls on "automatic." All was quiet on the other side of the front. Not even the flak tried to disturb us. But the cloud deck, which initially had been at 3,000 meters, sank lower and lower. The mountains of the Caucasus had completely disappeared into the clouds.

My element leader flew deeper into Russian territory. The cloud layer there was down to about 400 meters. We flew right beneath it. Suddenly we saw a Russian airfield directly in front of us. As we circled I saw several light courier aircraft parked at the edge of the airfield.

Hunting fever seized me. I was just about to ask permission to descend, when I heard in my headset: "We're going to make a low-level attack. Stay close and fire with me!" Oblt. Denk peeled off and flew toward one of the parked crates. I waited a moment before diving on the same machine. As I got closer, however, I saw that it was already burning and fired on the next aircraft, but scored no hits. I was going too fast to correct my aim. I therefore pulled up after my element leader and followed him down for a second attack.

In the meantime life had appeared on the airfield. Men ran here and there. Then a string of red pearls zipped past my left wing. Aha, the lads are firing! But one machine gun firing wildly could not put us off our plan. This time I scored effective hits on the target aircraft. It went up in flames. On the third pass we were met by tracer from every end and corner of the airfield. It was impossible to stay with my leader on this attack. I turned away to the right and circled the airfield.

Oblt. Denk set another aircraft on fire, but then when he pulled up something terrible happened. He was at 200 meters when his 109 took a full burst from a quadruple machine-gun and exploded. Burning pieces of his aircraft fell in the middle of the airfield. I was almost paralyzed with shock. What should I do? Could I salvage anything here? – And how was I supposed to find my way home now?

I circled the airfield twice at a safe distance and then, with shaking hands, tried to find my map, which was jammed beneath my seat. When I had retrieved the map I tried feverishly to orientate myself. One thing was clear – I had to get away from this terrible place. Without referring to the map again I began following a railway line which led in a southeasterly direction.

If only the clouds had been higher I would have been able to find may way. But I couldn't climb above 400 meters, which complicated orientation colossally. After a few minutes flying time I began to doubt that I had flown in the right direction. The mountains had to be to the south, but there the clouds hung down right to the ground. I couldn't go that way, so I reversed course and flew northwest by compass. Perhaps I could reach Rostov. But I soon abandoned this idea as well. If there was to be salvation it would have to lie, as always, to the west. By heading west I must reach the Sea of Azov, and if my fuel ran out I could turn inland and make a forced landing.

Again an icy chill went through my limbs. I looked at the clock and saw that I had been in the air more than an hour; the red light had probably been burning for some time already. I had completely overlooked it. When this red light on the instrument panel lit up there was at most enough fuel left for ten minutes flying. If the death of my element leader had brought me to the verge of a nervous breakdown, this latest discovery was enough to make me lose my head completely. Below me there were only Russians, who stared up in amazement at the lone aircraft.

Was that really land below me, or was I already over the bays of the Sea of Azov or the flooded Kuban? I saw a great deal of water in which chunks of ice and snow were floating and a few small, dark areas of land. Then an idea struck me: "If you ever want to get back to German territory, you will have to select a spot, land and take off again after finding out where the front is." It was a truly absurd notion, but I saw no other way.

While I looked for a suitable field, I once again weighed my chances: for any beginner taking off and especially landing the 109 was a minor feat. I was about to attempt it here without regard to wind direction and surface conditions.

I was going to land. It was clear to me that the wheels might sink into the softened ground causing the aircraft to overturn. I dared not think about the difficult takeoff.

Before me was a large, black field, across which was moving a horse-drawn wagon carrying two women and a man. "Now show your courage!" I said to myself. "The odds are 95:5 against you!"

I circled the field once and then made one of the most difficult decisions of my life: prepare to land! Radiator flaps open, landing gear down, flaps down, propeller pitch on automatic, trim tail-heavy and straps tightened. The aircraft set down in a three-point landing and rolled out without the tail swinging once. Luckily the ground had only thawed to a depth of about five centimeters. I opened the throttle and taxied toward the wagon, which tried to escape the cloud of dust as quickly as possible. When I caught up with the wagon the driver stopped. I let the motor run, released my straps and climbed out, my pistol at the ready.

With my pistol trained on the occupants, I asked in Russian: "Are there German soldiers nearby?" They repeatedly answered, "*Dallikoa, dallikoa*" and pointed in one direction. That really wasn't much to go on. However the landing had one positive result: it gave me a chance to calm down and the successful landing increased my self-confidence greatly.

There was no time to lose. I climbed in. The takeoff went smoothly. The heading that could save me was southwest. After about five minutes of flying at ground level I again saw Russian soldiers below me. They threw themselves to the ground when the recognized the swastika. From the number of soldiers I deduced that I must be near the front. Suddenly I was over a city. Flying jut beneath the clouds, I counted the railway lines leaving the city, in spite of heavy anti-aircraft fire. There were five of them, spreading out in a star shape. In an instant I realized I had been here before. I scanned my map and compared. By my third circuit I had figured it out: I had to be over Timoshevskaya. Only that city, near the front and ten kilometers inside Russian territory, had five railway lines.

I soon picked out the railway line I had to follow if I was to reach the German lines. I descended almost to ground level. My aircraft would be able to make the last 15 kilometers. Below me Russians jumped down from the railway embankment to the left and right and hastily took cover. I gave them no thought as I had other worries.

Finally, somewhere between hope and despair, I saw the first field-gray uniforms. I was finally over German territory. Now let come what may. I pulled up and searched for a suitable place to land. Again I was over a large town. It had to be Krasnoarmeyskoye.

My brave Messerschmitt had saved me and I therefore didn't want to put her down on her belly if I could help it. I was determined to make a wheels-down landing. It had worked the first time, so why not here in German territory. I selected a field which appeared suitable. At an altitude of 100 meters, still over the city, I lowered the undercarriage and landing flaps.

Suddenly the aircraft fell off into a steep left turn. It would not respond to the controls and in an instant I realized that only by putting the nose down and opening the throttle all the way could I get myself out of this dangerous situation. A house seemed to rush toward me at tremendous speed. While fully aware that certain death was racing toward me I felt not a moment of fear, there was simply no time.

Instinctively I placed my left arm in front of my head and hauled back on the stick with my right. I saw that the aircraft was coming out of its dive, then the house was there and I closed my eyes. There was a terrible crash and I thought: so this is death!

There were several more crashes and then all was still. I hadn't lost consciousness even for a second. I felt a light breeze and risked opening my eyes. I couldn't believe that I could still think and was therefore still alive. Seconds later I climbed from my smoking cockpit – that was all that was left of the 109 – like a phoenix rising from the ashes. I felt myself all over and then began to laugh loudly. The infantrymen who rushed to the scene must have thought I'd gone mad.

I had forgotten to strap myself in when I took off from the field far behind Russian lines. I tried to do so during the flight, but I discovered that my harness was jammed under the folding hood. I dared not open the hood in flight, and so I had crashed into the cottage without being strapped in. The Me had made a three-point landing on the roof of the cottage, during which the tail and wings must have broken off. The heavy engine, together with the fuselage to a point just behind the cockpit, had smashed through the roof and floor of the house. The engine itself remained stuck in one of the walls and only the cockpit section, with me inside, continued into the open, where it ended up in a garden near some apple trees.

What a sight the cockpit was! The canopy glass was shattered, the instrument panel was demolished and almost all the cables were ripped out. Actually only the parachute, on which I was sitting, and the control column, which I was holding with my right hand, remained undamaged. Everything else was smashed and destroyed – except me. I escaped with two bruises on my left forearm and a huge lump on my head. Luck had been with me again; without luck it would have been all over.

That evening a truck drove me to the airfield, which was only 15 kilometers away. The road was so bad that we had to drive with the lights on to avoid becoming stuck in the morass. The lights were soon spotted by a Russian bomber, which dropped its load to the left and right of the road. The driver initially wanted to shut off the lights and stop, but then we drove on and arrived undamaged at the *Gruppe* mess after midnight.

In addition to Oblt. Denk, three other pilots had failed to return that day. Morale was below the zero point when I arrived and made my report. The *Kommandeur*, Hptm. Steinhoff, was happy that at least one of the missing had returned. After a few glasses of champagne I had to tell all about my wanderings. The "old hands" had never heard anything like it. Had it not happened to me, I would scarcely have believed it myself. But the ruins of the destroyed house and the wreckage of my machine were proof of at least the last part of the drama.

We didn't stay long at Slavyanskaya. Out of the blue, orders came to move to Kerch. This airfield was not nearly so muddy as Slavyanskaya and there was even some grass, but there too the radiators were sprayed with a great deal of muck during takeoff. As a result we had to fly around with our radiator flaps open at a cost of about 20 kph. It was from this base that I saw my first real action. Usually I was in the air twice, sometimes three times per day.

On my 39th mission I flew as wingman for young Uffz. Waldmann, who had made a name for himself at Slavyanskaya by shooting down seven Russian aircraft in two days.

We took off together at 1410 on February 25. It was a dreary, wet, gray late winter day. The clouds hung very low. It was actually no weather for fighters, but Il-2s had been reported from the front. The Il-2 was a heavily-armored close-support aircraft which the Russians were deploying everywhere in great numbers. I knew this ship only by name.

From Kerch we rattled across the straits to Taman. There was no one in the air but us. Beyond Taman to the east the cloud deck rose to about 300 meters, although several strands hung down almost to the ground. As we were in the immediate vicinity of the front, we ceased our lively conversation and concentrated on what was going on around us. We had just flown through a low-hanging cloud when I saw several machines above me and to the right. They were flying in the opposite direction just beneath the clouds.

"Over own territory, so low, no flak, they must be our aircraft," I thought to myself. Their shape resembled that of the Ju 88 as far as I could tell. So as to let my element leader know that I was on the ball, I reported: "Six one from six two. Several Ju 88s behind and above us!"

Waldmann's only response was "*Viktor*, *Viktor*!" Then he made a leisurely right turn and climbed up to just below the clouds, trailing black smoke – this was the sign that he had selected full throttle. Because of the poor weather I was sitting only about 20 meters to his right and slightly behind. I now saw the other aircraft directly in front of me. They began a gentle turn to the left and I heard Waldmann's voice: "Lovely 88s, they're Russians – IL-2s!" This *Unteroffizier* had nerve! How could he be so cool! I was so excited I nearly caught up with Waldmann, who had reduced speed to increase his firing time and now calmly moved in behind the last of the six Il-2s. I saw his burst of fire disappear into the fuselage of the enemy aircraft, then I was carried past him by my excess speed and found myself sitting right behind the Il-2. All I could do was press down on all the triggers. All three of my guns fired but the fellow flying in front of me seemed to take no notice. There were flashes all over the enemy aircraft. He lost a lot of small pieces and in an instant began trailing a long, gray banner of smoke, but he flew on and before I knew exactly what was happening, began sending strings of pearls back at me.

At first I though flak was firing at us from the ground, but then I heard Waldmann's voice: "Watch out, they've got rear gunners. Don't let them get you!"

Firing everything I had, I plastered the Russian as best I could for several seconds. He had become terribly large and I had the feeling that if I didn't break away now I'd fly right through him. I couldn't pull up, therefore I dove away so that I could move in behind him again. I saw one of the enemy aircraft which had steamed off toward the east explode in a flash of flame. At the same time I heard Uffz. Waldmann call "*Abschuss*!"

Before I could shout "*Viktor*" a second time I was behind my Russian again. I moved in and opened fire, ignoring the tracer flashing from the rear gun. Having learned my lesson the first time, I slowed down to match his speed and thus had more time to fire. He lagged farther behind the others and the smoke trail became heavier. The return fire had ceased and as I pulled up and over him he made a belly landing. One wing came off and the fuselage broke into pieces.

Without worrying about Waldmann I made a strafing run on the aircraft lying on the ground. Finally Waldmann observed that that was enough as the Russians wouldn't be able to repair it, and when he assured me that it was obviously a kill I was happy.

That was number two. Satisfied, we flew home, and I waggled my wings twice for my two kills, having forgotten to do so out of excitement the first time.

Several days after this success I went up with Uffz. Barnickel. Our orders were to patrol the airspace over Novorossisk. The older, more experienced pilots warned us that we should not fly low over the land or water if we wanted to stay alive. We therefore flew light-heartedly over the Black Sea and arrived over Novorossisk at 4,500 meters. There were no Russians in the air. As it almost always was, the weather was splendid with outstanding visibility. As we flew a little farther along the coast Barnickel pointed out Gelendschik airfield far below us.

It was a fighter base containing large numbers of our comrades "from the other side." Two dust clouds down below certainly meant that two Russian fighters had just taken off. We were discussing the opportunity that was now offered us, when there was a frightful bang. My aircraft was tossed upward abruptly. The sudden change in direction pressed me down into my seat hard; afterward I was so badly shaken that I couldn't see or hear.

Where was my element leader? In place of his Me and all around me were large black clouds. "Damn," I thought, "to be bracketed by flak like this while doing 420 kph!" All due respect to the skill of the gunners. There was nothing left but to get out of the danger area. I rolled left until the aircraft was on its back then hauled back on the stick. I dove away toward the sea.

Then I heard Barnickel's voice: "I'm behind you on your left. Join me!"

Just then I sighted my element leader. "*Viktor*, I'm coming!" I answered. I pulled up and turned left until his Messerschmitt was visible beneath my wing. Then I dropped down and settled into position.

Far below us – we were still at 3,000 meters – and somewhat farther out to sea, the two Russians who had taken off were maneuvering and struggling to close with us, nervously aware that they were still flying in their own anti-aircraft fire zone. We climbed slowly to 5,000 meters and flew far out to sea, keeping a sharp eye on the Russians. When they were at about 4,000 meters Barnickel placed himself in the sun and made his first attack.

I stayed close behind him, continually reassuring him that I was still there. In this way he knew that I was watching our rear and that he could concentrate on the target.

Unfortunately the two Russians had already noticed us and before we were within range they turned quickly and came toward us. Now we began turning and soon I was so involved in the dogfight that I scarcely noticed what was up and down, where my leader was and where the flak bursts were.

Finally I got behind one of the Russians and stuck to him, but he wasn't about to allow me to get off a shot. The lad turned so well that it was all I could do to stay with him. In the meantime Barnickel headed off the other Russian, who for his part was trying to shoot me down. It was thus a merry, colorful chain, in which each was doing his best to close with the other. I was sweating and cursing profusely; each time my opponent dodged out of the way before I could press the triggers. The dogfight went on for perhaps a quarter of an hour, with neither side wanting to give in or break off the battle.

I was slowly becoming uncomfortable. This was the first long air battle I had participated in and I was feeling rather fatigued. I wouldn't be able to hold out much longer, but I didn't want to be the first to withdraw. The turning match went on until my opponent had had enough; he stood his machine on its nose and dove into the midst of the anti-aircraft fire. But I was so furious that scarcely anything could have prevented me from diving after him, especially since I knew that my machine was heavier than his and that I could certainly overtake him. Hopefully I wouldn't be hit by flak in the process.

The Russian in front grew larger and larger and soon he filled my gunsight. I pressed the triggers and saw my tracing ammunition disappear into his fuselage. There was a flash of flame. Then the enemy aircraft, which had taken no evasive action, reared up and dove toward the land at an increasingly steep angle.

I followed the aircraft for some time repeatedly shouting "*Abschuss*!" Then I noticed that the flak was becoming quite active again and I hauled my machine around and headed out toward the safety of the sea. As I turned away I saw the blazing enemy aircraft crash into the ground in a cloud of dust. As my red light had lit up, I quickly set course for home. On the way I asked: "Six one from six two. Did you see my kill?"

It was a while before Barnickel answered: "Six two from six one. I'm above and behind you. Come up. I saw your kill!"

Strangely, I was in rather poor spirits afterward. The element leader was to confirm his wingman's victory, although he had been unable to score a kill himself. The *Kommandeur*, too, was astonished when I reported my kill. "Now then," he observed, "perhaps we'll make a fighter pilot of you yet Lipfert. But don't go too fast. Give yourself time and first amass the necessary experience. Otherwise you'll go the same way as many others who didn't want to admit that they still had plenty to learn!"

Several days after this February 28 I flew again with Uffz. Barnickel, still as his wingman as I had flown only 44 missions. There was nothing going on in the air, and it was no fun to sail around in such dreary, misty weather at 4,000 meters where there was nothing to be found. In my recklessness I convinced Barnickel that we should descend to ground level and frighten the Russians on the far side of the front with our sudden appearance.

We roared along a railway line at high speed, Barnickel left of the tracks and me right, both below the telephone wires. Unaware of any danger, I saw a dot appear in the distance in front of me, followed seconds later by a second. They both grew larger rapidly and turned out to be two aircraft. They were at perhaps 300 meters and were coming toward us.

But what kind of ships were they? The aircraft had to be Russian. Barnickel had seen them too. We dropped lower, so as not to be seen and let them fly past above us. In fact it was two Russians, probably courier or training aircraft.

"*Horridoh*"[5] and after them. As we pulled up we realized they had spotted us. They turned away from the railway line to the right and descended. It almost looked as if they were about to land. We couldn't believe our eyes, but the Russians were in fact seeking a place to land.

We closed in before they could reach safety. Barnickel was first in range. He took aim at the leading aircraft and opened fire. Sitting almost beside my element leader, I was now in position behind the other and raked him as best I could while he was

perhaps five meters off the ground. That was still too high for the enemy pilot. He apparently wanted to get on the ground the quickest way possible. The Russian put his aircraft down nose first, whereupon it smashed to pieces.

[5] *Horridoh*. Battle cry of the German fighter arm.

The aircraft under attack by Barnickel made a smooth landing. The three occupants were in such a hurry that they leapt from the machine while it was still moving, rolled on the ground and left the aircraft to its fate. Even before the Russian aircraft, which was smoking slightly, came to a halt, Barnickel came and fired until it burst into flames.

We circled twice and waved to the occupants, who were fearfully trying to hide behind a haystack. Then we set course for home. We congratulated each other and celebrated because we had each scored a kill.

We had taken off early in the morning and the weather had deteriorated somewhat in the meantime. Visibility was now about one and a half kilometers. Then something happened which once again showed that I really must have had more luck than many other pilots.

I was perhaps 50 meters behind Barnickel when I once again saw a shadow coming toward me from ahead and to the right. I recognized the enemy aircraft, made a slight correction and pressed the triggers almost in an instant. The Russian exploded before my eyes and the pieces fell burning to the ground. Uffz. Barnickel had seen nothing and not until I shouted "*Horridoh*" did he turn around. He shook his head and had to admit that I had beaten him to it once again.

We cheerfully flew home and waggled our wings over the airfield. All my comrades congratulated me on my double success. Only *Feldwebel* Sachsenberg, who was later to become my closest friend and comrade, couldn't help saying: "He won't last long!"

But "he did last"! And how "he lasted"! My days as a wingman were over and from then on I was allowed to become an element leader and received a new Bf 109. Then a dry spell set in and there was not a single "carcass," as we referred to it in pilots jargon, to be seen in the air. I used this time to learn to fly properly, get used to my new Messerschmitt and familiarize myself with the terrain. I also worked hard on studying the enemy aircraft types, because I did not want to have to report a kill again without knowing what type I had shot down.

The pilots' quarters in Kerch, which we referred to as the "officer's mess," consisted of two rooms. In the rear one were the pilots' eight steel-frame bunk beds. They almost filled the place, leaving little room for personal belongings. Most fighter pilots had little baggage with them anyway, but even this small amount had to be stowed somewhere.

Usually it lay more or less picturesquely beneath the lower bed or hung on the bedposts.

In spite of this the quarters were usually relatively clean. In addition to the mess cook we had an orderly for all the pilots, who helped keep things tidy. And what would the 6 *Staffel* mess have been without these two *Obergefreiten*, Twardy and Klingel! I myself got along well with Twardy. Now and then he even stooped to polish my boots, which he never or very rarely did for the other officers. Even our *Staffelkapitän* at that time, Ofw. and Knight's Cross wearer Nemitz, a veteran pilot, received no special treatment.

The other two officers, Lt. Günther Kurz and Lt. Klaasen, had no orderly and had to look after their own things. We three *Leutnants*, "Patriarch" Nemitz and the senior NCO, Ofw. Gustav Bolinski, were in the adjoining room, the actual mess room, in which stood a large table and several chairs. During periods of bad weather we lived there in close quarters.

Most such days, after the unit IVa (rations and accommodations) had paid a brief visit, were spent drinking and singing and playing skat. Actually there was no set sequence. Naturally there was plenty of talk as well – about flying and women, as usual in the service. We all looked for any excuse to dodge training lectures, inspections or other such fun.

# CHAPTER III
# Battle Zone Caucasus

On March 13 we moved to Anapa. Although I had been flying as an element leader since my fifth victory, and I did this with passion and devotion, all my efforts to find Russians in the air came to nothing. At this time I was usually flying three missions per day – except when the weather was too bad. Unfortunately there were few *freie Jagd* missions, instead we flew escort for Stukas, for us a ticklish and uncomfortable assignment.

We fighters were responsible for the Stukas we were escorting no matter what. Even if one of these aircraft was shot down by flak they tried to put the blame on us. Often there were difficulties in rendezvousing with the Stukas. While there were occasions when we failed to arrive in time, the opposite was true just as often. When this happened there was nothing for the formation to do but circle until the dive-bombers arrived.

Things worked out best when the Stukas flew over our airfield on their way to the front. In such cases we were usually sitting in our aircraft waiting, and we took off immediately and soon caught up with the slower dive-bombers. Afterward we climbed to about 300 meters above them and stayed as close as the Stukas wanted.

Even more uncomfortable, especially for less-experienced pilots, was the assignment: "Fly along the coast of the Black Sea, if possible to Tuapse, and reconnoiter over the sea!" It was more than 200 kilometers to Tuapse and we had enough fuel for about 500. Therefore if there was any kind of incident, if one became involved with enemy aircraft on the way back or somehow lost his way, it was definitely critical, at least for a beginner.

Such thoughts were always on my mind when I headed out on a sea patrol. Often I flew out to sea with clenched teeth, so far over the water that I could just glimpse the land in the distance.

Any roughness in the engine made me think that I could smell something suspicious in the cockpit and that an engine seizure was not far away. But what then? Should I come down in the sea in such an event or land in Russian territory? The possibilities caused me to become quite warm, even at 6,000 meters where it was very cold.

Nevertheless I flew the missions when ordered to do so, just like all the others.

At this time I flew a mission with Lt. Günther Kurz. Günther, who already had three kills, and I agreed that we would take turns as element leader. But what harmless pilots we were, what raw beginners! And what childlike naivete we displayed in charging into a formation of eight Airacobras without any idea of what was in store for us. The Airacobra, supplied by the USA, was the best Russian fighter at that time.

I was flying as element leader, but Günther was the first to sight them. Without worrying about a favorable attack position we dove on the "Indians"[1] from a slightly higher altitude, happy that we were once again in combat. Actually the enemy should have realized what green novices they were dealing with and shot us down easily, as the Airacobra was almost a match for our Bf 109. Perhaps they were startled that only two machines dared to attack the whole formation.

Naturally we both tried to shoot down an enemy aircraft but failed to do so. At first Günther and I attacked the eight Russians together. However I didn't get into the formation as I had intended. The aircraft I had selected turned away just in time and I found myself sitting in the midst of the enemy formation. Günther, who was right behind me, and I now began flying in a circle with the Russians. We went round three, four, then five times without anyone being able to cause any harm to the other.

We turned with the Russians without success for probably half an hour. Then it seemed advisable for us to break off the battle so as to get

[1] Indians (*Indianer*). Radio code word for enemy fighters.

home safely.

The morning of March 14 found Günther and I at the airfield very early. Intelligence had reported the day before that the Russians intended to attack our airfield in the coming days. Usually they made their attacks in the morning, at noon or in the evening. Therefore we were there at the right time and waited by our aircraft. It wasn't long before they came. Our alert *Rotte* had already dived into the many Il-2s, Yaks and LaGGs. We climbed into our machines in spite of the falling bombs and gunfire and took off between the bomb craters after the enemy. Throttles wide open, we chased after the Russians along the coast in the direction of Novorossisk, almost to Gelendschik. There was no sign of the enemy anywhere.

"Those boys have landed again, Günther. Let's fly down to Novorossisk and then up the valley into the mountains. Perhaps we can catch a couple of stragglers there."

We put the noses of our aircraft down, then roared over the city at high speed and through the small valley, leaping over every tree and house and waving to our infantry below. Halfway between Novorossisk and Krimskaya I suddenly spotted a hole in the solid cloud deck, through which we climbed. Once on top of the cloud layer I made a full circle to make sure that no Ivan could drop down onto my tail, and then began a slow, spiral climb.

Suddenly a lone Il-2 appeared in front of me in a trough in the clouds, but he immediately disappeared into the clouds again. Then I saw him again, ghostlike, through the mist.

As I dove I saw that the Il-2 was just emerging from cloud again. Before he was all the way out I hit him with a burst from all guns. There were several flashes on the enemy aircraft. I continued firing until I was almost within ramming distance. The Russian flew straight ahead and acted as if this wild shoot-up had never started. Damn it, he was stubborn!

My speed was too great and I was forced to break away to avoid ramming him. I heard Günther's voice over the radio: "Watch out, Indians left and behind you! I'll stay above. Make another attack, that fellow hasn't had enough yet!"

Another pass! I hauled my aircraft around. Reduce speed and approach slowly! I opened my radiator flaps fully and then pressed the triggers. By now the Russian had noticed what was going on. Although his aircraft was now smoking heavily, he twisted and turned very skillfully, making it difficult for me to score any more hits.

I slowly drew closer, now he could do what he wanted. I poured a stream of fire into the aircraft, which shed pieces and began to emit more smoke. But he simply wouldn't fall! It was noteworthy that the Russian didn't try to escape into the clouds, because I wouldn't have been able to attack him there.

Finally, while I was lining up for a third pass, he dropped through a hole in the clouds and headed toward Gelendschik. But I was soon on him again and let him have it with everything I had. It was amazing the punishment the enemy machine could take. As I overtook the Il-2 for the third time I saw that large pieces were missing from its fuselage and wings. The engine was burning slightly. Soon the enemy aircraft went into a steep dive. Just short of Karbadinka it crashed into the water and sank, while I pulled out and flew out to sea to escape the enemy flak.

"*Abschuss, Abschuss*!" I roared. Günther confirmed my victory and congratulated me. I thanked him for the outstanding cover and promised to do the same for him next time.

Things did not go well for II *Gruppe* at Anapa. There were few contacts with the enemy but many losses. And it was not just the beginners and young pilots who failed to return, but some of the old hands as well. The *Gruppe* consisted of about 35 pilots at that time and within a few weeks lost the following personnel: Ofw. Nemitz (78 kills), Ofw. Kiworra (38 kills), Fw. Gleissner (34 kills), Oblt. Ritzenberger (21 kills), Lt. Smiatek (6 kills), Lt. Kirnbauer and Lt. Baumann (2 kills).

In addition to these veteran fighter pilots a number of wingmen were also lost whose names I can no longer remember. In those days it was a daily assignment to fly cover for the ferries operating between Anapa and Kerch. That meant that a pair of aircraft had to circle over the sea somewhere and escort two or three tubs sailing below for an hour until relief came. Among other things these ferries brought our mail to Anapa and were therefore very important to us. We did have a lot of fun though taking forbidden gunnery practice.

Halfway between Anapa and Kerch lay a wrecked ship and every fighter pilot had a go at its smokestack. None of us would pass without giving it a burst. It was a welcome target, and the way it was riddled spoke for our accuracy.

My "dry spell" continued. I scored no further victories. Once I flew an early morning mission with Ofw. Nemitz. We climbed over Anapa to 6,000 meters and busied ourselves with the weather. Then to my right I saw a single machine flying aerobatics and then realized that it had to be a Pe-2, a Russian multi-role aircraft.

At first I wasn't going to report it to Nemitz, but then I did, as I was the wingman this time and was supposed to at least inform my element leader of my intentions. Nemitz called me and said that shooting down a Pe-2 was a risky business as the aircraft had two rearward-firing machine-guns. I assured him that it made no difference to me, but he moved in and attacked anyway. The enemy aircraft began burning brightly after Nemitz' first attack. Moving in close behind him, I dared not open fire. This, too, annoyed me.

At this time Lt. Baumann, the 27-year-old *Staffelkapitän* of the 4th, failed to return from a mission. As one of the *Gruppe*'s oldest officer pilots it fell to me to take over command of the *Staffel* for a few days. It was with reluctance that I left 6 *Staffel*. But it too had received a new *Kapitän*, after our "Patriarch," Ofw. Willi Nemitz, likewise failed to return from a mission. Soldiers in the front lines saw a single Bf 109 dive out of the clouds and crash into one of their trenches. When a Knight's Cross was found in the wreck it was clear that it could only be that of our missing Nemitz. His death meant that II *Gruppe* had lost its oldest and most experienced pilot.

Oblt. Ritzenberger, who was appointed to command 6 *Staffel* after Nemitz, lasted only a few weeks. He was shot down by a Yak over Novorossisk and crashed into the sea. After his death I took over as leader of 6 *Staffel*.

There are several things from this period that must be told. One was the affair over the champagne: there were huge cellars just in front of the Russian lines, near Lake Abraum, in which lay thousands of bottles of Crimean champagne.

We were allowed to help ourselves so as to deny the wine to the advancing Russians. At that time the cellar of one *Staffel* contained 600 bottles. Naturally everyone was quite pleased. Unfortunately this noble drink, which was enjoyed in great quantities, produced a terrific diarrhea. Nearly every pilot could tell stories of how he had withstood this illness while in the air.

After consuming the terrific Crimean champagne one could fly like a young god. Everything was so easy and ethereal. Only rarely did I shoot down anything in this condition, but I frequently came home with a bullet-damaged aircraft. Naturally it was strictly forbidden to fly if even slightly intoxicated, but this ban was sometimes ignored.

On March 30, 1943 the entire *Gruppe* took off together and carried out an exercise over the Krimskaya-Novorossisk-Taman area at an altitude of 3,000 meters. All did not go well and our *Gruppenkommandeur* at that time, Hptm. Kühle, raged at us. After three-quarters of an hour he had had enough and ordered us to break up into *Schwärme* [2] and fly *freie Jagd* in the area until our fuel ran low and we were forced to fly home.

Scarcely had my *Rotte* [3] separated from the formation, when I saw a lone Yak flying far below me. Without worrying about the rest of the formation, I dove on the Russian and shot him down on the first pass, all this before the others knew what was happening. Not until I yelled over the radio that I had scored a kill did they arrive and marvel at the fire where the Yak had crashed. In the meantime my wingman, Ofw. Kuhn, had spotted and reported a second enemy aircraft. Like vultures, ten or more Messerschmitts swooped down on this poor fellow. Everyone tried to show up the others and in consequence just got in each other's way.

I had moved off somewhat and observed the dangerous affair from a distance. The Russian was a very good pilot and was able to keep away from the pack of hounds through his outstanding turns.

In the course of his efforts he flew right in front of me. I caught him with a long burst in a left turn. The Russian raced away with one undercarriage leg down and trailing a long banner of black smoke. Before I or one of the others could shoot at him again he had made a fast split-S and landed his mill, which was by now burning, on a road. Before stopping it rolled between two trees, losing both wings in the process. The wingless aircraft then plunged into the ditch at the side of the road and broke apart in a cloud of dust.

---

[2] *Schwarm*. Standard four-aircraft formation used by the German fighter arm. Adopted by RAF and USAAF, which called the formation the "finger four."

[3] *Rotte*. Element of two fighters. Two *Rotten* made up a *Schwarm*.

My comrades flew up and congratulated me even though I had snatched a certain victory from in front of their noses. One can imagine how triumphant I felt. The entire *Gruppe* had been in the air with all its experts, and it was I, the beginner, who had scored two kills.

The mechanics at the dispersal were more than a little amazed when I waggled my wings twice, and naturally there was an appropriate celebration afterward.

April 19. That day I flew with a new wingman, Lt. Smiatek of 4 *Staffel.* He was a cheerful fellow and a daredevil but lacked flying experience. We took off and met a lone Russian flying at low altitude in the valley near Novorossisk, well inside German territory. At first I thought it might be a Bf 109 coming toward us. But when I saw the huge Soviet star I hauled my machine around and rammed the throttle forward, leaving a dense, black cloud of fuel in the air behind me. The Russian increased speed as well and pressed on through the valley, making minor heading changes as he went.

Soon I was upon him, but my rate of closure was so great that I only had time for a brief burst. The enemy pilot then turned so tightly that Smiatek also had only a brief opportunity to fire. I climbed steeply and made a half split-S.

Then the Russian, who had flown a full circle, flew past beneath me. I dropped down behind him and reduced power, opened the radiator flaps slightly to act as brakes and ended up sitting behind the enemy at almost the same speed. But I opened fire too soon. I began blazing away from 200 meters. Naturally I hit nothing and the Russian was warned. He flew in such a way as to make accurate firing impossible. All I could do was spray bullets in his direction.

I saw hits flash now and then but the fellow in front of me seemed to pay them little attention. When I finally got into position 100 meters behind him all my weapons had jammed. There was nothing I could do but order Lt. Smiatek to move in. While he set about making things hot for the Russian I carried out a regular St. Vitus's dance in the air. I shook the machine back and forth, laid it on its back, stood it on its tail and twisted and turned until my efforts showed results. One of the machine-guns was working again.

In the meantime Smiatek had carried out a third attack. The Russian had slowed down and was leaving a faint trail of gray smoke. Then I was behind him again. This time I didn't fool around, instead I flew up behind him and opened fire. My speed was now matching his. I saw that I was scoring hits. Large pieces of his aircraft's skin whirled through the air but he simply refused to go down.

Before I noticed what was happening the fellow had throttled right back and I couldn't prevent myself from overtaking him; no amount of side-slipping and fish-tailing helped. I even found myself in front of his nose for a second in the narrow valley. Luckily the Russian wasn't thinking about firing and I breathed a sigh of relief.

I climbed while Smiatek made another pass and in no time I was on his tail again. Once again I opened fire with my single machine-gun.

I broke away and Smiatek prepared to attack again. Suddenly and without warning the Russian landed his aircraft in a field. Apparently he ran into an obstruction, because there was suddenly a large cloud of dust down below. When it settled there was nothing left of the Russian aircraft but wreckage. I looked at the clock: exactly 1500.

It was anything but an air victory. I felt sorry for the poor lad we had forced down in this fashion. I would dearly have loved not to report the kill at all, but the ground station had been monitoring our transmissions and knew that something must have happened in the air. With this ninth victory I met the conditions for the award of the Iron Cross, First Class.

At the same time they were looking for an experienced pilot to serve as a fighter instructor with the Rumanians. The choice fell on me and there was nothing else to do but prepare my few things for my departure for Tiraspol. Today I know that this transfer probably saved my life, because it was with the Rumanians that I learned to fly the Bf 109 properly and master it completely. When I returned to II Gruppe two months later it was no longer so easy for them to find fault with me.

Much had changed at Anapa in the meantime. The *Gruppe* had lost several more good pilots, including two *Staffelkapitäne*. I once again took over my beloved 6 *Staffel*. There was little flying, much like it was at the time I left for Tiraspol. The Russians were seen in the air only rarely.

We pilots took things easy. Every third day was a rest day due to a growing shortage of fuel. So we went hunting in the Caucasus, looked for parachutes, tortoises, snakes and doves or swam in the nearby lake. We were quite happy in Anapa.

There were cherries, apricots and peaches in abundance. However in the neighboring village of Gostagayevskaya there were no cherries. Based there was I./JG 52 and my friend Herbert Deinert. Once he asked me to come over and bring him some cherries. By a fortunate coincidence I received a new machine the next day. I asked Hptm. Kühle for permission to make one of the necessary test flights in this Me to Gostagayevskaya. My request was granted.

The whole affair wouldn't have been especially worthy of mention had it not resulted in a belly landing in the new 109. I stowed a large ammunition crate full of cherries in the baggage compartment and set out cheerfully across to Gosta. On my arrival I buzzed the "Picnic Ground"[4] so enthusiastically that the *Gruppenkommandeur*, *Major* Wiese, was close to having me court-martialed for this breach of Paragraph 92.

When I had roared over the field I began a risky steep turn prior to landing. Everything was going well and smoothly. Near the ground, however, I noticed that the machine was floating. Then the propeller blades began mowing the grass. At the same instant it was clear to me that I'd forgotten to lower the undercarriage.

To those who came hurrying over I explained that in spite of all my efforts the undercarriage refused to lower and I had thus been forced to decide on this belly landing. When asked why I hadn't flown back to my own base at Anapa and crash-landed there, I could only stammer that I was returning from a combat sortie and was low on fuel.

Fortunately no one discovered the cherries, otherwise I would have been in trouble. Later, when the crowd had dispersed, I lifted out my cargo and gave it to Herbert. I must have looked pretty silly, because Herbert laughed heartily.

I returned to Anapa by vehicle. Hptm. Kühle had already learned of the affair by telephone and ordered me to report. Under questioning and cautioned to tell the truth, I said: "*Herr Hauptmann*, I forgot to lower the undercarriage. The machine sustained 9% damage and can be repaired. Responsibility for the crash is mine alone."

Kühle looked at me for a second and then replied: "Let that serve as a warning to you! The matter is closed."

---

[4] Picnic Ground. Radio code word for airfield.

And truthfully these words had more effect than any punishment. From that time on I was never again found at fault in a crash.

Things went somewhat differently with my interrupted "ascension to heaven party." On the advice of Fw. Heino Sachsenberg, known as "*Wimmersal*," I had left 200 Marks in the mess cash box with instructions that it was to be used to buy drinks should I fail to return, so that my soul could arrive in fighter pilot heaven in style. Yes, traditions were so strong there! As Heino repeatedly let me know that I wouldn't be around much longer I increased the fund to 250 Marks just to spite him. In fact Heino could have been proved right had I not been unbelievably lucky once again.

During an air battle near Krimskaya an Airacobra succeeded in shooting me down for the first time. The Russian came at me from directly in front. I didn't like that much, because on the one hand the 109 was easily damaged there, and on the other because it was extremely uncomfortable to look into the enemy's flashing guns. This time there was no getting away as there were enemy aircraft behind me as well.

So I pressed all the triggers and fired everything I had. Just as we were about to collide the Russian suddenly pulled up. At the same instant there was a thump and oil covered my windscreen.

There were still enemy aircraft behind me. I rolled my aircraft onto its back and hauled back on the stick. It was a successful Split-S, but I had no idea where I was and in what direction I was flying. The compass had not yet settled down and I couldn't see the ground. If the Russians were still behind me then heaven wasn't far away. I opened a side window to get my bearings and saw by the tracer flying back and forth that I was over the front. I climbed to search for a field in which to land. I didn't have long to choose, as the windscreen was now completely obscured by a thick layer of oil, the entire crate stank and shook so badly that I could barely keep it under control. I therefore made short work of things and put my Messerschmitt down in a vineyard. It was belly landing number 3.

It was well that I was strapped in tightly, because the machine bucked and bounced as if it had gone wild. The wild ride finally ceased, but not before I had banged my head against the gunsight several times. I climbed out quickly and looked around. Was I really in German territory? Yes, I must be, at least according to the entries on the map.

Then half a dozen German soldiers came running and helped me extinguish the flames in the engine compartment.

With their help I removed my radio, dashboard clock and the battery. I clamped my parachute and the map under my arm and trotted with them in the direction of the nearest command post. I had to wait until evening for a vehicle to come and fetch me.

I walked into our mess at Anapa at about two in the morning. And now came the highlight! All of the *Staffel*'s pilots were there and under the leadership of Sachsenberg they were drinking to my hide. None of them could believe that I was back again. 150 of the 250 Marks had already been spent and I didn't want to be a killjoy. What was there left for me to do but make the best of a bad thing. So I celebrated with them till the early morning. Only instead of my "ascension to heaven" we celebrated my "salvation."

There was one other high point for me at Anapa. I was awarded both Iron Crosses, First and Second Class, on the same day. Once I had made a firm promise not to go on leave until I was wearing these decorations. Now that I had done it there was nothing holding me at the front and I prepared to go home. But first there was another session with the "beer bomb," and once again the instigator was Heino Sachsenberg.

The vast supply of champagne we had at Anapa finally ran out. We therefore tried to brew schnapps from the dregs of the wine with the help of our landlord, an old, experienced Russian. But the stuff was horrible, it smelled awful and burned terribly. When one of the pilots suffered a mild case of blindness we swore off the stuff, preferring to endure our thirst.

But in the long run such a thirst is also not a good condition, so Heino promised to provide relief. He had to go to Nikolayev and reported from there that he would be arriving in the afternoon and would bring sufficient quantities of beer with him. Naturally everyone assembled punctually at the command post. It wasn't long before the 109 came roaring toward the field. Under its belly was a huge bomb – or at least that's what it looked like.

We knew what it was, but we kept quiet and smiled knowingly. The laymen were astonished. Although he had to pull up and go around three times, and then just stopped the aircraft right at the end of the landing field, Sachsenberg in fact managed to land safely with the dangerous thing. We hurried over and were amazed that Heino had managed to do it. The beer keg, because that was what it was, had at most five centimeters ground clearance and occupied fully the narrow space between the undercarriage legs. Heino had taken off from Nikolayev with this keg and delivered it to Anapa without incident. It was a masterful feat and naturally he received a fitting amount of praise.

I now had 17 kills and thus was far ahead of Lt. Kurz, who had only nine at this time, and Heino Sachsenberg with seven kills. 167 combat missions and 17 kills; now I could allow myself to be seen at home. On July 26, 1943 I left the front for my first home leave. Mother was always fearful and more than anything she wanted me to stay home. But what mother didn't think exactly the same way.

The way to the front once again took me though Krakow. The forward directing center was located there, as was the delivery center for new aircraft, which was there for some time. Every pilot on his way to the front had to go through Krakow to find out where his unit was located.

I happily swung myself into a brand-new Bf 109 G-4 and easily covered the approximately 1,500 kilometers in two days in splendid weather. On August 29 I arrived back at Anapa. The place appeared dead, empty and strange, not at all as I expected.

A few days after my departure the *Gruppe* had transferred up into the central sector and all I found at Anapa was a small base party. The *Gruppe* was supposed to return soon and I was to stay in any case. But what was I supposed to do at Anapa without my comrades? Nothing could hold me back, not the vineyards and the magnificent sea, not the Caucasus and the outlook for a pleasant, lazy life.

The next day I climbed into my aircraft, which was equipped with an auxiliary fuel tank, and took off. I flew across the foul lake[5] up to Stalino. By this I mean that I didn't land at Stalino rather came down twice in the immediate vicinity of my destination. After taking off from Kerch I had climbed to 7,000 meters and flew above the clouds to Melitopol. There I refuelled, took off again and climbed up to the same altitude. I flew by dead-reckoning until I was over Stalino and descended through the thin layer of cloud. Before me lay an airfield. I landed and

[5] Foul lake. This term refers to the Sivash, a shallow body of water with numerous islands and lagoons, separating northern Crimea from the mainland.

cautiously asked a mechanic who came running up: "Is this Stalino airfield?"

But the mechanic laughed and informed me that I had landed about 20 kilometers away from the place I was seeking. "Well now," I thought to myself, "it can happen to you too." In any event I had my aircraft refuelled and checked. Then I took off again.

Once again I missed Stalino and landed at Makeyevka, four kilometers away, but in the end I managed to reach my destination.

There were many new faces in II./JG 52, and a considerable number of the old pilots were missing. The war was still claiming its victims. In the meantime my comrades had far surpassed my score. Lt. Günther Kurz now had more than 20 kills and Fw. Heino Sachsenberg 38. However Sachsenberg cracked up after his 38th due to mental stress. They had to put him in a straightjacket and send him home. He really had gone half mad.

At the time I could almost have laughed about it, until the same thing nearly happened to me. It just wasn't a game this combat flying.

I flew only one mission from Stalino and I could have come within a hair of getting lost on this flight too had not my wingman brought me back. Oh yes, there was that too! The next day we moved again, this time to Karlovka, southwest of Kharkov. Here there were a series of encounters with the enemy. Four sorties a day was normal.

My first victory while flying from Karlovka was a LaGG-5. Our *Staffelkapitän* at that time, Oblt. Heinz Schmidt, who had 175 kills, confirmed this kill. We had flown far behind the front in the direction of Akhtyrka. We saw no enemy aircraft while prowling around there. Not until we were over the front again did I see two LaGG-5s far below.

I waggled my wings briefly to alert my companion and dove, but Oblt. Schmidt failed to notice. But the Russians had spotted me and turned for their lives. I called my wingman and pointed out the enemy, after which Oblt. Schmidt joined the battle. Before he arrived I scored effective hits on one of the Russians. The LaGG trailed a visible banner of smoke.

Both of my opponents were excellent fliers. I had to manipulate the controls skillfully just to get into firing position. Just as Schmidt arrived on the scene I caught up with the Russian again in a turn. I pulled on the stick with all my strength, aimed well in front of his nose and let him wander through my stream of bullets. That did it. The LaGG went down in an ever-steepening dive and crashed into the ground. It was my eighteenth kill.

I cast a quick glance at the machine and then climbed up after the other enemy aircraft. Damn, could he turn! Finally I was sitting behind him. I turned so tightly that condensation trails formed behind both wingtips and my Me shuddered on the verge of a stall more than once. Fortunately the Messerschmitt I was flying turned extremely well.

The whole air battle took place at very low altitude. I sat behind the Russian like a shadow, and now and then I succeeded in hitting him. The enemy pilot climbed to about 400 meters in a turn and I dived briefly in order to catch him from behind.

He probably saw the danger and began a Split-S. In fact he succeeded in pulling out a few meters above the ground. I couldn't follow this maneuver as the Bf 109 required at least 700 meters of altitude for a Split-S.

Trailing a visible banner of smoke, the Russian climbed again and in doing so flew right in front of Oblt. Schmidt's guns. All he had to do was press the firing buttons. The enemy machine literally blew apart in the air.

One day Oblt. Schmidt failed to return from a sortie and in him II./ JG 52 lost one of its most outstanding fighter pilots. So once again I assumed command of 6 *Staffel*. Every leader of this *Staffel* I had known had one day failed to return: Hptm. Resch, Oblt. Denk, Ofw. Nemitz, Oblt. Ritzenberger and now Oblt. Schmidt. All of these men had been lost in the period from December 18, 1942 to September 10, 1943. If they had all been lost, what chance did I have of surviving this war?

Not much happened in the days from August 31 to September 10 while we were at Karlovka. I succeeded in scoring a total of three kills during 35 sorties in this time. This brought my total to 20 and I was recommended for the goblet instituted by Göring. (Lipfert never received the goblet.)

Our accommodations at Karlovka consisted of large tents. As a protective measure in the event of air attack we erected these over approximately two-meter-deep excavations. These quarters offered excellent protection against bomb splinters. The wisdom of our actions was soon confirmed. It was early in the morning and we were still lying in our "beds" when a hellish racket began. I am a cautious man and the sound of explosions and whistling bombs caused me to jump from my bunk onto the floor and crawl to the deepest hole. The other pilots did the same. Outside all hell seemed to have been let loose. One explosion followed another and machine-gun bullets pierced the roof of our tent and smacked into the side walls. The bombing ended after a short time but the shouting continued.

I stuck my head through the wall of the tent during a lull in the firing and with one look spotted about 20 Russian aircraft circling our airfield. They were just preparing to dive on our dispersal. Four machines raced toward our tent. I quickly let myself fall back inside so as to take cover with the others before they began firing. This was repeated several times and the Russians chased us around the tent from one wall of the pit to another for a good five minutes. They apparently had fun doing it and were able to go about their work peacefully as we had no anti-aircraft guns which might have been able to change their minds.

After the Russians had finally left we were filled with a mighty hatred and everyone hoped to be able to pay them back soon. But it was some time before our chance came.

Just as the difficulties on takeoff and landing and the factory on the approach to Rostov-North had once brought me to the verge of desperation, here it was problems finding the airfield which gave me considerable difficulty. I was so unsure in the air that I stayed aloft only three-quarters of an hours so as to have the last fifteen minutes to find the airfield. In the Crimea and at Anapa it was not difficult to find one's way back to the "Picnic Ground." One had only to fly south to reach the sea. But here, where the terrain looked the same over wide areas, I often had great difficulty finding my way back.

So I was happy when we transferred to Poltava on September 11. The city had a fine, large airfield. Unfortunately autumn set in with a rainy period of unsuspected heaviness and duration, so that we were scarcely able to get out onto the field due to the mud and filth. Only tracked vehicles could move on the airfield, everything else got stuck. As a result the pilots often arrived late, if at all, and our flying activities were thrown into confusion as a result.

For this reason we left our houses and once again pitched tents at the edge of the landing field. But in spite of the double tents and continuous bailing everything was wet the next morning. None of the pilots had a single dry piece of clothing. We had to fly wearing damp things.

Naturally under these conditions I flew few combat missions from Poltava, but there is one I still remember today. It took me up to the northwest, far beyond Lebedin, where the *Gruppe* had once been based but which now was occupied by the enemy. On the return flight my wingman and I went as high as the cloud cover allowed and flew leisurely along the railway line in the direction of Poltava.

About 50 kilometers from base my wingman reported: "*Herr Leutnant*, you're leaving a black smoke trail!"

One look at the instrument panel was enough for me to realize that the temperature was a little too high, even though the radiator flaps were fully open. Initially I placed the blame on mud which had probably been sprayed into the radiators on takeoff. But I became suspicious when the temperature continued to climb slowly, especially as the smoke trail became heavier.

Something unpleasant was definitely in store. It was fortunate that we were at 4,000 meters. If the motor held out a little longer I should be able to make the remaining 40 kilometers. As a precaution I switched off the ignition, set the propeller pitch to the gliding position to reduce drag and sailed on with 20 degrees of flap and the engine off. Sure enough, the temperature slowly dropped. Of course I steadily lost altitude as I had to put the aircraft's nose down in order to maintain flying speed.

At 2,000 meters the temperature had returned to normal. I switched on the ignition again, changed the propeller pitch and let the slipstream turn the blades. The motor immediately sprang to life, although it ran somewhat less smoothly than before.

While I retracted the landing flaps I implored the engine to hold out a little longer, as I couldn't be too far from our airfield. By the time I reached 3,000 meters the smoke trail behind me had intensified. The engine rattled and shook. I detected the familiar smell of burning in the cockpit. There was nothing left to do but switch off the ignition so as to prevent the crate from catching fire.

So I wobbled along the railway line, my left wheel over the right track. I was down to 500 meters when I finally saw Poltava ahead. I switched on the engine again and climbed to 900 meters. Then there was a loud bang and the propeller blades froze. Seized piston!

In an instant oil was running into the cockpit and over my legs, which I withdrew quickly to avoid being burned. The windscreen was almost completely opaque. Forward visibility was almost zero, nevertheless I wanted to try to land on the airfield. The machine went lower and lower. Quickly I lowered the undercarriage and wobbled along only a few meters above the houses.

Finally, just as I was about to stall, I managed to put my crate down, oblivious to the landing direction or activity at the airfield. Fortunately the landing field was clear and there was no danger of ramming another aircraft. I climbed out with shaking knees and inspected the damage. As I suspected, it had been a piston seizure with the subsequent failure of the camshaft. Although the engine was a write-off, I had managed to save the aircraft.

On September 18 we transferred to the beautiful city of Kiev on the Dniepr and for the first time in a long while took up quarters in a barracks. From the beginning Kiev, the city and the airfield, was very sympathetic to me. Flying from there I scored five kills in ten days.

There was contact with the enemy right from the beginning. On the first day my G-6 sustained 23 flak hits and had to spend several days in the repair shops. It came out again on the 21st and I carried out a test flight the same morning. I was scarcely off the ground when I heard over the radio: "To all cyclists (German fighters)! Air battle with many Indians over xyz at '*Hanni*'[6] 3000!"

Quickly I orientated myself. Then I shoved the throttle forward all the way and roared toward the scene of the combat as fast as my 1,800 H.P. could take me. Moments later came the report: "Indians flying away to the northwest. Air battle ended!"

Disappointed, I turned around and flew back in the direction of Kiev. On the way I climbed to 5,000 meters for orientation by major landmarks. As I flew along I spotted a single dark dot far to the northwest about 1,000 meters lower. At once my suspicion was aroused. It could only be an aircraft, perhaps even a Russian one.

I instinctively opened the throttle and closed quickly with the other aircraft, which appeared to be practicing aerobatics. As I could not yet make out the type, as a precaution I enquired over the radio: "Any Cyclists over Koseletz at *Hanni* 4,000?"

[6] *Hanni*. Radio code word for altitude. *Hanni* 2,000 means altitude 2,000 meters.

No one answered and I repeated my question. Again there was no reply. So I positioned myself in the sun and observed. Then I saw the Soviet star.

This time I was going to wait until I was in the most favorable position. I wanted to make only one attack and it had to be on the mark. While the Russian continued to cavort lustily 1,000 meters below me, I transmitted a report: "To all Cyclists. A single Indian over Koseletz in quadrant xyz, *Hanni* 4,000. Apparently engaged in aerobatics training."

"Cyclist from five one. *Viktor*, *Viktor*! I'm coming, am in your vicinity. I can see you."

I responded: "Attention, I am attacking. Please stay on the alert! I am on a test flight and have no wingman."

I now opened the radiator flaps halfway, placed my Me on its nose and let it dive. I pulled up about 500 meters below the Russian at more than 600 kilometers per hour and came up behind the unsuspecting enemy just as he began an Immelmann. When he levelled off I was right behind him. I forced myself to wait a second and opened fire when I couldn't miss.

Almost all my rounds smashed into the wings and fuselage of the enemy aircraft with immediate effect.

There were several flashes and large pieces flew off the Yak. Dense black smoke poured out of the fuselage. At the same time flames spurted out and I ceased firing and climbed up to one side. The Russian aircraft spun toward the earth like a blazing torch.

Then I heard the voice of Lt. Petermann: "Five one here. Terrific kill. I congratulate you!"

That was victory number 21 and the next was soon to follow. Together with my wingman, *Gefreiter* Wüst of 4 *Staffel*, I flew off to seek enemy aircraft reported by another pilot. However we were unable to find any sign of an air battle. After a long search I finally saw a Bf 109 beneath me. It was chasing a lone machine and turning with it, without being able to pose a serious threat however. This Russian had to be an outstanding pilot, because he handled his aircraft magnificently. The Messerschmitt behind him was unable to do much, no matter how much he "flew around the corners."

I wanted to try my luck and ordered my wingman to remain above and make sure that no other enemy aircraft could sneak up behind me.

The two machines below me continued the chase.

Once again I dove below the enemy aircraft and approached from below. When the Russian straightened out his machine I pressed the triggers. While firing I saw the huge radiator of the machine in front of me and recognized it as a fighter of American origin, a Curtiss P-40.

After a few hits it rolled onto its back and dove toward the earth in that attitude at an angle of 45 degrees. The aircraft made no move to pull out and a huge fire marked the spot where it struck the ground. It later turned out that it had been Uffz. Hoffmann who had driven this kill in my direction.

My 23rd kill was achieved without a shot being fired. Once again I was flying with Lt. Günther Kurz. We had spotted several LaGG-5s and were trying to approach them. They saw through our intentions, however, and tried to escape to the northwest. We rapidly closed the range and Günther opened fire from 400 meters, causing the Russians to continually change positions. Before we were within proper firing distance two of the LaGGs separated from the other, one to the left and one to the right. Günther immediately set out after the left one. I pulled up, turned as tightly as possible and let myself drop down behind the other one. The latter turned so tightly, however, that I was unable to fire. I was about 100 meters behind him and could clearly see the pilot looking around for me.

The two Russians completed their 360 degree turns and arrived back at their starting point. Since both were looking for their pursuers, they forgot about each other and collided wing to wing. Both machines spun away "with their ears pinned back."

On September 30, 6 *Staffel* transferred to Usin, southeast of Kiev. The airfield was excellent for takeoffs and landings but brought the *Staffel* no success whatsoever. One day Lt. Kurz failed to return from a sortie from Usin. His wingman told us that Kurz had been shot down by a LaGG-5. He went down vertically from an altitude of 3,000 meters. The engine of his machine buried itself five meters deep in the ground. The loss of my friend was a shock from which I recovered only slowly. Günther's fate was still bothering me when we transferred to Novo-Zaphorozhye. I had lost some of my confidence and in spite of daily contact with the enemy was able to achieve little success.

All hell had broken loose in this area along the Dniepr. Even if one climbed to 6,000 meters he could be certain that he would be jumped by the Russians from an even higher altitude. One of our pilots in particular distinguished himself here – Lt. Obleser of III *Gruppe*. Every day he shot down two enemy aircraft. He had a special tactic. He climbed up to 7,000 meters and waited until he saw Russians beneath him. Then he came from above like greased lightning, shot down one of the enemy and then climbed back up to a safe position using his great speed.

I tried to emulate this tactic, but I couldn't seem to get the hang of it. With so much speed I couldn't fire accurately enough to knock down the enemy aircraft. I was more of a close-in fighter. For this reason the Russian pilots, who flew very well here, usually picked on me. They were never able to shoot me down, however, as I was always able to escape at the critical moment. I was thus relieved when 6 *Staffel* was moved back to Kerch. There we were to support I *Gruppe*, which had three *Staffeln* in action.

October 8, 1943. It was five in the morning and the sun was not up yet, but we were already on our feet, tending to our machines with the mechanics. The three *Staffeln* of I./JG 52 were also up and about. As the Russians made the air unsafe from morning to evening here, we had to try to have all available aircraft ready to take off. The *Staffeln* of I *Gruppe* had a somewhat easier time of it, as they had all their technical personnel with them. We, on the other hand, had brought only a third of ours with us, and the majority of our people were forced to stay behind at Novo-Zaphorozhye due to a shortage of transport capacity. As a result each pilot helped service his own machine.

On this day we were supposed to fly in *Rotte* strength only, and I had assigned my eight pilots accordingly. I wanted to take off with *Gefreiter* Dinius and the first *Rotte* as soon as the fog lifted a little. I called Dinius to me and briefed him on the situation. Once again I went over his duties with him. Dinius was a young pilot with almost no front-line experience. For this reason I had him fly with me.

In the middle of our discussion came a report that large numbers of Russian aircraft were approaching Kerch. Everyone raced to the aircraft. The mechanics turned the starter cranks while the pilots strapped themselves in, and the inertia starters sang their familiar song. Quickly I checked my seat parachute, put my helmet on and plugged in the radio lead. Then I switched on the ignition, operated the hand pump and pulled the starter handle. The engine started immediately. A few seconds to warm up and we could go.

I looked over at Dinius and raised my hand. He returned the signal. We were ready to take off. In the meantime radio reports on the enemy aircraft continued to come in. I signalled to Dinius that we were to take off together. He acknowledged. I opened the throttle and began to roll. Both aircraft lifted off simultaneously.

Dinius was in position at once, and we established radio contact while raising the undercarriage and switching the radiator flap controls to automatic. As soon as I made the first turn I could see that Dinius was on the ball. I could risk taking him into a scrap. We headed out across the Straits of Kerch – the narrows linking the Sea of Azov and the Black Sea – and soon we were approaching land – Taman – again.

Visibility was poor. I had just passed 1,000 meters on the altimeter when another report came in: "Many light Furniture Vans[7] and Indians over Taman at *Hanni* 200!"

I levelled off and looked around, especially behind and above, to ensure that our tails were clear, and then began scanning the area while circling. Nothing! Once again the Russians were reported over Taman. What the devil was going on! I cursed loudly but it did no good – the Russians remained invisible.

"Dinius, we're going lower," I called to my wingman. Dinius held position well and repeatedly reassured me that he was with me.

The shoreline of the peninsula came toward us rapidly. I dove steeply in order to build up as much speed as possible, so as to be able to regain altitude quickly should there be trouble brewing. Soon I was at ground level, roaring along just above the terrain at 600 kilometers per hour. I opened the throttle to maintain speed and scanned the airspace above me, as there were unlikely to be any Russians below. Finally I spotted a machine to my right and about 200 meters higher. It had just dropped its bombs. The heavy German anti-aircraft fire seemed not to bother it.

Hunting fever seized me. With a glance I checked weapons and gunsight and shouted over the radio: "Dinius, do you see the stinker?

[7] Furniture Van (*Möbelwagen*). Supposed to indicate friendly twin-engined aircraft, but in this case apparently refers to enemy bombers.

Fire at him when I pull away no matter what! It doesn't matter who shoots him down as long as he goes down!"

The enemy aircraft grew surprisingly quickly and then I noticed that he was coming straight toward me. No, I couldn't let him fly past my nose, because with his heavy weapons he was more dangerous to me than I to him. I quickly dived to ground level again. He failed to notice me and I let him fly overhead to the side. Then I hauled back on the stick and climbed without losing sight of him. Now I was above him, but I noticed that we were no longer alone. The airspace around us was swarming with aircraft: we two, somewhat lower the lone Il-2, and 200 meters lower an entire Il-2 unit.

It was noteworthy that the other Il-2s had a brown, green or dark camouflage finish. Only the one with which I was closing rapidly was white. Apparently it was the unit leader's aircraft, which excited me greatly. Before I attacked I took one more look behind and above. Dinius was still with me.

When I dived on the Il-2 it commenced a gentle turn to the left. I hauled the nose of the Me around and searched for the firing button with my thumb. The enemy aircraft grew in my reflector sight. The rear gunner must have spotted me long ago, but he didn't fire. I hesitated a moment then fired all weapons. The cannon and both machine-guns spat fire and the smell of powder filled the cockpit.

My first shots passed to the right of the Il-2. I corrected. There were flashes all over the aircraft and its wings and fuselage began to smoke. Large pieces separated and flew past me. All the while I continued to pour fire into the aircraft, which stubbornly continued flying straight ahead. The first flames were already visible when the Russian finally tried to dive away. My speed was too great to stay with him. "Dinius," I roared, "shoot!" As I pulled up I laid my Messerschmitt almost on its back and saw the *Gefreiter* sitting behind the Il-2 raking it with fire. Then he was within ramming distance and had to break away. While Dinius raced upward past me I cast a quick look around. Above us were a large number of enemy machines which fortunately took no notice of us. I dove again and came down on the Il-2, which was burning slightly and trailing a long banner of smoke. The enemy aircraft was steadily losing altitude.

I opened fire again. The Il-2 nosed over and dove steeply into a pool.

There was a huge splash. Then I saw pieces of the aircraft sticking out of the water.

I heard Dinius shout "*Abschuss*," but I stayed quiet. The thought that one of the Russians flying around a few hundred meters above could still dive on us was unsympathetic to me. I dove down to ground level again and Dinius and I raced at maximum speed northwest toward the foul lake. Dinius flew quite close beside me. I saw his beaming face and realized that in spite of the low altitude he let go of the control column in order to wave to me with both hands. "I congratulate you on your 30th victory," he called.

We reached our airfield quickly, dove toward 6 *Staffel*'s tent and waggled. Mechanics and pilots came running toward us as we taxied in. 6 *Staffel* had scored the day's first kill.

We weren't on the ground long when an aircraft of 3 *Staffel* arrived. It waggled its wings too. One after another the remaining Messerschmitts began returning, but none of them came home with any kills.

I took off four times that day and scored five kills, the highest total I ever achieved in one day. Now I had a name, I had become Lipfert the fighter pilot.

Unfortunately our stay in the Crimea was again a short one. The next day we transferred back to Novo-Zaphorozhye and from there to Beresovka. I began well there, scoring a double on October 10. Then began a period when we flew Stuka escort missions almost exclusively. We were all less than enthusiastic about this. I scored four more kills, which brought my total to 40, when we were transferred once again, to Fedorovka in the Ukraine. Two of these last four kills are worthy of mention, because in both cases I ran into pilots who knew how to protect their skins and who gave me a good fight. In neither encounter was the outcome a foregone conclusion.

As was so often the case, on October 21 I led the early morning weather reconnaissance flight. I had assigned several pilots for the first takeoff the night before, but when I saw them sleeping peacefully in their beds the next morning I couldn't bring myself to wake them both. Instead I took just one, *Oberfähnrich* Thomas.

The weather was rather poor – cloud cover down to 300 meters. At the front it was no better. Climbing on top was certainly futile, as the clouds had to be at least 4,000 meters thick. So the two of us prowled about rather aimlessly at low altitude near the front. We flew here and there until finally that became too boring. If we wanted to find a Russian we'd definitely have to look in Russian territory. So over we went.

Still on the German side, we climbed up to just beneath the clouds and then dove across the front at high speed. For about ten minutes we patrolled parallel to the front three kilometers deep in Russian territory. Then it seemed to me as if two shadows were coming toward us from the east. It had to be two enemy aircraft, because only Russians could romp about so lustily in the air. We maintained heading, flying almost "under the sod" until both aircraft were over German territory.

It was two Yaks. Their pilots either didn't know that they were flying beyond their own lines or were "experts" who felt very sure of themselves. Both machines continued steaming south, "direction Germany."

Then we tried our first attack. They must have seen us as they began turning. Nevertheless, with my greater speed I got behind the Russian wingman. When I opened fire all three weapons failed. Lucky for the Ivan! I couldn't get Thomas to fire at the enemy machines, perhaps he didn't understood my transmissions.

The other Russian had turned around and now sat behind us, but still too far back to shoot. The battle started at an altitude of 300 meters. The Russians could fly, I noted that right away. While we continued to chase the second, the first drew ever closer. The situation was not without danger to us. I cocked the guns again and shook my machine about. Then the Russian in front of me was in my gunsight again. Once again the guns refused to fire. Damn! What bad luck!

I roared at Thomas to stay behind the enemy and if possible shoot him down. Then I pulled out of the turn toward the south. The other Russian stayed behind my wingman. When he had passed behind me I pulled up and climbed in a tight spiral to just beneath the clouds. Skirting the bottoms of the clouds I approached again. Even if my weapons failed to fire again, I wanted to at least be present if my wingman scored a kill or to help him if necessary. And damned soon that seemed to be the case.

The trailing Russian drew ever closer to Thomas' aircraft. I had to try and force him away before he opened fire. I dropped down and came so near to the enemy aircraft that I could clearly see the pilot turning in his seat. When he saw me he was so terrified that he abruptly rolled his

Yak onto its back and began a Split-S from an impossibly low altitude. The Russian pilot must have realized that his situation was impossible.

He tried desperately to recover, but the earth was coming up too fast. Leaving behind a dense vapor trail, the Russian raced earthward. He might even have pulled off the maneuver had it not been for a small hill. I hadn't followed the Russian, but simply flew a descending turn and watched as he hit the ground, skidded about 50 meters and finally smashed into a farm cottage.

As I pulled up I saw flames shoot up from the collapsing hut and then race back along the path the aircraft had followed over the ground. Both the hut and the ruts left by the crashing aircraft were ablaze. Apparently the Russian's fuel tank had burst when his aircraft struck the ground. When the machine exploded in the cottage the fuel caught fire.

In the meantime Thomas had rejoined me. We circled twice over the fire. Then we flew back to base as there was no sign of the other Russian.

Early in the afternoon Thomas and I took off again. This time were in a *Schwarm*, or a four-aircraft formation. A *Rotte* from 4 *Staffel* accompanied us. Soon after takeoff we became engaged in a tough battle with six LaGG-5s. We had not encountered this type often, and the fellows with the radial engines were not too sympathetic to us. Ten aircraft twisted and turned. In an instant our *Schwarm* had split up. Each man had to fight for himself and accordingly had to watch out for himself as well.

Thomas flew around among the Russians like a wild man. He fired from the most impossible positions, and I couldn't help thinking that he was pressing the firing buttons to give himself courage. There were other, experienced fighter pilots who had done the same thing.

In the meantime a Russian flew right in front of me, range about 50 meters. I pressed the triggers and to my dismay my guns failed to fire for a third time. The first thing I did was make a fast Split-S and dive for home as fast as I could go. I checked the weapons once again. I could scarcely believe it! I had forgotten to switch on the weapons!

At that instant a regular hail of tracer flashed past my cockpit. I stepped on the rudder pedal with my left foot and hauled the machine around. A LaGG-5 raced past my tail with all guns firing. It had followed and overtaken me, and had he not given himself away by opening fire too soon, this would certainly have been my last flight. But now, furious at myself and the Ivan, I turned back and set out after him.

At first the Russian flew west in a straight line, but he soon noticed that I was closing on him. He turned and I followed every movement. The enemy pilot was unable to shake me off and I got behind him, but held my fire at first. I wanted to have him for sure. Realizing his dangerous situation, the Russian began a Split-S from only 500 meters, which he pulled off successfully. I followed immediately, but could not prevent him from increasing the distance between us. Flying close to the ground, he raced back in the direction from which we had just come, with me behind him.

Then suddenly he pulled up and was again in the middle of the dogfight between the other Russians and my comrades. I tried to stay with him. In desperation the enemy pilot stood his aircraft on its tail in an effort to escape into the clouds. He was several meters into the safe grayness when his aircraft stalled and he dropped back out of the cloud. This maneuver allowed me to get into firing position. He had just recovered and was heading for the clouds again when I opened fire from point-blank range.

After only a few shots he blew apart in a tremendous flash of flame. Wreckage sailed through the air and spun toward the earth.

I heard several voices: "*Abschuss*!" "Congratulations on your kill!"

The other Russians suddenly disappeared as if a broom had swept them from the sky. We saw none of them again.

# CHAPTER IV
# On the Black Sea

Once again 6 *Staffel* was transferred. After Novo-Zaphorozhye and Fedorovka we moved to the airfield at Askania-Nova. But the Russians were soon pressing there too, and finally we ended up in the fighter pilot's paradise of the Crimea. The entire *Gruppe*, 32 machines, landed safe and sound at Bagerovo, near Kerch. As a good omen I brought my 44th kill with me, having shot it down during the transfer flight. The move to Bagerovo marked the beginning of a very successful period for me. During the five months we spent in the Kerch area I shot down 46 enemy aircraft.

As before, I was almost always the first one in the air each morning. Perhaps there were also such people among the Russians, because often when we had been at a base for some time and I ran into an enemy aircraft while on weather reconnaissance, the way he flew looked familiar.

When such an opportunity failed to result in a kill because the enemy spotted me in time, there was scarcely any point in turning with him. The other side's weather reconnaissance pilots flew at least as well as we. Several times I attempted to dogfight them. I would send my wingman to altitude and order him to keep a watchful eye from there. Sometimes the Russian did the same. The result of this was that both wingman stayed above without attacking, circling peacefully while a life and death battle raged below. Each man tried every conceivable trick to get the other in front of his guns, but always without success.

Russians who allowed themselves to get involved in such experiments were experts and handled their machines magnificently. The only result of such a forty-five minute air battle was both pilots flying home at the end with shaking knees and sweat-soaked clothing. The claim that the Russians were poor flyers is false. I can only repeat that the beginners among the German fighter pilots were just as awkward in the air as the Russian beginners.

On December 5, 1943, the young *Feldwebel* Manfred Stolpe accompanied me on a weather reconnaissance sortie. Takeoff was at 0710. The command post reported two "Indians" east of Kerch at 2,000 meters. Instead of flying east right away, I headed west to gain some altitude. When we had reached the 2,500 meter mark, we took up position just below the clouds and turned east toward the enemy.

The Russians were supposed to be over the Straits of Kerch, so we entered the clouds over Kerch. This was of course a dangerous move, because my wingman and I had to fly wingtip to wingtip in order to stay in visual contact. These clouds were more like a high mist, however, and allowed us to fly in close formation. But we didn't stay long in the dense grayness and soon dropped out of the bottom.

At first I saw nothing, even though I turned and twisted around in my seat, but when I placed the aircraft on its back I saw two Russians flying directly beneath us on the same heading. Still inverted, I closed the throttle, opened the radiator flaps and waited until the two appeared in front of my nose. Then Stolpe and I dove steeply and approached the two unsuspecting Russians from behind. Before either of them realized what was happening the element leader had already lost his left wing. I had aimed so well from close range that there was no escape for him. His wingman circled around the spinning aircraft as it went down. He still hadn't caught on to what was going on.

I closed to point-blank range again and fired at the second enemy aircraft until its right wing suddenly broke away. The element leader hadn't yet reached the surface of the water when his wingman plunged after him. Neither pilot was able to take to his parachute. The other two kills I scored on December 5, 1943 were not so easy. Both were Il-2s which I shot down from a large formation. On this occasion I flew with *Gefreiter* Ewald for the first time. It was my 347th combat mission.

I took off from Bagerovo at 1023 with Ewald, a young daredevil who was to be promoted to *Leutnant* and win the Knight's Cross in a very short time. It was my second sortie that day. As we were on a *freie Jagd* sortie, we flew down to Eltigen, south of Kerch, and romped about happily in a blue, cloudless sky at an altitude of 5,000 meters. I was just telling Esau – that was what we called *Gefreiter* Ewald – about my last air combat. All the while I kept a sharp eye on the Russian bridgehead at Eltigen. If the Russians came, it would probably be from that direction.

My hunch did not disappoint me. We spotted them climbing far below us, swarms of Il-2s, LaGGs, Yaks and Airacobras.

"Come on," I called to Ewald, "we're going to have a closer look at this bunch!" Then we put the noses of our aircraft down. While diving I began transmitting running reports to our aircraft. "To all Cyclists, to all Cyclists! Many Furniture Vans and Indians over the Strait of Kerch at *Hanni* 1500 to 2000, heading west."

I intended to allow the Russians to fly a little farther into German territory before attacking. Meanwhile the first of our comrades arrived and began a dogfight with the highest swarms of enemy aircraft. Then I saw the first burning aircraft and a parachute in the sky. Unfortunately the Russians had now been warned, and my first attack was foiled. The Russian I had selected spotted me in time, swung around and at the same time climbed steeply.

I didn't bother with him any further, because Ewald was sitting behind him. It was his job to watch the Russian, who was now above us. The next enemy aircraft I selected also saw me coming. He turned away so sharply that no matter how hard I pulled on the stick I couldn't get him in my sights. And then we were in the midst of the swarm. There were so many machines around us that being rammed seemed likely. Everyone fired at everyone else and tracer flitted everywhere.

Getting down to the Il-2s was quite impossible. I still had plenty of speed and climbed back up in order to try and hold the fighters in check and perhaps separate them from the bombers. If the Il-2s then flew on alone it shouldn't be too difficult to shoot down several. I therefore left the melee and climbed.

But in the meantime two Russians were sitting behind us and firing, although they were still too far away to possibly hit us. Nevertheless they forced us to turn. More Russian fighters joined the first two, and as they came from above and had more speed, they closed rapidly. Finally we had no other choice but to pull the stick back, tramp on the left rudder pedal and spin away.

I gave Ewald a quick briefing and outlined my intentions. Ewald stayed with me. Once again we dropped through the beehive, rolling as we dived until we were at ground level. Then we pulled out and climbed toward the north. It was my intention to dive into the swarm again once we had built up enough speed. We didn't dare make an attack from below. I might have tried it had I been alone, but I was responsible for my wingman and couldn't risk his life.

During my second approach I could see that the Russian bombers had failed to reach their target. They turned around and dropped their bombs in the water before reaching land and the German lines. That didn't happen very often. Usually these Il-2s flew on to their assigned target and dropped their bombs even if the aircraft were already on fire. But this time I saw the last bombs exploding in the water before the machines disappeared at low altitude. There was no sense whatsoever in chasing them.

The Russian fighters were unable to disengage, however. They had to keep turning to avoid being attacked and shot down from above. I approached at full throttle. Another one fell burning from the sky and from the cry of "*Abschuss*!" I could tell it was an enemy aircraft. Then I dove through the swarm, pulled up far below and climbed toward the combatants at a speed of probably 700 kph.

Apparently the Russian I was attacking was looking only above. He didn't notice me at all as I roared toward him. Unfortunately I repeated the typical beginner's mistake and opened fire from 250 meters. I scored a few hits but nothing serious. The Russian hauled his machine around and I roared past him.

I immediately turned my attention to the next one. He came down from above and immediately began to fire. It was an aircraft with a radial engine. I ducked and pushed the nose down, so that the bursts meant for me passed over the canopy. Then I was on the third one, who was climbing eastward trailing a banner of black smoke. With my great speed I closed on him rapidly. Just as I was preparing to fire the enemy pilot looked around. He went into a tight turn, vapor trails streaming from both wingtips. This fellow was an experienced pilot.

*Lt. Lipfert in the cockpit of his Bf 109 preparing to take off on a sortie in early 1943.*

*Lt. Sturm and Lt. Lipfert in the Crimea. Sturm, Kapitän of 5./JG 52, was killed on 22.12.1944 when his Bf 109 collided with a truck while taking off from Csor, Hungary.*

6./J.G. 52. 31.1.1943

Abschussmeldung

30.1.1943 12.47 Uhr.

1 km N Malaya-Balabinka Pl.Qu. o8 693

1200 m

1. Lt. Lipfert

Lagg-5

U.d.S.S.R.

Sowjetstern

senkrechter Absturz

Aufschlagbrand

jenseits d. Front

senkrecht Aufschlagbrand

Hptm. Resch 6./J.G.52

--

1

in Linkskurve

200 m

aus der Überhöhung

--

Pz.,Pzspr.,Pzbr.,Brdspr.,S.m.K.,P.m.K.,B.-Mun.

1oo Schuß M.G.151/2o, 8o Schuß M.G.17

3 M.G.151/2o, 2 M.G.17

BF 1o9 G-2 mit 3 M.G.151/2o u. 2 M.G.17

--

--

--

Hauptmann und Staffelkapitän

*Victory number one. After two months in action with 6./JG 52, Helmut Lipfert scored his first kill on his 18th combat mission. Staffelkapitän Hptm. Resch witnessed the victory.*

*On March 11, 1943, Ofw. Willi Nemitz, Staffelkapitän of 6./JG 52 and at 32 years of age one of the oldest fighter pilots on active duty, received the Knight's Cross following his 81st victory. Only one month later Nemitz was shot down and killed near Anapa. With his death II./JG 52 lost one of its outstanding pilots.*

*Lt. Walter Krupinski with 6./JG 52. Krupinski went on to command II./JG 11 and III./JG 26, and ended the war with JV 44 with a total of 197 kills.*

*Lt. Krupinski's "Yellow 5," photographed in summer 1942.*

*Oblt. Barkhorn, leader of 4./JG 52, and Lt. Schmidt (in white sheepskin jacket) on the snow-covered airfield at Slavyanskaya, March 1943.*

*Three pilots of 6./JG 52 — three fates. From left to right: Lt. Klassen (KIA 22.4.1944), Lt. Kurz (KIA 11.10.1943 after shooting down a LaGG-5), Ofhr. Mohr (KIA 11.4.1944). The photo was taken at Anapa in the Caucasus in May 1943.*

*Lt. Nikolaus Jeschonnek was the nephew of the Luftwaffe Chief of Staff of the same name. He was killed during an air raid on Anapa on 5.8.1943.*

*A Russian Yak-7 which was forced to land by 6 Staffel. Crimea 1943.*

*Ofw. Sachsenberg was able to force another Yak-7 to land at Bagerovo. Afterward he and his mechanic posed for a photograph in front of the unique trophy.*

*Three photos of Taman airfield, situated on the Black Sea, which served as 6./JG 52's base of operations in the spring and summer of 1943.*

*Top: 6 Staffel's "command post." Center: Staffelkapitän Oblt. Ritzenberger, killed in air combat over the Black Sea on 24.5.1943. Bottom: The wooded hills in the hinterland.*

*The Ilyushin Il-2 armored close-support aircraft. This type was well known — and feared — on the Eastern Front as a robust and dangerous opponent. 40 of Helmut Lipfert's 203 kills were Il-2s.*

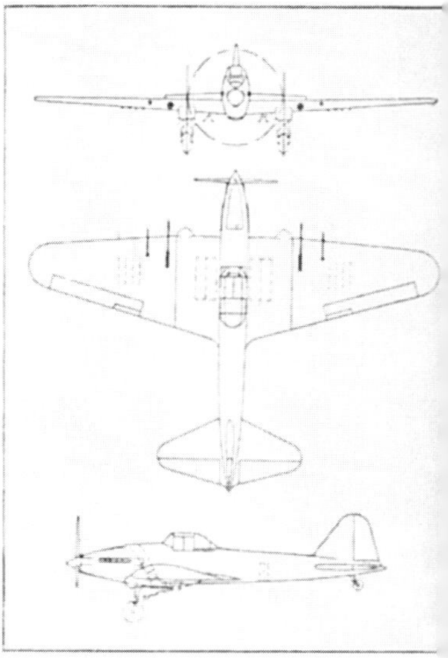

*Mechanics work on the engine of "Yellow 10," a Bf 109 G-2. Summer 1943.*

*Another lucky escape. Flak damage to Helmut Lipfert's Bf 109 G-6.*

*Anapa, summer 1943. From left to right: Fw. Pilz, Oak Leaves wearer Hptm. Schmidt, Lt. Jeschonnek, Fw. Sachsenberg, Fw. Waldmann, Uffz. Otten.*

*Hptm. Schmidt, Ritzenberger's successor as Kapitän of 6./JG 52. Schmidt went missing in action near Markor on 5.9.1943 while flying his Bf 109 G-6 "Yellow 7." His score at the time of his death stood at 173. It was assumed that Schmidt was shot down in error by a Hungarian fighter. The photo shows Schmidt as a Leutnant.*

**Entwurf** f 13. Abrd. d. Staffel,

6./J.G. 52. 3.5.1944

Abschussmeldung XXXXXXXXXXXXXXXXXXXXXXX

11.4.1944

15 km NW Dshankoj, Pl.-Qu. 46 181, 9,25

Bodennähe

100. Lt. Helmut Lipfert

IL-2 m.H.

U.d.S.S.R.

Sowjet-Stern

Einzelteile weggeflogen, brennend in der Luft

Einzelteile weggeflogen.

Aufschlagbrand

diesseits der Front

Aufschlagbrand steiler Winkel

tot.

Uffz. Heinz Krah, 6./J.G.52

\- - -

1

von hinten oben

6o-4o m

Überhöhung

nicht beobachtet

Pzspr., Pzbrd., Brdspr., M.-Mun., Pzgr., Brdsprgr.

25 Schuß M.G.151/20 und 7o Schuß M.G.131

1 M.G.151/2o und 2 M.G.131

Bf 1o9 G-6 mit 1 M.G.151/2o und 2 M.G.131

\- - -

\- - -

\- - -

Lipfert

Oblt. und Staffelkapitän

*Lipfert's 100th victory, this time an Il-2. The cooling system of Lipfert's aircraft was damaged in the combat and he had to make a forced-landing near Karankut in his "Yellow 1."*

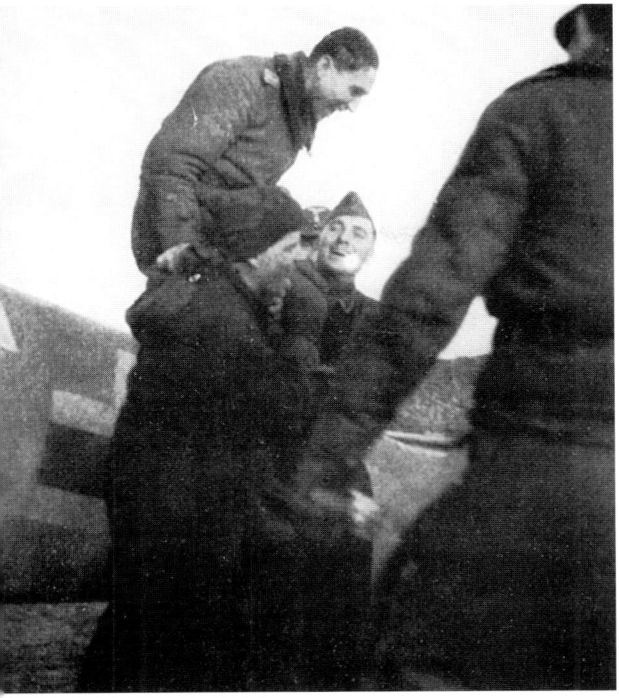

*Now the Knight's Cross is due. Lt. Lipfert at Bagerovo airfield on December 11, 1943 following his 75 kill, a Yak-7. The victory was witnessed by Uffz. Fritz Haas of 5 Staffel.*

*Confirmation of Lipfert's 100th victory. The kill was also the 713th for JG 52's II Gruppe.*

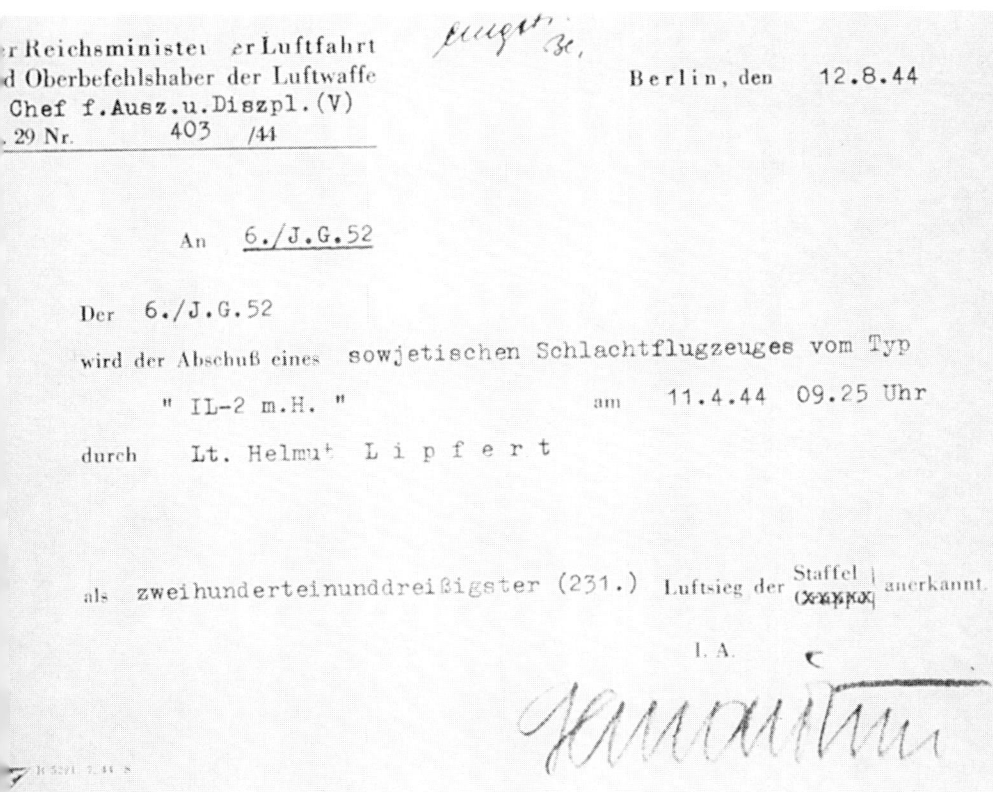

r Reichsministe er Luftfahrt
d Oberbefehlshaber der Luftwaffe
Chef f.Ausz.u.Diszpl.(V)
. 29 Nr. 403 /44

Berlin, den 12.8.44

An 6./J.G.52

Der 6./J.G.52

wird der Abschuß eines sowjetischen Schlachtflugzeuges vom Typ

" IL-2 m.H. " am 11.4.44 09.25 Uhr

durch Lt. Helmut L i p f e r t

als zweihunderteinunddreißigster (231.) Luftsieg der Staffel anerkannt.

I. A.

*The "Sixth" at Khersonyes, autumn 1943. From left to right: Uffz. Peiper, Ofhr. Thomas (KIA 12.1.1944), Ofw. Nietschmann, Lt. Lipfert, Uffz. Otten (KIA 10.1.1944), Fw. Pilz.*

*In June 1944 6./JG 52 was based for a time at Manzar, Romania. The pilot with his arm in a sling is Uffz. Wester, who was wounded in combat and bailed out of his aircraft on 3.6.1944.*

*The Crimea, early 1944. Gruppenkommandeur Hptm. Barkhorn (2nd from left) with the three later Knight's Cross winners Sturm, Batz and Fönnekold (from left to right).*

*Oblt. Wilhelm Batz in April 1944. Two months later he took over command of III./JG 52 and at the end of the war was Kommandeur of II./JG 52.*

Lt. Hans Waldmann joined 6./JG 52 in the summer of 1942 and in February 1944 was awarded the Knight's Cross after his 84th kill. Later in the war Waldmann was transferred to JG 7, equipped with the Me 262 jet fighter. He was killed on 18.3.1945 near Kaltenkirchen when his aircraft was rammed by another Me 262.

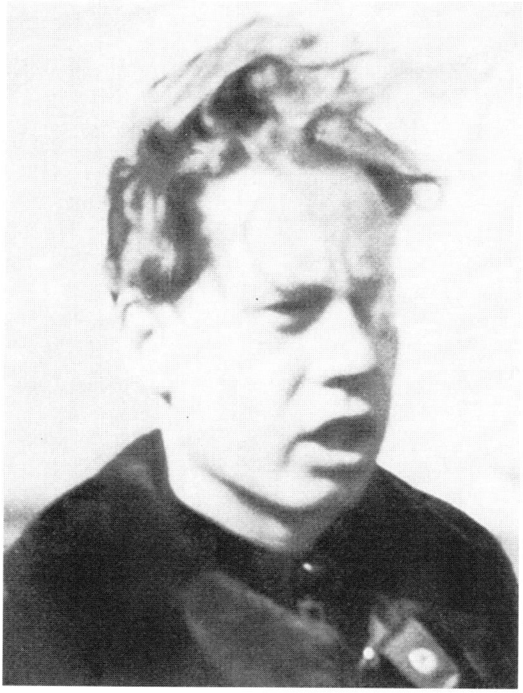

*Personal insignia on Lt. "Dackel" (Dachshund) Waldmann's Bf 109 G-6 (6./JG 52).*

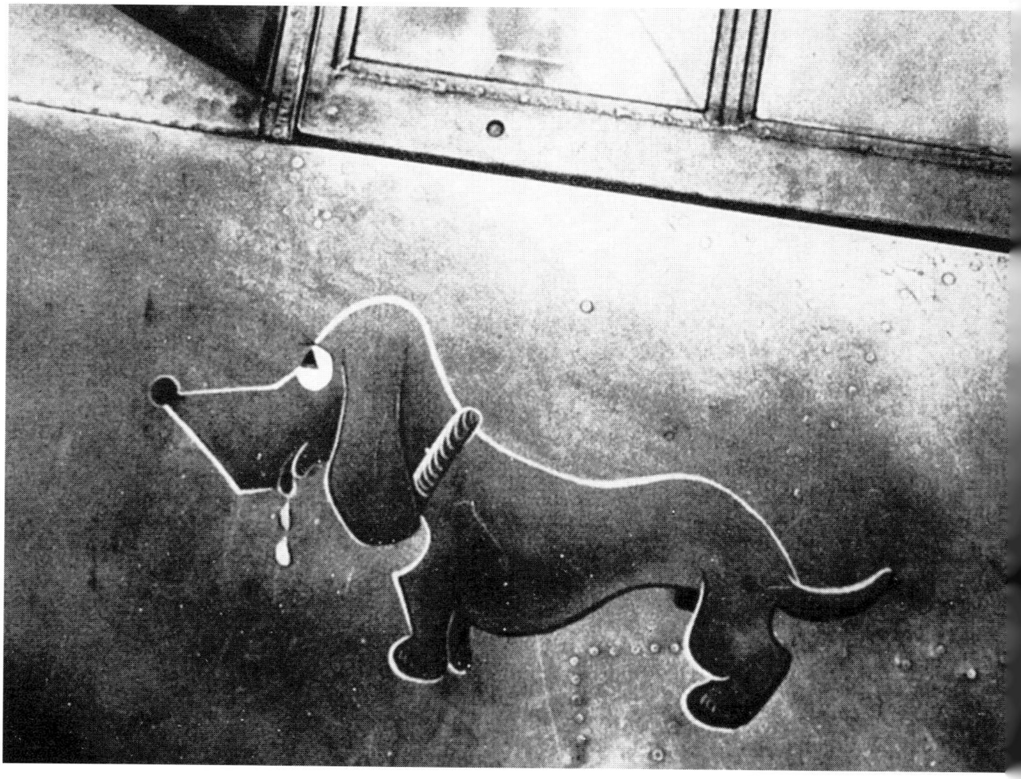

*"Yellow 1," the Messerschmitt Bf 109 flown by Leutnant Heinz "Wimmersal" Sachsenberg.*

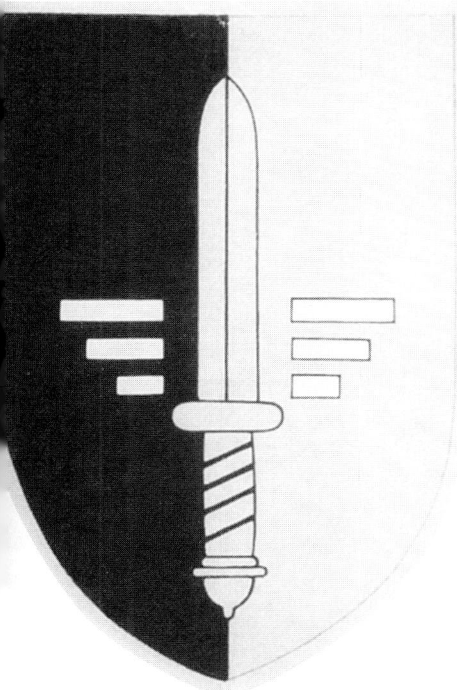

*The emblem of Jagdgeschwader 52.*

*Lt. Otto Fönnekold, Staffelkapitän 5./JG 52. Fönnekold was shot down and killed by a USAAF Mustang while trying to land at Budak, Romania on August 31, 1944. At the time of his death Lt. Fönnekold had 136 victories to his credit.*

*Lt. Heinz "Esau" Ewald, one of the best young pilots in JG 52 and longtime wingman of the Gruppenkommandeur, Hptm. Barkhorn. Ewald was awarded the Knight's Cross in early April 1945 following his 84th kill.*

After glancing up quickly to check for other aircraft, I immediately pulled up into an Immelmann turn. The Russian dove away and, turning beneath me, tried to escape to the east. I ordered Ewald to stay above and keep my tail clear. During my next attack the Russian observed me closely. Nevertheless he flew on calmly on an easterly heading until I was within firing range. Then he turned hard toward me. I broke away and called to Ewald to come down.

Ewald attacked but the Russian evaded him. Instead of flying east he now turned toward the west in the direction of the Crimea. He raced along at an altitude of 200 meters then dropped even lower. The Russian was just above the wavetops, Ewald about 600 meters behind him and I about 1,000 meters above.

Before the enemy aircraft reached the land I descended, while Ewald, as agreed upon, climbed. As I dove I saw that the battle was still raging over Eltigen. By now I was just above the water, like the Russian in front of me, and, as expected, the enemy pilot hauled his aircraft around again. But I turned with him, so tightly that I began to black out and the whole aircraft shuddered. Nevertheless I stayed on his tail.

There now began a tremendous turning contest. The Ivan must truly have been an expert. He simply refused to allow me to get in a single shot, even though I was only 30 meters behind him. We flew one complete circle after another, while Ewald repeatedly assured me that he was 300 meters above and covering me.

Every time I flew over land the Russian anti-aircraft guns opened fire, but none of us worried about that. There was nothing the enemy pilot could do but keep turning and I would rather have been shot down by the flak than give up. I hung on bitterly, but I realized that I couldn't close with the Russian like this. I had to try a different approach.

I climbed to 100 meters, rolled my aircraft onto its back and came down on the Russian in a steep descending turn. This maneuver perplexed him so that he made an ill-considered move. He dove away and in doing so gave me a chance to fire. I seized the opportunity and scored my first hits on him. Then he was gone again, while I had difficulty pulling out before my machine struck the water.

As I was about to repeat my maneuver I saw flashes on the engine in front of me and heard several blows. I hauled back on the stick desperately, because it was clear that there must be an enemy aircraft on my tail. But before I could take Ewald to task for neglecting his observation duties, a Bf 109 roared past me, blazing away with all guns. What an idiot! "You beginner," I called, "are you blind? Do you want to shoot down one of your own?"

I had to abandon my pursuit of the Russian. He saw that this might be his chance and tried to make tracks. Then Ewald got on his tail and he had to go back to turning again. While Ewald chased him around in three circles several 109s assembled above us. Their pilots gave good advice on how to shoot down the fellow, who must have been bathed in sweat by now. I said nothing, rather let myself drop into the circle a second time and got quite close to him. I opened fire from point-blank range and saw pieces fly off the enemy aircraft. Then he straightened out and headed for a small island in the Strait of Kerch, Kossa Tusla.

Although I kept firing I couldn't prevent the Russian from making a smooth belly landing on the enemy-occupied island. As I roared low over the aircraft the pilot jumped out and ran away. The belly landing justified claiming the machine as destroyed, but this kill nevertheless gave me no peace. I was not satisfied with it, although I had allowed a brave pilot to escape with his life. During my first sortie the next day I flew back to the island with Ewald and strafed the Russian machine. It finally caught fire after three passes. Not until we returned to base did I report my kill.

The Russians were forced to evacuate the Eltigen beachhead surprisingly quickly. Under such adverse conditions their bravery and determination meant nothing – the German superiority was too great. The narrow beachhead south of Kerch, barely one square kilometer in size, was squeezed ever tighter and finally split apart. The Russians began their withdrawal across the Strait of Kerch during the night. When the first *Rotte* appeared over Eltigen the next morning, the last Russians were reaching land on the other side.

We fighter pilots lost an "Eldorado" with the elimination of the Eltigen beachhead, because from then on scarcely any Russian aircraft came across the Strait of Kerch any more, and even over Taman there were few enemy aircraft to be seen. The next days passed without any contact with the enemy, and the *Gruppe* received orders to transfer to another location.

My next victory would be number 75, which would mean a

recommendation for the Knight's Cross. The "leading members of the administrative body" – the senior NCO, paymaster and the 6 *Staffel* orderly room – came out to the field every time I flew, ready to congratulate me. And day after day they had to withdraw with their flowers and champagne without having fulfilled their mission. Finally it all became too much for me. When the senior NCO, G. Bolinski, tried to steal away from the field with his entourage and gifts following an unsuccessful sortie by me, I called him over and made him do fifteen push-ups. As I explained to him, it was punishment for trying to push me. I wanted it badly, but no one was going to force me to get this 75th kill.

During this dry spell I once again had a stroke of unbelievable luck. Even though there was no contact with the enemy we still had to fly escort for the He 111 units the next day. I led the four aircraft of the third *Schwarm*. The Heinkels dropped their bombs unmolested and flew home. Not a single Russian showed himself no matter how hard we strained our eyes.

I took leave of the bombers not far from our base at an altitude of 4,000 meters. I wanted to fly back to the front with my *Schwarm* after the other eight machines had descended to land.

We climbed slowly to 5,000 meters. My wingman reported two aircraft approaching from the west at high altitude. Two Russians? I was electrified, but enquired cautiously on the frequency: "Any Cyclists flying east over picnic ground at *Hanni* 6,000?"

No answer.

I repeated the question, but before I fully realized what was happening the two machines peeled off and dove on our bombers. We did the same at once. Although we were closer to the Heinkels than they were, they got their first on account of their greater speed in the dive. Ignoring us, they closed in on the trailing bomber and opened fire with everything they had. I saw pieces fly off the He 111.

The Russians pulled up for a second pass, but now we were there. The trailing Ivan forgot about our bombers; instead he abandoned his element leader and dove away. I had to open fire even though I wasn't close enough, otherwise the Russian would have fired on the last He 111 a second time.

He ignored my bursts of machine-gun fire at first, until he was hit several times. Then he turned sharply, leaving a heavy vapor trail, and dove away toward the northeast in the direction of the foul lake. I cut him off and closed in at high speed. My airspeed indicator was showing more than 750 kph and I could scarcely hold my machine on course. I was applying almost full right rudder and had to hold the stick forward with both hands in order to keep my Me behind the Russian.

I had never experienced this from a Russian before. Usually 600 kph was their limit. The lightly-built enemy aircraft then pulled out on their own without the pilot being able to anything about it. With a good Bf 109 G-6 one could dive to more than 850 kph. Past that the aircraft very rarely responded to its pilot. The resulting control forces were enormous.

As already mentioned, I could only hold my machine behind the Russian by using the strength of both arms. The enemy aircraft grew larger and larger. It almost filled the gunsight; I had to open fire now.

Slowly, without reducing pressure on the control column, I felt for the firing button for the machine-guns and moved my thumb onto the cannon button. The Russian still seemed not to notice that I was sitting behind him, believing he had long since shaken me off with his wild dive. The very first shots I fired were hits. The exploding cannon shells produced small black puffs of smoke on his fuselage.

The Russian suddenly pulled up and then dove even more steeply. I couldn't follow as my speed was already more than 850 kph. Instinctively I pulled back the throttle and opened the radiator flaps, then I threw the Messerschmitt on its back with some difficulty. Just then I saw the Russian passing beneath me. He was smoking slightly and his left undercarriage leg was down. My speed had dropped in the meantime and so I attacked again.

This time I first trimmed my machine nose-heavy, as the Russian was still diving, although not as steeply as before. I got on his tail again at 3,000 meters. This time he saw me but continued to fly straight ahead. I opened fire rather too soon, but he didn't change direction, instead he put his nose down briefly so that I was suddenly a level higher than he was. I put my nose down as well, but as I was about to fire he pulled up again, and this time I ended up below him. The Russian carried out these maneuvers with such skill that I was simply unable to fire. As well he constantly changed his speed, apparently in an effort to force me to overshoot. Had he succeeded, this skilled pilot would certainly have swept me from the sky or at least scored some hits.

But I was careful enough not to get too close to him. I pressed the triggers now and then and sprayed bullets around him. My aim was not precise but he took one hit after another. After a time he gave up on his defensive tactic and began to turn.

My red lamp was already flickering. A quick look around revealed that there were no other aircraft in the air besides us. Powder smoke seeped into my cockpit and excited my nerves, if that was at all still possible. Shot up and with one undercarriage leg hanging down, the Russian turned for his life, proving through his skill that the enemy had outstanding fliers and fighters too.

Again I laid my machine on its back, dropped down into his turn and fired with plenty of deflection. He took evasive action, but I nevertheless hit his wingtip, which immediately broke away. Now he was finished. His movements were too badly hindered for him to mount an effective defense. I hit him with a full burst. A cannon shell blew off his entire tail and then he went down in a spin, burning. I wiped the sweat from my brow, opened my flying suit and followed the enemy aircraft until it crashed into the foul lake a few hundred meters from shore.

"Cyclist from five two, I saw your kill. Congratulations!"

The pilot who congratulated me on my 75th kill was Lt. Haas of 5 *Staffel*. Now it was time to go home!

Before reaching our base I climbed and then dove toward the command post of 6 *Staffel*. As I roared overhead I saw everyone running out onto the landing field. All of 6 *Staffel* had gathered when I taxied in. I was lifted from the cockpit and carried on their shoulders to the command post. The senior NCO was there again with champagne and flowers.

After this victory there was a quiet period. My *Staffel* and I transferred for a short time to Karankut, deeper in the interior of the Crimea. But I returned to Bagerovo and during this time scored another notable kill, six days after my 75th.

December 17 promised to be a clear day. The sun was not yet up but we were already sitting in our cockpits, waiting for the order to take off. My new wingman, Fw. Mohr, was rather impatient. I told him that it was quite unlikely we'd run into any enemy aircraft today. A messenger came running out of the 6 *Staffel* command post tent waving his arms wildly. The mechanic knew at once what it meant: "You can take off now, *Herr Leutnant.*"

"Stay close, Mohr. I'll explain a little of the front to you." We flew across the Strait of Kerch at 600 meters, dawdling along, in economical cruise so to speak. I had never taxied out for takeoff so calmly as on this day. Perhaps it was just because I was now one of the "old hands." Perhaps I was already too old to be a fighter pilot. There were very few pilots flying at the front at 28 years of age.

We were approaching land – Taman. The first strings of pearls from the Russian anti-aircraft guns snaked up toward us. Turning all the while, we wandered eastward, where the sun was just appearing on the horizon. As there might eventually be Russians in the air as well, we descended toward land, racing along at low level and staying on the look-out. We saw nothing. Our beloved wreck appeared just off the shoreline, and I intended to fire a few test rounds to see if my guns had been bore-sighted properly. But first I sent Mohr down to show what he could do. Then it was my turn. Satisfied with the results, we flew on. There was still nothing to be seen or heard.

We climbed into the sun. The snow-capped Caucasus Mountains shone in the distance, and I could make out Anapa quite clearly. After about an hour the red light came on: time to think about going home. We reached the Strait of Kerch in a shallow dive. And because we had not exchanged a word for the past few minutes, I was slightly startled when I heard the voice of the ground station: "To six one. One Furniture Van over the airfield at *Hanni* 6,000, heading east!"

"6,000" I had to think. "I'm at 2,500 and have only a little fuel left. My wingman must therefore have even less."

Should I try it anyway? Would I even be able to find the enemy aircraft?

"Six two from six one. What is your fuel state?"

"Six one from two, my red light is on," replied Mohr.

Reports continued to come in on the position of the Russian. He was maintaining his easterly heading and was descending slowly toward his own territory. He was reported at 5,000 meters over Kerch. We had meanwhile reached 3,200 meters and were south of his position.

If I reversed course and climbed we could perhaps catch him over Taman at 4,000 meters. I considered sending my wingman home, but he asked permission to stay as his red light had only just come on.

Suddenly we caught sight of the Russian, a Pe-2, to our left and about 600 meters higher. The machine descended in front of me at high speed and dove toward Taman. I set out after him but the distance between us became greater rather than less because of his greater speed in descent. I rammed the throttle forward and dove after him so quickly that Mohr was unable to keep up. The Russian, on the other hand, grew larger in front of me.

Would my fuel hold out or would my comrade and I have to make a forced-landing in Russian territory? But who knew what important reconnaissance information the enemy aircraft might take home if we let him fly on unmolested.

Now we were at low level, with me 800 meters behind him. I left Mohr at a higher altitude so that he could glide home if all else failed. I was only seconds from overtaking the Russian, but before I reached proper firing range the bomber's dorsal gunner opened fire. Tracer flew past my ears, and I tried to make myself as small as possible because the fellow fired damned well. There were two thumps and two sizable holes appeared in my left wing. I couldn't wait any longer, I had to open fire.

The first burst passed over his cockpit. I corrected my aim, but while doing so the cannon failed. I scored several hits with my two machine-guns, but the dorsal gunner kept firing back. The Russian pilot held his aircraft on a steady course and I was able to aim precisely.

Then one of my two machine-guns failed as well. Only precise shooting could help me now. For the third time I hung behind the enemy and cursed the failure of my weapons. Then I pressed the trigger.

Almost every bullet struck the fuselage of the Pe-2. Pieces flew off and flames darted out, but the Russian kept flying. Luckily the dorsal gunner had stopped firing, apparently I had wounded him. Now I flew even closer. 60, 40, 20 meters. I bounced around in his propwash. My aircraft shuddered and I had to pull up. I dove again immediately and hit him from above and to the side from a range of 20 meters. Not a bullet missed.

The Pe-2 exploded and the tail unit and part of the fuselage broke off. The rest fell to earth like a fiery bullet. I ordered my wingman to take the quickest way home so that he could at least land relatively safely.

Then I had to worry about myself. I dared not fly over Taman at low level, because everyone there had been alerted by the combat. The Pe-2 had surely transmitted its exact location and alerted the Russian fighters. Climbing slowly, I flew south toward the sea. They wouldn't be expecting me there.

I prayed that my fuel would hold out. I turned west and was about to climb higher when I saw several dots far off to the right. Now I had to stay low, as my aircraft would have stood out clearly against the bright sky. So I flew on, hovering between hope and despair, my glance alternating between the fuel gauge and the airspace around me. I crossed the Strait of Kerch south of Eltigen at an altitude of 700 meters. Now it didn't matter; even if I couldn't reach my airfield I was still over friendly territory.

Then Mohr informed me that he was about to land. That was one less thing to worry about. I maintained altitude to base and saw Mohr's aircraft below, sitting on the landing field. The engine of my brave Messerschmitt quit on final approach, but it had brought me home. I made a smooth landing at precisely 0705.

There was another lull in the action for a few days following my 76th victory. It was not just me who was affected; all of II./JG 52 had no contact with the enemy. Nevertheless we celebrated Christmas.

On December 27 I took off on a sortie with Uffz. Middeldorf. I was flying a new aircraft armed with two machine-guns and three cannon – a so-called "gunboat." First we had a tussle with four Airacobras over the Strait of Kerch. On this occasion we had to "take to our heels" as this time the Russians were really good and their aircraft faster. We had to dive away and disappear quickly. Then we flew a wide arc over the southernmost tip of the Crimea, Cape Takyl, toward the sea.

From an altitude of 1,000 meters I spotted a wake beneath me. I followed this to its origin and discovered a small, fast-moving vessel. I ordered Middeldorf to stay above and descended alone to inspect the ship more closely. As I approached, the thing in the water began to zigzag. It changed course and headed for the open sea.

Even at a range of 100 meters I wasn't sure if it was friend or foe. But I did see the two twin machine-guns on deck, and the sailors behind the weapons training their barrels at me. But not a shot was fired. At that moment I didn't know what to do. As I turned away I heard over the radio that it was a Russian motor torpedo boat. Soon thereafter the ground station, which was right on the Crimean coast, gave me the order to attack.

I was all too conscious of the threat such a boat posed to me, especially after having had such a close look at its defensive armament. Again I asked Middeldorf to stay above initially and provide top cover, and then I made my first attack. I didn't fly directly toward the vessel, rather I acted as if I still hadn't seen it. I dove at high speed toward a point off to one side of the boat. When I was just above the waves I changed course and flew toward the ship.

Again all weapons were trained at me, but I had to attack somehow. I opened fire when I was still about 200 meters away. I could scarcely miss. There were flashes all over the ship's deck and side. The Russians must have been startled for a second, because they didn't fire back until I turned away just in front of them and flew away aft of the ship. But then they showered me with a veritable hail of bullets. Tracer flashed all around me and I was forced to twist and turn like an eel. Luckily only three bullets hit me, two in the fuselage and one in the right wing.

The boat emitted smoke and steam, but kept on going, its speed undiminished. I called Mitteldorf down for the second attack. He was to attack the boat from the left, while I approached from the other side. In this way the defenses would have to engage two targets at the same time, preventing them from concentrating on a single machine. And that is how it happened.

Again I descended to just above the water and opened fire from farther back, correcting my aim as I closed in. Before I reached the target I saw Mitteldorf roar over the vessel and pull up. Now the boat was smoking rather heavily. The Russian defensive fire ceased abruptly. I closed the throttle and opened the radiator flaps to reduce speed and then aimed carefully at the forward third of the ship's side. Then I was in ramming range and was forced to break away. Looking back, I saw a huge detonation on the ship. Large, dense clouds of gray and white smoke rose into the air, and as we formed up over the ship at 800 meters it slowly listed to one side and began to steam in a circle. Before it completed the circle a tremendous fire broke out on board. After two more circles the motor torpedo boat sank in a matter of seconds.

Two days later Mitteldorf and I managed to sink another torpedo boat in almost the same spot. Like the first one, destruction of the ship was seen by land observers and confirmed.

One could suppose that with the many kills I made, I was often presented with the same situation. But that was not the case. Kills achieved through surprise attack were often similar in their initial stages and a very few differed only in detail, but nevertheless no two were exactly the same. One kill which was rather different was my 77th.

The entire *Gruppe* had been assigned to escort an He 111 unit and the formation flew out over Kerch at an altitude of 4,500 meters. After successfully bombing targets on the coast, the bombers flew away to the northwest. So far everything had gone as planned. The fighters' assignment was to stick close to the bombers and escort them on the return flight as well.

Scarcely had we turned away, first toward the north, then west, when a single machine appeared over the bomb release point. It could only be a Russian. I waggled my wings briefly, a signal to my wingman that he should follow me, but he didn't react. Without a moment's hesitation and without informing the *Kommandeur* in advance, I dropped out of formation and flew back. As I wanted to return to the formation again as quickly as possible, I didn't try to climb above the enemy aircraft before attacking. I rammed the throttle forward and locked it there. Then I dove another 500 meters and, using the speed built up in the dive, approached the enemy aircraft, which was flying toward me about 1,000 meters higher, from below.

I climbed almost vertically, allowing plenty of lead. As quickly as the altimeter climbed, the airspeed indicator fell. By the time my aircraft was almost stationary and on the verge of stalling, the Russian was 150 meters directly in front of me. I fired in front of his nose at first and then into his fuselage. And then my tricks were over. The Messerschmitt fell away and plummeted earthward the way it had just come.

As I dropped away I saw a white-gray smoke trail coming from the fuselage of the enemy aircraft. I had just regained control of the Messerschmitt and brought it out of its dive when, a few hundred meters to one side, I saw the Russian machine going down in a vertical dive trailing a dense plume of coolant.

I was going to have to claim the kill as a "victory without witnesses," but then I heard the voice of the *Kommandeur*: "From Radetzki – Who just made a kill?"

Dutifully I answered: "Radetzki 1 from six one. Kill was made by six one."

Instead of the expected confirmation, I heard: "Report to the command post immediately after landing!" This I did. *Major* Barkhorn had probably seen my kill, but reproached me severely for not carrying out my assignment, namely escorting the He 111s. A month later the *Kommandeur* confirmed my kill and even my unauthorized action was forgiven, especially since there had been no negative consequences.

I also shot down another R-5. This was one of those harmless courier aircraft which caused no harm by day and only became unpleasant by night. Then these slow machines were employed as harassment bombers, and they deprived us of many hours sleep. Thus the R-5 I shot down was not quite so harmless.

I took off that day with Uffz. Middeldorf as my wingman. We were sweeping over the northern Russian bridgehead at low level when I saw a dot in front of me. Because of our high speed we closed on it quickly, and I soon recognized it as an R-5. The enemy aircraft quickly grew larger. Before I knew it, tracer was flying toward me. It was only then that I realized that the machine was coming toward us and not, as I had thought, flying away from us. I fired a short burst from close range, then pulled up and felt quite clearly the turbulence one experienced only when one flew over another aircraft very close. Looking back, I saw the R-5 crash into the sea in flames and sink quickly. "Damn," I thought, "that could have ended badly."

By now the enemy anti-aircraft gunners were awake and letting us have it as we flew along at treetop height. So heavy was the fire that we were forced to twist and turn, making one "flak waltz" after another. Middeldorf was hit five times; I myself escaped with a fright.

At this time the Russians had fortified the northeastern part of the Crimea and were holding their bridgehead against all German attacks. The front was at a standstill. Dense concentrations of anti-aircraft guns were set up along the front lines on both sides. Attempts to fly into the enemy hinterland were usually punished with hits. The Russian 20mm anti-aircraft guns in particular made life difficult for us. The only way to get into the bridgehead relatively unscathed was to approach over the sea. I nearly flew into the water on several occasions after misjudging my altitude due to poor visibility. After that I wasn't quite so eager to fly out over the sea.

Like most of us, I often stayed on the German side of the front lines just below the clouds and beyond the range of the Russian anti-aircraft guns. For a full hour we would fly seven kilometers to the north as far as the sea, then turn around and fly seven kilometers to the south. The Russians did the same thing on the other side.

In the beginning I now and then made an attempt to dash over in order to have a go at an enemy aircraft, but the Russian flak soon put me off that. So we played "non-intervention" until it all became too boring and stupid for me. One day, instead of flying east where the front was, I flew west until I found a small gap in the clouds. I climbed up through this hole and flew back to the front. There the clouds were only about 400 meters thick. The airspace above was clear. So I headed back to the west, dropped through the hole and fetched my wingman. My battle plan was complete. The two of us observed the Russians, with whom we flew parallel to the front for a time.

Just short of the point where the Russians turned south, I led my wingman up through the clouds again. We turned and flew east for barely a minute before returning to a southerly heading. Then I dove at high speed through the clouds, hoping desperately that we would come out behind the Russians. There was of course a chance of ramming one of them as we dove through the clouds, but I didn't want to think about that.

Emerging from the grayness, I had to pull up immediately to avoid flying into the ground. I saw that I was on the Russian side and raced along at low level. Scarcely 500 meters in front of me and somewhat higher were the unsuspecting Ivans.

Fw. Mohr, my number two, had descended through the clouds with me and was now flying next to me about ten meters away. The enemy flak could do nothing against us, because we were flying very low and enjoying the element of surprise. We closed in on the enemy aircraft at high speed. I would gladly have told Mohr to attack the second Russian, but my radio refused to function during these critical seconds.

Then I was beneath the trailing Russian. I pulled up and fired from close range. The machine staggered immediately. Before I was forced to break away the enemy lost almost his entire tail. I was so happy about the success of my tactics that I gave no thought to disappearing up into the clouds. And as the Russian flak was still silent, I remained below the clouds to watch the crash of the aircraft I had shot down.

The Russian spun about 100 meters, then he recovered, flew a short distance, went into a spin again and finally crashed. He had ended up over German territory and came down in a courtyard surrounded by walls. The aircraft stayed in one piece, only the wings were badly rippled. German infantry hurried to the scene and pulled the pilot, who appeared to have sustained only minor injuries, from the aircraft.

While we observed the downed machine – an Airacobra – the number one Russian had turned around and was now behind us. I wanted to lure him a little farther over our territory and flew toward the west. The Russian sent a few bursts after us and then disappeared on an opposite heading.

I scored several more kills this way, but the Russians soon caught on and from then on they became very cautious.

Then came a time when there was scarcely any flying. The entire Crimea, especially its eastern extremities, was covered with low cloud. Cloud cover was 10/10 and extended down to 300 meters. Only rarely did it break up to reveal blue sky.

On December 29, 1943 I made an extraordinary kill. It was a Douglas Boston and at the same time my 80th victory.

6 *Staffel*'s command post at Bagerovo, a few kilometers from Kerch, was in a small underground shelter. I was sitting with Ogfr. Dautz, who was writing up the report of my victory from that morning, when the telephone rang shrilly. It was the *Gruppenkommandeur*, Hptm. Barkhorn:

"I have a special assignment for you. This morning signals intelligence has learned that a high-ranking Russian officer is going to visit the bridgehead at about noon today. Take a *Rotte* and wait over the Strait of Kerch. You are to shoot him down!"

As it was already 1030 we had to hurry, because who could say at what time the general from the other side would deign to come. My wingman, Fw. Mohr, and I therefore had long-range fuel tanks installed so as to be prepared for any eventuality. We were able to take off shortly after 1100.

The sun had burned off the fog and by the time we were airborne it shone from a cloudless sky. We climbed higher while still over land and reached the Strait of Kerch at an altitude of 6,000 meters. South of the bridgehead we positioned ourselves in the sun and patrolled from the southern tip across to Taman and back again. There was no talking.

Time passed slowly. The better part of an hour had gone by when I waved to Mohr and indicated that he might empty his auxiliary tank so that we could jettison them as quickly as possible. It was always a touchy situation to have to fly an attack with the auxiliary tank. Not only did it reduce the aircraft's speed by about 40 kph, it also limited maneuverability. Besides, a hit in such a tank immediately turned the Messerschmitt into a blazing torch.

With time my eyes began to hurt, as the constant and strenuous searching for the enemy soon had a negative effect on the optic nerve. I frequently had to look over at Mohr's aircraft so that my eyes could focus on another range.

The Russian had to appear soon. If he did come, it would have to be over the foul lake in the north or directly from the east across the narrowest part of the Strait of Kerch. Suddenly I thought I saw a shadow gliding over the water of the bay north of Taman. But where there was a shadow there also had to be something to cause it. I was still doubtful whether I should leave my favorable altitude because of this shadow, but it gave me no peace, especially since it was wandering westward in the direction of the Crimea. I waved Mohr over and pointed downward. He nodded. We were going to have a closer look at this shadow.

At 4,000 meters there was still nothing to be seen of an aircraft. However the shadow was so large that it definitely couldn't be from a fighter. At 3,500 meters I was finally able to make out the aircraft. The machine which approached from out of the east was quite large. It had to be the general's aircraft we were so eagerly awaiting. Mohr, too, had spotted the enemy. Was it possible that such a large aircraft was flying alone, without fighter escort? I strained to spot possible escorting aircraft. Finally I discovered them. Eight fighters were perched close above the twin-engined machine.

If we wanted to get at the "fat one" we'd have to dive through these fighters. There was no time to lose. The Russian and his whole entourage were over the middle of the Strait of Kerch. I waggled my wings briefly and Mohr, who knew me well, moved in close. "If possible, open fire when I do," I called to him. We didn't have much time, because if the Russian fighters realized what was going on it might be too late.

Mohr sat beside me at the same altitude, no more than five meters away. Now, radiator flaps open to reduce speed and increase firing time. I checked my weapons once again; my heart was in my throat. Then we dove on the Russians. As we came out of the sun, the fighter escort failed to notice us. We could easily have shot down two of the unsuspecting Russian fighters as they flew past in front of us, but that was not what we wanted. Our eyes were fixed on the fat bomber.

We dove straight through the midst of the fighters. They finally noticed us and tried desperately to dissuade us from our plan. But they were unable to do so, because our superior speed let us pull away from them quickly. To be sure, we couldn't stay behind the "fat one" too long, or else the fighters would catch us from behind.

One thing was clear. We had time to make just one pass at the twin-engined machine and then we'd have to scurry across the bridgehead at low level. The flak and fighter escort would make things hot enough for us.

The Boston quickly grew larger in my gunsight until it filled it. I held my fire, although my limbs were trembling with excitement. I finally opened fire with all weapons from a range of about 400 meters and blanketed the enemy machine. There were flashes, sparks and smoke in front of me. I was so close that every burst was on target. The Boston's propeller wash seized me and bounced my machine around, making accurate aiming impossible.

Pieces from the Russian aircraft flew past me. It belched flames and I was forced to pull up to avoid flying into my kill. I flew over the Boston, then dove to just above the water and in a few seconds was over land.

I was greeted by a real display of fireworks from the Russian anti-aircraft guns. I exploited every valley, every hedge and every house to avoid the heavy defensive fire. In spite of this hellish inferno and the other dangers I found time to risk a look to the rear. Mohr was behind me. He was beaming. And then farther behind I saw the doomed enemy aircraft hit the water. It bounced off the water and made a great leap over the ten-meter-high coastal bluff, where it finally broke apart.

The anti-aircraft guns ceased firing, apparently they had lost us. But now the Boston's eight escort fighters were on our tail, and if seemed to me that they were closing. Mohr turned to the right and then pulled ahead, while my Messerschmitt simply refused to go any faster. Then I remembered that I had opened the radiator flaps. That could have been my undoing, because the Russians weren't that slow and would definitely have overtaken me had I not spotted my error in time. With the radiator flaps closed, I pulled away from them.

We were still flying low and were possibly already over friendly territory. The next look behind revealed that the Russians had turned away. I called Mohr over. Then we turned to the left and began to climb. I had to know what had become of the twin-engined machine. In scanning the sky I spotted a huge pall of smoke above the eastern tip of the Crimea, in the area where I assumed the Boston had crashed.

We first turned toward the east, then north, and spotted the wreck of the Boston. Russian soldiers were swarming around the burning machine, apparently trying to rescue something. Mohr and I dove down, although I could see that Russian fighters were circling the fire. We opened fire on the Boston from 1,000 meters in order to ensure that there was nothing left for the Russians to recover.

As I pulled up I felt a powerful jolt which tossed my machine up into the air. As it still answered the controls it couldn't have been a serious hit. Racing low over the ground, I looked back and saw a huge smoke cloud over the fire site. The Boston must have blown up in the same instant I flew over it, and it was the shock wave from the explosion which had tossed me into the air.

This time no Russian fighters came after us as we raced away at about 700 kph. Once over German territory again, I pulled up and looked at the inferno blazing in the distance. Our mission had been a success.

Naturally this kill was widely talked about. I can remember very well the words of Heino Sachsenberg, that I had long since passed my peak as a fighter pilot and was unlikely to get much older. He was almost right a second time. A few days after shooting down the Boston I met a real ace Russian fighter pilot. It was only through luck that I escaped with my life.

As was so often the case, I saw two Russians over the Strait of Kerch and climbed after them without regard to my position. In an instant we found ourselves in the loveliest dogfight. In front of me was an enemy fighter, behind me a young *Unteroffizier* who was on his third flight as my wingman, and behind him the other Russian. After the third circle I realized that this was becoming dangerous for my wingman. The Ivan behind him was closing, while I was unable to gain on the aircraft in front of me.

On my order, therefore, my wingman pulled out of the circle and dove away toward German territory. At the same moment the Russian in front of me straightened out and tried to fly away in an easterly direction. A look behind convinced me that the second Russian couldn't fire yet, so I dove after the first machine. We both dove toward the large flak island in the Strait of Kerch. Things were getting a little too ticklish and I veered off. I was now flying west at 500 meters.

All the while I observed the other Russian. First he flew over me and then, when he had passed me, hauled his machine around and dove at me. There was nothing for me to do but turn. I waited a moment until he was in range and then hauled the Messerschmitt around so hard that I began to black out and the machine trailed two long vapor trails. The enemy aircraft immediately levelled off, turned with me and began another pass. The Russian closed in and I had to dodge quickly again to avoid catching a burst of fire.

This time the Russian turned with me. He turned as tightly as I and was now directly behind me. He was so close that I could see the muzzles of his guns. But he came even closer. The nose behind me grew larger and larger, and I slowly grew more uneasy.

Now it didn't mean too much to be pursued by an enemy, especially if one was turning. The pursuer had to turn even tighter and allow for deflection if he was to score hits. Otherwise the bullets would pass behind the tail of the aircraft being pursued without inflicting any damage. The vast majority of Russians that I met fired in such situations and wasted their ammunition. Once they had expended all their ammunition they broke away and disappeared.

This enemy pilot reacted differently, however. He let me wait and just by doing that made me feel very insecure. I raged and pulled on the stick, trod on the rudder pedals, dodged, sideslipped and never stayed still for a moment. But I couldn't shake off the Russian; he sat behind me like a shadow. I couldn't climb away from him because his machine climbed as well as mine. Diving away, which could have been my salvation, was out of the question because our altitude was only 300 meters.

So I turned for my life, cursing and sweating. Land, and thus German territory, was only about 1,000 meters away. Not far for a fighter, to be sure. But this Russian behind me didn't give me the slightest chance to get closer to land, at least not by the shortest route. I tried a sharp bank and then flew straight toward the German lines for as long as possible. I hadn't gone more than 100 meters when I was forced to start turning again to avoid being shot down.

I managed to make a half-loop from the turn, and as my machine had almost no speed I turned practically on the spot. As a result of the steep bank the enemy had fallen behind somewhat, but after the pitch-up he was even closer than before. And still he didn't fire. That made me almost beside myself. If I flew straight for only a second or stopped turning I was a dead man.

I worked the stick and rudder pedals until my machine was dancing. The game had been going on for ten minutes already without the Russian firing a shot. He was now sitting only 20 meters behind me. Only luck could save me now.

Just then three Bf 109s passed overhead, perhaps 1,000 meters higher. I shouted into the radio: "People, come down. Directly beneath you. Shoot this bastard off my tail, the fellow is about to finish me!"

But no matter how hard I shouted, my comrades didn't answer. The Russian stuck behind me like a leech and still he did not fire. I simply couldn't take it any more and placed everything on one card. Once again I made an Immelmann and let my Messerschmitt roar toward the safety of the shore.

"Why doesn't he fire?" I thought. "And if I come down in the water at least I won't be dead. Better to lie in the water than to endure this torture much longer." Scarcely had I ended my thoughts, when there was a pinging noise in my crate. At least the tension was broken. There was so much tracer flying past my ears that I didn't know which way to turn.

Instinctively I pulled up briefly and then dove sharply at the instant that he fired. I heard the hammering of his guns again and dove away once more. Then I was over land and raced into the midst of the German flak barrage. Which was better, to be shot down by the enemy or one's own anti-aircraft guns?

It was a real hell. Tracer reached for me from every side, but I roared straight through. Then, abruptly, the whole shooting match came to an end. I looked behind; the Russian had disappeared. I was overjoyed. I didn't know if the enemy aircraft had turned away or been shot down. All I knew was that the flak had saved me.

I came home and even managed to land my Messerschmitt. Totally soaked in sweat, I climbed out and stood weak-kneed on the wing. I was so all in that I couldn't walk. Twenty-six bullet holes in my machine were proof of the Ivan's gunnery skills. I had never been so outclassed in the air. I couldn't bring myself to get back into an aircraft again that day. I learned my lesson from this encounter. Never again did a Russian catch me from above at low altitude.

By the next day I had pretty much recovered from my fright and was even able to fly my beloved weather reconnaissance mission. I arrived over the Strait of Kerch at a safe altitude, 5,000 meters, and just then spotted two Russians about 1,000 meters below me. I left my wingman above and attacked the two Yak aircraft. They must have spotted me, because they immediately tried to turn away.

I imitated the Russian from the day before and didn't come all the way down after them. Instead I pulled up and immediately made a second attack. The two Ivans turned tightly, condensation streaming from both aircraft. I dove beneath them, climbed to the side until I was above them and then made my third pass. I let my 109 stall, laid it on its back and pulled around sharply. I came down close behind the trailing enemy fighter. The latter rolled over onto its back and began a Split-S.

Having learned from the events of the day before, I didn't dive after him, rather I latched onto the tail of the other Russian. Apparently he was too proud to make a Split-S like his wingman. He let me approach almost to firing range and then hauled his aircraft around with all his strength. As I was expecting this maneuver, I turned as well and stayed behind him. When he then flew straight for a brief moment and I scored my first hits on him. The Russian immediately began turning again.

I turned a little tighter than my opponent, aimed in front of his nose and fired. Again I hit the Russian several times. While he turned the most amazing figures in the air, I flew straight ahead, cut him off and scored more hits. Unfortunately my cannon had failed after the first shots and the enemy was able to withstand plenty of hits from my two machine-guns, as it turned out.

During the wild dogfight the other Russian had climbed back up and was getting ready to fall on me from above. He was still too far away to be a threat, but I had to hurry if I was to shoot down the one in front of me. The fellow was not a bad flier either. He pulled out all the stops and didn't allow me to get into firing position.

We had been turning for more than ten minutes when the pilot in front of me straightened out and dove away steeply. That is what I had hoped and waited for. As the Messerschmitt was heavier than the Yak I closed rapidly and then pressed all the firing buttons. In the next instant there was an explosion in front of me and all that fell into Kerch harbor was wreckage. The Russian pilot swung down beneath his parachute.

There was a heavy blow in my machine as I turned away. Aha, I had completely forgotten that there was another one behind me. I dove away immediately. The Russian didn't fire again and I didn't see him behind me any more. I kept diving toward Kerch. At 1,500 meters and 600 kph I pulled back on the stick to recover from the dive. It came back surprisingly easily. At the same instant I realized that I was still diving and that the elevator was not responding. I immediately rejected the idea of jumping, because at this speed I wouldn't be able to get clear of the aircraft.

Kerch came ever closer and in a few seconds I must crash into the middle of the ruined city. Then a thought struck me: the trim. Damn, the trim! I had set it to "nose-heavy" when I began the dive.

As fast as I could, I turned the trim wheel with both hands. I levelled off over Kerch. That was close!

As I flew on I looked over my machine and discovered a bullet hole in the wing, right at the near end of the aileron. I was shocked when I pushed the stick to the left and discovered that the aileron was jammed and would move only slightly. But how was I going to land without elevator or aileron control? But that was not all. I managed to find the airfield and was about to begin my approach when the aircraft nosed down as the airspeed dropped below 300 kph.

Meanwhile I had arrived at the field from the side. I was already too close for a belly-landing at 300 kph, but it was clear that I would have to make one. I jockeyed my machine around until I was again lined up with the airfield. Its full length lay before me and I was lucky that no one was about to take off or land at that moment.

I descended carefully toward the "Picnic Ground" and chopped the throttle just as I was about to touch down. The propeller blades immediately struck the ground. The machine bounced and came down with a crash, then bounced into the air again before touching down once more. This happened several times with the bounces becoming ever smaller, until the aircraft finally stayed on the ground and skidded along on its belly. It finally came to a halt in front of a small hillock at the edge of the landing field.

I climbed out and surveyed the damage. This time I had only been hit twice – but in this case I couldn't have taken any more.

My wingman landed after me. He had seen everything and confirmed my 84th victory. His confirmation was unnecessary however, as the command post was already well aware of my battle. They even knew far more than I did, and I was able to learn several interesting facts, including that I had just shot down one of the best-known Russian fighter pilots. Our listening post had discovered the frequency being used by the two enemy fighters and had overheard the following scraps of conversation: "Watch out. Two "Messers" (Russian designation for the Bf 109) above us. We're being attacked! Turn! Attention, attacking again! Stay close! Keep turning!" – "I have to dive away or he'll shoot me down!" – Pull out. He's not following you! Hurry, I've been hit!" – "I've been hit again! Hurry up and fire at that miserable 'Messer'! Help me! Help, help! I am M..., help me, I'm married and have a wife and children! Help, help!"

There was nothing I could say. I felt sorry for the poor fellow, especially as I could understand how bad it must have been for him. I had been close to calling for help the day before. Perhaps the matter would have bothered me for some time had not the same listening post brought news four days later that my comrade M... was again racing lustily about the sky. He had come down safely by parachute and had then been fished out of the water by his comrades. Perhaps he later shot down some of us.

At this time my friend Heino Sachsenberg was again the subject of conversation. He hated and despised dogfighting. He refused to spar with the enemy, instead he made his kills with elegance and superiority. He always maintained: "I am the highest of all. Should I fly somewhat too low, inadvertently or from necessity, then I'm faster than any other!"

Yes, Heino had his peculiarities. They began at takeoff. He always climbed into his machine the same way and three times went so far as to climb out of his Messerschmitt, which was running, and not take off because his crew chief, Ogfr. Rommel, had not waved to him as he was about to taxi out for takeoff. Once in the air his first act was to reach for the "snorkel," or oxygen mask. Heino maintained that he couldn't fly without oxygen and always wore the mask.

Once I was allowed to fly Sachsenberg's aircraft. During the flight I was unable to find a speed at which his "Yellow 8" would run smoothly. But why? Quite simply, Heino knew only one position for the throttle in the air – wide open!

The Crimean weather was also not to Heino's taste. The clouds usually hung quite low, and so he flew close beneath the clouds at full throttle.

We flew together in a *Schwarm* on one of these dreary winter days when the ceiling was at 2,500 meters. The four of us climbed out and arrived over the Strait of Kerch. Heino had no desire to fly out over the sea and abruptly turned around with his wingman in order to steam south along the coast while hanging just below the clouds. As Russians were reported in our assigned area, I wanted to press on at least as far as Kossa Tussla, the small island in the middle of the Strait of Kerch. Unfortunately the enemy didn't turn up anywhere. We therefore turned around as well and flew leisurely toward the coast on a southwesterly heading.

Then I saw a lone aircraft. Suddenly another aircraft dropped out of the clouds and fired at the first. "Aha," I thought, "that's Sachsenberg." While the first aircraft stubbornly maintained its heading, the second made a second attack, broke away and attacked again. The aircraft in front was already trailing a huge banner of coolant and headed off in the direction of our base. The Russian – it must have been one – disappeared into the clouds again.

While approaching to land I saw a charred, smoking Messerschmitt on the landing field. It was Heino Sachsenberg's "Yellow 8." This is what had happened: conscious of his speed and altitude, Heino had thought, as always: "No one can touch me!" He stopped looking behind and concentrated on finding an enemy aircraft, certain that he couldn't be surprised. But then the Russian dove out of the clouds behind him and had all the advantages. When things started ringing in Heino's machine he didn't think anything was wrong: "What's up with the engine, it's certainly knocking today!" Not until the third pass, when a burst almost shaved off the left radiator, could Sachsenberg no longer overlook the Russian. He noticed the enemy's fat, red nose right behind his aircraft and started taking evasive action. He saved his life with a skillful Split-S.

His Messerschmitt was ready for the scrap heap, but he brought it back to base. There he jumped out and ran before the ammunition exploded.

# CHAPTER V
# Retreat in the Crimea

On January 25, 1944 I scored my 87th and 88th kills in one sortie. That was the end of operational flying for me until I went on leave on February 2. Recently the fighting in the air had grown in intensity. Every week several of us failed to return. I was "all in." But I was about to learn that a flight home and back could be almost as dramatic as a real combat sortie at the front.

As requested, a "transfer machine" sat ready in front of the 6 *Staffel* dispersal. The aircraft was no longer fit for combat and was to be ferried to Germany for overhaul. But first I had to fly to Grammatikovo, where two *Staffeln* of our II./JG 52 were based. This rather short trip from Bagerovo to Grammatikovo almost finished my already jangled nerves. As soon as I lifted off the machine began to turn and slip; I had to work just to keep it in the air. I had so much to do that any Russian novice could have shot me down easily.

Sweating profusely, I finally landed at Grammatikovo. There was no way I wanted to get back into that aircraft, but I wanted to get home as quickly as possible and travel by train was out of the question as the Russians had completely isolated the Crimea. The long way around to Rumania by sea also seemed too dangerous to me. So I handed the beast over to the mechanics, "ironed out" and fixed what I could and then tried a test flight. The aircraft still didn't fly normally, but I was ready to risk the flight to Nikolayev.

Together with an *Unteroffizier* who had likewise received permission to fly home on leave, I climbed out immediately after takeoff and we approached the Russian front near Perekop at 5,000 meters. We swung out slightly to the west toward the sea. I wasn't all that happy about flying over the sea, because my crate was vibrating so badly that I didn't have to worry about getting cold. When I finally reached 6,000 meters I remembered the five bottles of champagne stowed in the fuselage. Later, after landing at Nikolayev, I was relieved to find that they had survived their high-altitude flight.

There things reached the stage where the machine had to be stripped down. The mechanics were amazed that it could fly at all.

I received another crate in which to continue my journey. It was not significantly more confidence-inspiring, a fact I realized immediately after the first test flight. I was definitely not happy that our *Oberzahlmeister* Freygang packed so much mail, parcels and provisions in the fuselage. I warned him. No reasonable man could believe that this mill would reach Germany. Unfortunately I paid too little heed myself to my forebodings. Had I listened I would at least have spared myself a terrible fright which was to take the pleasure out of flying for me for some time.

I was so cautious after departing Nikolayev that I undertook no long route legs. At first I was satisfied with the 150 kilometers to Tiraspol. And there I sat. Outside the weather was so bad that one wouldn't have sent a dog into it. Even the large quantities of red wine given me by *Prüfmeister* Renke could not cheer me up. My aircraft sat in front of the door, my leave pass was in my pocket. There was nothing to do but wait.

On the fourth day the weather improved. The ceiling was high enough, but it was snowing. The weather technician warned that the flight was possible but risky. Nothing was going to hold me back any longer and I took off. My next destination was to be Proskurov. Under normal conditions it wouldn't have been difficult to find my way there. All I had to do was follow the railway line and I'd reach Proskurov in about 40 minutes.

I flew along the railway line and checked the map at every intersection. Things went well for about 35 minutes. On the way I'd flown through several snow showers and had dropped down low over the tracks. Then there came a heavier shower. It became dark. Visibility dropped to perhaps 50 meters. I swore. Finally it became brighter and I was able to go somewhat higher. But where was Proskurov?

I had been flying for 45 minutes already, then 50 and 55. I became contemplative. I couldn't have lost my way because the tracks were below me and my heading was correct. Had I flown over the city in the heavy blowing snow? I continued northwest for another two minutes and then discovered that I must be almost halfway between Proskurov and Ternopol.

Reaching Ternopol seemed impossible because of my low fuel state. My only chance was to reverse course and find Proskurov. In any case there was a good chance that I might have to make a forced-landing beside the railway line. The red light came on punctually after an hour's flight time. Twelve minutes later I saw an airfield below me, from which a Ju 52 was just taking off. Several other Junkers were sitting on the landing field. I saw a small barracks which was probably flying control.

The landing field was very short for a Bf 109, but I would be able to make it if I could touch down right at the perimeter. As I turned on final approach a red flare was fired from below: "pull up and go around!" I checked all the instruments and as they were all in order I couldn't understand why I shouldn't land. As my fuel was about to run out any second, I decided to land in spite of the repeated red flares. I approached under power and touched down almost exactly at the edge of the landing field.

I rolled about 200 meters, then suddenly the tail began to come up, quite slowly, and no amount of hauling back on the stick or trimming could stop it. It was clear what was about to happen. I quickly reached for my harness straps with both hands and pulled them as tight as I could. Then came the expected crash. The aircraft's wheels had sunk into the soft snow and it had flipped over. Luckily the cockpit remained intact. I had banged my head somewhere and strained my back. Hanging upside down in my straps I was unable to free myself from this awkward situation. Around me all was quiet.

In my excitement I released the straps and naturally promptly fell on my head. I was thus in a worse situation than before.

Then finally I heard voices. Someone shook the aircraft and called: "are you still alive?" I hastened to confirm that I was. Then I felt the machine being lifted somewhat and the canopy was opened. It took an eternity for the people to get me out. A Ju 52 took me to Proskurov, where I was supposed to spend three days in the dispensary because of my concussion and compression injuries.

But this lasted only one day, then I seized the opportunity and flew to Breslau in another Ju 52. From there I took a train home. On my return to the front I was ordered to pick up a new Bf 109 at Krakow. I took off in the new machine for Lvov. But fresh misfortunes seemed to be awaiting me there. The entire airfield was covered with bombs. They lay practically everywhere, and only one runway had been left clear. It was difficult enough to land a Bf 109 on a concrete runway because of its tendency to swing. Added to this was the fact that I was back in an aircraft for the first time in weeks and as well I was frightened by the bombs stacked close to the runway.

When I turned final they fired so many red flares that I pulled up and went around. Too much crosswind! I had no other choice, I had to land here as I didn't have enough fuel to reach an alternate airfield. I made a wide circle while ambulances and fire trucks drove into position below. Which should I try, a landing outside the airfield or an extremely risky landing on the concrete runway?

The wind sock on the flight control building was almost horizontal. If the machine swung on account of the strong crosswind and I crashed into the stacked bombs it would mean an a trip to heaven for sure. I concentrated only on the landing. I succeeded in keeping the aircraft from swinging in spite of the wind. When I climbed out, pale and trembling, I had made up my mind that I wasn't going to fly back to the front, at least not in a machine I had to pilot myself.

At Lvov I met Oblt. Krupinski, a III./JG 52 "ace" with more than 150 kills. "Graf Punski," as he was called, welcomed me warmly and showed me a good time. He certainly kept me from getting bored. However I was eager to get back to the front. Then I developed a boil on my neck overnight, which made me unfit for combat for the time being. But when the opportunity came to hop a ride in a general's He 111 to Nikolayev and then to the Crimea, I took it. I had to make the last 200 kilometers to Grammatikovo by train.

On April 1, 1944 I took off on my first sortie after returning from leave. The Russians had flown in near Feodosia and attacked the harbor, which lay far in our rear on the east coast of the Crimea. When I arrived over Feodosia with Uffz. Haas, the Il-2s had already dropped their bombs and flown away. A number of Yaks were still there, dogfighting with several 109s. The Russians made repeated attempts to turn away toward the east, because they couldn't stay long over the target area if they were to make the 200-kilometer return trip to their base.

Our Messerschmitts forced the enemy aircraft to keep turning. I dropped into the swirling mass from an altitude of 3,000 meters and was fortunate to find right in front of me an Ivan who was being chased by another 109. The Russian had made an Immelmann in an effort to escape the German fighter and in doing so flew right in front of my guns at low speed. I fired from point-blank range. The enemy aircraft immediately began to burn brightly. Apparently I hit the pilot, because the machine went straight down, crashed into the water and sank.

Then I climbed back up again, first leaving behind all the Yaks below me. I turned in behind the last Russian. The Ivan failed to notice me. Although he banked left and right and climbed and descended, he didn't turn, rather flew stubbornly toward the east. He had good reason to do so. I wouldn't have wanted to be in his shoes, 200 kilometers from base, far behind enemy lines and then the last of the whole group. I wonder if he knew the old saying that the last one gets bitten by the dog.

As I moved in closer I saw aircraft being shot down to my left and right. It was quite a picture: in front about 20 Russians low over the water, behind them the Messerschmitts. I opened fire from 100 meters and immediately scored hits. There were flashes all over the enemy aircraft's fuselage, wings and tail. But he didn't go down. He tried to stay with his formation, although his aircraft was a blazing torch.

I ordered Haas to come down and finish off the Ivan. Wingmen needed gunnery practice too. But Haas' guns jammed after firing a few rounds. So I came back down and fired until the Russian turned toward land. Then I broke away and in doing so made the mistake of overshooting him, as the enemy had apparently cut his throttle. Quite a determined fellow, I thought. He pulled up behind me and opened fire. Tracer flashed past my machine. I immediately turned sharply and saw the enemy aircraft fall backward and crash into the sea, where it sank.

The *Gruppe* scored a total of 16 kills that day with 11 aircraft. Unfortunately our *Gruppenkommandeur*, G. Barkhorn, was also shot down and forced to make a belly landing away from base.

On April 7 and 8 I scored two kills on single sorties each day. The first two kills were witnessed by one of the sharpest of my contemporaries, Oblt. Batz, *Staffelkapitän* of the Fifth. He already had more than 100 victories.

On April 7 I flew to Feodosia with *Feldwebel* Mohr. While we were prowling around a report came in that there was heavy air fighting going on over the Sivash, about 100 kilometers away. We couldn't miss out on that! On arriving we saw the old familiar scene. In front two Russians, behind two Messerschmitts. The 109s were on the attack, but they weren't making much headway as the Russians were flying well and turning magnificently.

When we were above them the two Me's separated. One attacked and the other waited above to possibly foil an attempt at flight. But the Russians evaded every attack by turning tightly just above the ground. After observing this game for a while, I dropped down into the circle, positioned myself close behind the last Russian, allowed plenty of lead and fired. Once again my cannon failed to work properly, but the few rounds it fired must have been on target. I must have hit the pilot, because the machine spun away immediately and crashed into a swamp.

The other Russian was seized by fear. He tried to get away. But both of the Bf 109s were behind him and forced him to turn. I was about to attack again when I heard over the radio: "From five one. Where are you? *Oberleutnant* Batz here!"

"*Viktor*, Willi, did you see my kill?"

"Oh it's you is it? I believe you want the other one too," came the reply.

In the meantime I was closing fast on the second Russian. But he must have seen me, because he turned so tightly that I thought he must stall. I climbed above him, rolled onto my back and pulled harder on the stick. I lined up right behind him again. This time he couldn't turn away from me. He had lost a great deal of speed after the first turn and could only turn feebly now. That was his undoing. I fired my first burst from close range. This caused him to dive away trailing white smoke. But I was on his tail right away and fired again. The Russian probably realized that there was no escape. He dove to ground level and tried to make a high-speed belly landing.

At first I pulled up over him, but as he was in Russian territory and not yet burning, I asked Batz to help me set the aircraft on fire. After the third pass it was blazing fiercely and we could head home. Although we were good friends Willi Batz never forgave me for snatching both Russians from under his nose, although he did confirm both kills. They were victories 91 and 92.

I scored another double on April 8. This time one of them was an R-5 for a change. I shot down my 95th, a Yak, on April 9. We were flying Stuka escort and the Russians let nothing keep them from nibbling around the Ju 87s. I closed in on one of the Russians while he was busy firing at a Junkers; several bursts and he fell from the sky in flames.

My 96th victory came deep in German territory. The aircraft warning service had located a Russian reconnaissance aircraft, a Pe-2, approaching our base at 6,000 meters. Two of us took off and reached 6,000 meters safely, almost hanging on our propellers as we climbed. There was no trace of the Pe-2. Fortunately the ground station was on the ball and informed us that the enemy aircraft was still above us. Then we spotted him. He was about 1,000 meters higher and on course for our base.

We climbed higher. Directly over the airfield I got into position behind him undetected. My aim was poor on the first pass and I had to break away before inflicting fatal damage on the Pe-2. As well, the dorsal gunner was very alert and scored no less than nine hits on me during my first pass. Fortunately, all were in the wings.

When my wingman finally caught up I was already making a second pass. The Pe-2 tried to escape by diving steeply toward the north. I hung behind him. A regular duel developed between me and the dorsal gunner. The fellow shot devilishly well, but I had more weapons. Matching the bomber's speed, I pressed on and fired until the gunner threw in the sponge.

It was amazing the punishment this machine could take. Then the pilot began taking evasive action. He danced about the sky in his machine like a madman, but I sat clung to him stubbornly and refused to let myself be shaken off. We were deep in friendly territory and I had plenty of time, so I let him carry on. I waited for the moment when he would fly straight and level. Finally my patience was rewarded and I opened fire.

Apparently I hit the fuel tank, because there was a huge flash of flame and in no time, the Pe-2 was ablaze. I moved away. The enemy aircraft pitched downward, recovered and made a belly landing. One man climbed out and ran away. I circled the aircraft until I saw German soldiers hurrying toward the fire and watched as the Russian who had climbed out was taken prisoner.

Two hours after the battle, which had been watched attentively from the airfield, they brought in the Russian pilot. He was the only member of the three-man crew to have escaped with his life. We conversed as best we could and I poured him several glasses of schnapps.

In this way I slowly approached my 100th victory. I have always had a certain respect for all "anniversary kills." How could it have been different with my imminent 100th. But fighter pilots were a very superstitious lot. I had a very odd feeling before takeoff, and I wouldn't have been disappointed if my crate had developed ignition trouble or something similar which would have forced me to turn back. Luck was again with me, otherwise things would have turned out much worse.

Once again we escorted Stukas up to the Sivash. The Russians were laboring to build a raised roadway through the morass of the lagoons between the foul lake and the Black Sea to enable to them to reach the Crimea from the north. So far the Stukas had been able to frustrate this plan. There was thus plenty of activity in the air above the Sivash in those days.

As we flew in from the south with 15 Stukas and six fighters we saw a Russian formation of 30 Il-2s and twenty fighters approaching from the north. At first both sides concentrated on their assignments and the two formations passed one another about three kilometers apart, heading in opposite directions. On the return flight, when the bombers had dropped their loads, we met again.

Now there was a great mixup. Without warning the Ju 87s dove on the Il-2s, out-turned them, got behind them and fired until they were driven away by the Russian fighters or even shot down.

We engaged the Yaks and LaGGs and tried to make their lives more difficult. It really was a great scrap! It was impossible to look after anyone else. Each man had to look out for himself. Wingmen flew on their own, as ordered. There was a huge risk of colliding with another aircraft or being rammed. This milling crowd was too much for me. I waggled my wings to summon over another aircraft with a "Yellow 3" and left the scene of the battle as quickly as possible.

Unfortunately, as I dove away I overlooked the Il-2 below me, which was just about to drop its bombs. Apparently it belonged to a new wave of bombers which had just arrived. Like those in the Taman at that time, this one, too, was painted white. One simply couldn't miss it and I dove beneath it without worrying about the furious German anti-aircraft fire it was drawing. The rear gunner blazed away as I approached. I made myself as small as possible in the cockpit and decided not to see the enemy's tracer any more.

I hit the Russian so well that he immediately began to burn and raced away on fire toward the ground at a steep angle. Before he struck the ground two hard blows shook my machine. I knew at once what it was, especially since oil began spraying about my ears. A hit in the oil cooler or oil line! I disappeared toward the east at low level and quickly thought over my situation. It was about 100 kilometers to the "picnic ground," and I couldn't make that. There were no other airfields in this area so my only choice was to fly as far as I could and then make an emergency landing as near a road as possible.

Once I had convinced myself that no Russians were following, I climbed gingerly to 1,000 meters. When I came to a railway line I knew where I was. I turned to the right and found a road beside which I could land if it came to that. "Another forced landing," I thought to myself, "it certainly isn't the first." Pity that I had been hit by my own flak, otherwise this wouldn't have been necessary.

The engine began to stutter and it grew increasingly warm in the cockpit; I knew from experience what was soon to come. Therefore I quickly found a suitable place to land, three kilometers from the road. I touched down smoothly. Before the crate caught fire I removed the dashboard clock, unplugged the radio lead and clamped my parachute under my arm. Unfortunately I couldn't take the battery with me, because I had my winter flying suit on and I was sweating even before I began walking in the hot April sun. I plodded westward slowly in the direction of the road, over which many vehicles were streaming toward the southern corner of the Crimea.

The northern and eastern parts of the Crimea could not be held much longer as the Russians were too strong, and apparently my aircraft was also beyond saving. If that was the case I at least wanted to strafe it and set it on fire on my next sortie before it fell into the hands of the Russians.

It took me almost an hour to reach the road, but once there I was fortunate enough to find a truck which could take me to Karankut. Although I was aware that the truck belonged to the flak arm, I couldn't have suspected my "luck." This revealed itself during a conversation with the driver, an ancient *Stabsgefreiter*. He told me that at noon on the previous day his battery had hit and badly damaged a Bf 109. The German fighter had then flown away toward the southwest smoking heavily. I didn't want to tell him that it was I who had been flying the fighter. For me it was another hint that I shouldn't overdo it.

In the meantime the Russians had broken into the front in the north and, coming from Perekop, were threatening to cut off or encircle elements of the Wehrmacht still east of Kerch.

A great race began on the Crimea, at least for the ground forces. Initially everything proceeded in an orderly fashion, but with each new day the withdrawal increasingly degenerated into a headlong flight. In the end everyone's main objective was to find a way to get away to the southwest in the direction of Sevastopol. Most of the army units managed to withdraw to the southwest corner of the Crimea.

It was the beginning of a bad time for all those who had to hold out in the Crimea. II./JG 52 transferred initially to Khersonyes, located at the extreme southwestern tip of the peninsula, but a few days later it had to pack up and move again. The fighters had to make room for the Stukas and were sent north, as close to the front as possible.

Our new airfield was called Belobek. It was as narrow as a handkerchief and sloped gently toward the sea. Moreover there was only a single runway. If I as an experienced flyer felt a certain trepidation before every landing, how must the beginners among us have felt. Often we stood in front of the tent and watched the landings. About every third one resulted in a crash, especially since a barbed-wire barricade and a broad trench ran along the coast. At least three of our pilots became hung up in this obstacle each day. We lost a considerable number of machines in this way. In the short time we were at Belobek we lost eleven aircraft through landing accidents against only three victories.

Finally we moved back to Khersonyes. The airfield lay on a plateau, which in the south towered about 30 meters above the sea. In the west was an old lighthouse. The landing field was partially turf-covered, while the rest was sandy or stony ground. The technical personnel squatted in "one-man holes" or slit trenches around the airfield. By night everyone, with the exception of the sentries, drove to Sevastopol, where most of the pilots were housed in barracks.

I did not have a promising beginning at Khersonyes. On the day of the move my wingman, Uffz. Middeldorf, and I ran into a group of Il-2s during a Stuka escort mission. I inflicted serious damage on one of the enemy ships, but as I broke away the rear gunner hit me with more than ten bullets. Afterward I instructed my wingman to finish off the enemy aircraft. But my faithful aircraft was just about finished and had to spend some time in the repair shop. I received a new Messerschmitt. During my first test flight I found that the aircraft was totally out of trim. It was a bad start, and I had to pull on the stick with all my strength to avoid "going in." After a successful landing I set about fixing things myself, had the Me thoroughly overhauled and took off again that afternoon. This time things worked significantly better. The machine handled well in the air. I tested it thoroughly at a safe altitude of more than 3,000 meters. Last of all I wanted to test it in a dive. I therefore hung the aircraft on its propeller and climbed. At 5,000 meters I quickly checked the instruments again. All in order. Only the radio wasn't working; I had no contact with the ground station but I could do without that. I began the dive and observed the airspeed indicator and control forces very closely. At 4,000 meters I had reached 680 kph, when the machine began to bank slightly. I moved the stick to the right, but the bank grew steeper. At 3,500 meters and more than 700 kph, there was suddenly a jolt which caused me to bang my head on the cockpit roof even though I was strapped in. The machine then transformed itself into a vicious, bucking monster.

I now received such a blow on the left forearm that it still hurt a week later. My left leg was whipped against the instrument panel by the force of the gyrations and my shin began bleeding at once. And still I was unable to regain control of the machine, it did with me what it wanted. I let go of all the controls and opened the radiator flaps to at least slow the aircraft somewhat. In doing so my gaze fell on the undercarriage position indicator and suddenly it became clear what the jolt had meant: the light for the left undercarriage leg was on, thus the left gear leg and wheel were hanging down.

My attempt to lower the other undercarriage leg so as to balance the aircraft failed. And still the machine shook me to and fro. If I didn't settle it down soon I'd have to bail out, so I made another attempt. I closed the radiator flaps again, lowered the landing flaps and selected full throttle. Meanwhile I changed the trim – and the aircraft recovered. A glance at the altimeter showed that I was at 800 meters.

Having regained control, I dutifully looked around me and noticed that I had flown into scattered flak bursts. But I saw something else that caused me to quickly forget my fright. In front of me hung a dense cluster of Il-2s, and separated from the others by about 400 meters was a lone machine.

The recent events were now forgotten. The only thing was that one undercarriage leg was still down. But that wasn't going to bother me now. I moved in quickly behind the Il-2 and fired before the gunner could suspect trouble. Although I had to work hard to hold the enemy in my sight, my first rounds were on target and the Ivan burst into flames at once. I closed in to ramming distance. When I broke away the fuselage of the Il-2 was burning fiercely. It flew on like a blazing torch. Then the fuselage broke apart and both large, burning pieces fell toward the ground. The machine crashed a few kilometers from our base.

My landing proved difficult because the left undercarriage leg was still down. In spite of side-slipping and diving and pulling out, I could neither raise the one leg or lower the other. I gyrated above the airfield until just about out of fuel, then flew over my dispersal waggling my wings. I was relieved to see the fire trucks and an ambulance standing by. Then I prepared to make a one-wheeled landing.

I approached the field slowly under power, let the lighthouse pass to my left and then touched down on my one wheel. The landing was a success. The machine gradually sagged to the right. As long as I maintained speed I could compensate with aileron. But the more my speed dropped, the more the aircraft sagged, until the wingtip touched the ground. This caused a ground loop, but I never had the feeling that I was in serious danger.

My combat and kill had been observed from the airfield and there were plenty of people to confirm my 101st victory.

If it had not been clear to us before, we now realized that the final battle for the Crimea had begun. The front drew closer each day; the

Russians pressured and pushed so that we simply couldn't withstand it any longer. The German forces were driven steadily back toward the southern tip of the Crimea. Ferries were under way day and night to ensure the evacuation of the wounded and the most vital materiel. This was not so simple, however, because the ferries had to cross the 340 kilometers to Mamaia on the Rumanian coast. Moreover the Russian bombers were in the air continually and sank many of the vessels.

We were often sent up to protect the ferries. On April 22 I flew out to sea with Fw. Stolpe. Our assignment was to rendezvous with several German ferries about 150 kilometers southwest of the Crimea and watch over them. We found the ships following a long search and took up station above them at 3,000 meters. It was very difficult to pick out such small boats, usually we spotted them by the wakes they left on the water.

After about ten minutes the Russians suddenly appeared. They came from a higher altitude and when I first spotted them they were already diving. I attacked the first seven machines from the side and sprayed my tracer in front of their noses to put them off their aim. Meanwhile the boats below began zigzagging wildly so that the bombers were in fact unable to land any of their bombs.

Meanwhile the second group of six aircraft approached. Initially I let them through. Then I positioned myself behind the last Russian, closed in quickly and poured fire into him until Stolpe was beside me. Then I left the bomber and concentrated on the next one. Stolpe finished what I had started and shot the first bomber down in flames.

Unfortunately I couldn't concentrate just on the Russian in front of me. Instead I had to spray my bullets beneath him if I was to interfere with the others dropping their bombs. As a result I didn't score any victories, although all of the enemy aircraft received more or less effective hits. But I was successful in that none of the bombers were able to inflict any serious damage on the ships either.

While I was hanging behind the second group, still firing, the first formation had turned around and was about to make a low-level attack on the ships. The seven aircraft approached head on in close formation. We therefore left the formation in front of us, made a steep turn and attacked the seven bombers again. I selected the second to last and Stolpe the last. The bombers all opened fire as we approached.

I attacked my bomber from above and scored hits from 300 meters, but so accurate was the furious fire from its twin machine-guns that I dove quickly and tried to approach the Russian from below. The gunner must have been a sharp fellow, because he greeted me again, this time with a 20mm cannon. But I had closed to 200 meters and my shells were on target.

Large pieces separated from the bomber and flew past me. There was a bang and then the machine in front of me exploded. In an instant my canopy was covered with oil. There was no need to deliberate, it was a hit in the oil tank. I saw the Russian aircraft disintegrate in the air through the side window as I pulled away, but it did nothing to raise my spirits, because I had to prepare for an eventual bath.

I climbed using the speed I still had and immediately picked up a northeasterly heading. Fw. Stolpe had no idea why I did this, but he informed me that I was leaving a black trail. I answered: "Have a hit in oil tank. Do you see the Crimea?"

"No!" came the reply.

"Stay close to me. Fly a little ahead and lead me. Tell me as soon as you see the Crimea!"

My engine began to overheat at 1,500 meters. The water in the radiators must be boiling. I repeated the by now familiar routine: ignition off, propeller set for gliding, flaps down 15 degrees.

If I was to reach the Crimea at all, this was the only way. I had to creep along, switching the ignition on and off. I contacted the ground station: "Have hit in the oil tank. Please have a motor torpedo boat put to sea, unable to reach 'garden fence!'"

At 800 meters the instruments showed that the temperatures were normal again. I retracted the flaps, selected 12 o'clock on the propeller pitch control and switched on the ignition. The engine sprang to life at once. My Messerschmitt gained altitude. Then Stolpe reported that he could see the Crimea and that we had to steer somewhat more to the east. The oil and coolant temperatures began to climb again. I had to shut down the engine again before they reached the limit. I couldn't let the engine get so hot that a piston seized, otherwise nothing would be able to save me from taking a bath. We were now about 200 meters above the surface of the water.

Once again I switched on the engine and let the machine climb. The Crimea came ever nearer. Would we still make it?

I now intended to climb until the motor seized and then try to glide to the coast or at least close to it. As I climbed I saw the saving shore lying before me. If only the engine could hold out a few seconds longer, I might even be able to reach land for a belly landing.

Suddenly there was a jolt. The propeller stopped.

Unfortunately I didn't arrive from the west at the flat coast, but directly from the south at the 50-meter-high bluffs. There was only one thing to do if I didn't want to come down in the water: I would have to dive the last few meters before the coast in order to gain speed. If I was unable to pass over the bluffs in this way, I would have to chance a risky turn and land in the water at the foot of the bluffs.

I dove until I was a few meters from land, somewhat below the crest. The machine's speed had meanwhile climbed to 250 kph, and I pulled up and just passed over the edge. Immediately afterward my machine dropped and touched down just beyond the crest of the bluff. I had made it.

Anyone who lived through these final days on the Crimea will never forget them. Even though most of the soldiers were rescued from the hell of Sevastopol, our losses were enormous. With their vastly superior forces the Soviets tried to break through the German lines from the north and throw our forces into the sea. On our side ships were under way day and night, taking out mainly the wounded. In the beginning Ju 52s were still landing, bringing in food and ammunition. Once even a company of infantry came in by air, but they were not enough to halt the enemy advance. The front moved visibly nearer.

At that time our airfield was still beyond the range of the Russian artillery, but the enemy bombers and fighters made things difficult enough. They were in the air practically all the time. By night the Russians employed their Pe-2s as dive-bombers, which made our lives miserable.

Together with Oblt. Schuller, also of 6 *Staffel*, and Lt. Sachsenberg, I moved into a new night camp which had been hewn out of the rock. We thus were at least safe from the threat of bomb splinters, as the bombing attacks went on continuously. It was maddening, a hellish inferno!

The same scene awaited us each morning at the airfield. The Russians had bombed the runway and all available forces were hard at work trying to repair it. Usually the holes had not been properly filled when a new formation approached and dropped its bombs. Even though many bombs fell in the water, some always hit the target and inflicted more damage. So it was a difficult affair just to get into the air and once aloft one never knew if the airfield would be fit to land on an hour later. These conditions were terribly hard on the nerves and deprived me of my confidence in the air.

Almost more difficult was waiting at cockpit readiness. The Russians flew without pause. Only occasionally was there a break of one or two hours in their attacks. Then there was nothing to be found in the air and we wasted our precious fuel. Therefore we had cockpit readiness. The aircraft had to take off immediately when the Ivans approached. Often it happened that the enemy appeared suddenly over the airfield and dropped their bombs before the mechanics had cranked up our machines. The mechanics then disappeared from the wings as quick as lightning and the pilots were left sitting in their cockpits, strapped in and helpless. We didn't always get out of our crates quickly enough.

But usually the mechanics were able to get the aircraft going in time, and we took off through our own flak into the midst of the Russian formations. These came diving at us from all sides. Many pilots were shot down while taking off. I always dropped down to just above the ground or water immediately and never strayed outside our flak zones, as the Russians avoided these. The Khersonyes flak was exceptionally accurate.

In spite of the adverse conditions in the Sevastopol combat zone II./JG 52 was able to shoot down about 20 enemy aircraft each day and I myself did quite well also.

The climax and end of the tragedy were played out on May 7, 8 and 9, 1944. On the first day only six to eight kilometers separated us from the front lines. Had the Russians succeeded in breaking through during the night we would have been finished, because we wouldn't have dared to take off in the 109 by night, especially from such a narrow airfield as Khersonyes.

Only a very few sorties were flown during these last days and one never knew if he would be able to land again at the airfield. On May 7 I had another lucky day. I was waiting in my aircraft when two Russian fighters appeared over the airfield. We took off at once, but the two Russians gave us the slip and flew away to the north. Together with my wingman I patrolled several times along the front. Only the Russian flak paid us any attention. But we continually changed altitude and heading and they finally gave up. After an hour we returned and landed.

Give it time, I thought to myself, something will turn up!

I took off again at 0930. Two formations of Russian aircraft had been reported heading for our base. This time we waited until the enemy aircraft were sighted before taking off; soon we spotted the swarm of Russian aircraft in the distance. My wingman and I got airborne and descended toward the water on a southwesterly heading. As we did so the first formation was already releasing its bombs. I flew so low that the propeller tips were almost touching the water. The main thing was not to be seen by those above. Had we been spotted, one of us would have been in trouble.

Then we had enough speed and climbed steeply. The first group descended toward the sea directly north of us and headed for home. In turning I saw the other formation, which was just approaching the airfield.

We approached the Russians from behind from above and out of the sun. One pulled up, apparently to evade the anti-aircraft fire, and found himself right in front of me. I pressed the firing buttons and blew the canopy off the enemy machine. The now pilotless Yak climbed a little higher then spun down until it struck the water. Fw. Stolpe confirmed the kill at almost the same instant.

While the ground station was congratulating me, I saw another Russian leave the swarm and climb toward me. When he turned his nose toward us I knew what he had in mind and quickly put the nose down. The bullets meant for us passed by far above our aircraft. The Russian stalled and his nose fell back over his tail. I was behind him before he had regained control. Sadly I was only able to hit him a few times as his machine was always in motion. When he recovered, the enemy pilot began to turn wildly and showed that he knew something about flying. I sent my wingman above and began a wild dogfight with the Yak. Each time I got into position the Ivan hauled his machine around so hard that there was no point in firing. Once he dove after turning and came toward my flank from below, which made things awfully hot for me. But before he could open fire I hauled back on the stick, laid the Messerschmitt on its back and waited until my opponent must have flown past beneath me.

Then I sideslipped and dropped into position about 80 meters behind him at approximately the same speed.

Now the Russian couldn't escape. I followed every one of his movements. Suddenly the Yak put its nose down. After a flat dive of more than 2,000 meters it pulled up and climbed steeply, directly into the sun. When I recovered from my blackout I saw him about 500 meters above me. We were both on the verge of a stall, and although the danger existed that he might crash into me as he fell, I pressed the triggers. I saw hits flash just as the Russian tumbled backward.

The Yak began to burn immediately and plunged downward right beside me. I was really quite fortunate, because the enemy machine came within a hair of ramming me.

All of a sudden the flak began firing. We were still over our base, where the air battle had been played out, and tried to show to the gunners down there that we really were not Russian aircraft. But suddenly Ivan was there again.

This time Stolpe spotted the enemy machine, a lone Yak, first. Like us, it was flying straight toward the southern tip of the Crimea and was somewhat lower than our Messerschmitts. "Go on, Stolpe. This one's yours!"

I stayed at altitude and observed the airspace around and above us. The *Feldwebel* began his attack but, like most beginners, he fired much too soon. The Russian saw tracer whizzing past and pulled his aircraft into a tight turn. I moved in a little closer and gave my wingman instructions: "Make another pass. I'll tell you when to fire. Attack now – move in closer – still closer."

But once again Stolpe opened fire from 1,000 meters and warned the Russian. The latter now began to dance about the sky with my wingman clinging to him, firing wildly. I now positioned myself between the enemy aircraft and the land, somewhat higher, ready to prevent any attempt by the Russian to flee toward the Crimea. Then I summoned Stolpe and directed a new attack. It would have been his second kill.

Slowly he approached to the correct distance behind the Yak. I ordered him to fire, but Stolpe's weapons remained silent. He came so close to the enemy aircraft that I thought he might ram him. Then I heard a desperate cry: "My guns are jammed!"

As it later turned out, Stolpe's guns weren't jammed, rather he had expended all his ammunition in the previous attacks. When he needed it there was none left. Yes, how often had the same thing happened to me, how many sure kills had I lost in this way?

I had the *Feldwebel* cover the rear and flew toward the Ivan, reducing power and moving in cautiously. The Russian turned immediately but that didn't help him. During the second full circle I laid my machine on its back just above the water and sideslipped down into the Russian's circle. I allowed plenty of deflection and let the Yak wander through my fire. He blew apart immediately and plunged into the water of the Black Sea.

I flew one other sortie that day, without success. But three kills were enough.

On the next to the last day in the Crimea the Russians bombed our airfield four times. We were unable to get into the air and lost six machines through these attacks. Following a terrible night dawn came on May 9, the last day in the Crimea.

I had lost much of my confidence as a result of the terrible events of the past 36 hours. In the following sorties I was so at the end of my tether, like all the other pilots, that I was unable to score any further kills and in the end had to be happy that I hadn't been shot down myself.

I flew only one sortie on May 8, setting out full of listlessness and uncertainty. My wingman was forced to turn back early due to a mechanical problem. When I headed back to land about an hour later, I heard over the radio that the Russians were bombing our airfield again. Then I saw a giant cloud of smoke and dust. The ground station promptly advised me that I couldn't land.

My red light was already burning and the only choice left me was whether I should put my machine down in the bomb craters at the airfield or in the water near the shore. A belly landing in the uneven terrain of the bridgehead meant almost certain death. Then I remembered the small airfield just behind the front which the Ju 52s had used. I flew low over this airfield and saw only a few bomb craters and bumps. I made another pass to determine the landing direction and then made my approach, not lowering the landing gear until the last moment. I stood on the brakes with both feet and the machine teetered several times and threatened to nose over. But I made it and taxied over to a barracks, where I shut down the engine and got out as quickly as possible.

Russian machine-gun fire was already whistling through the area, but fortunately the barracks lay in a shallow depression which ran through the middle of airfield and was thus pretty much out of the enemy's sight. I crawled back to my Messerschmitt to get everything I could remove and take with me: parachute, oxygen mask, flying helmet, starter crank and dashboard clock. Then I ran to the positions lying a little farther back and found a vehicle there which took me back to Khersonyes. On the evening of the same day I returned with all my things, the accompanying fuel truck filled up my machine and after it left I took off over the heads of the Russians.

With nine bullet holes in my machine, but otherwise all right, I landed at our airfield as night was falling. But everything I had risked to preserve my brave Messerschmitt was for nothing. At dawn a direct hit by a bomb transformed the Bf 109 into a smoldering wreck. The *Staffel* was now possessed a total of three Messerschmitts. I selected the best one and took off on a sortie at 0430.

The air was teeming with Russians and I got into them immediately, but three hits in my own machine was all I brought home. As the holes in the fuselage were rather large, the machine had to go in for repairs right away. I climbed into the last Bf 109 but one and prepared to take off, but as I taxied out I rolled into a bomb crater and was unable to free myself under my own power. A vehicle had to be brought out to pull me free. This done, the mechanics cranked up the engine, but just then the Russians appeared overhead. Everyone took cover.

Miraculously my machine and I remained in one piece, but the howling of bombs left me feeling rather unwell. Finally the machine started. I had rolled about ten meters when I felt that the left tire was flat. Once again the aircraft had to be towed back to the dispersal. I simply couldn't get airborne!

I went to *Major* Barkhorn, our *Kommanduer*, and told him what I thought of further flying from this airfield. I also informed him that the *Staffel* had only a single machine left. We were to evacuate the Crimea that afternoon and transfer to Rumania. Did it make any sense to risk this single aircraft?

Barkhorn was under orders to put every possible aircraft into the air, and in this case I was to take off alone, which was normally strictly forbidden. The other *Staffeln* still had several aircraft, but it was 6 *Staffel* whose turn it was to fly. As I was left with only four young pilots fit for action, I took the mission, climbed into the last mill and took off. I didn't take any chances on this sortie, I just wasn't up to it. I landed between two bomb craters and had to flee to my foxhole as soon as I had climbed out. The Russians honored us with a visit for the sixth time that day.

Especially worthy of mention at that time was our flak. It was the anti-aircraft guns which were often able to keep the Ivans at a respectful distance. Many a bold enemy pilot had to learn the hard way that our anti-aircraft guns were quite capable of putting up a stubborn defense even in a hopeless situation such as this. The deeds of the flak soldiers are even more worthy of respect because these people were well aware that there was no way they were getting out of the Crimea.

When I climbed out of my hole my first thought was of my aircraft. But it was ablaze and beyond all help. The exploding ammunition forced me to take cover again quickly. And already the Russians were over the field again. I really saw no chance of getting out of there. Perhaps one of the machines in the repair hangar would at least be ready by evening.

Many of the pilots had already taken off for the mainland in the last few days and had ferried over all the aircraft which were not fully combat-ready. The first operational aircraft left for Rumania during the course of the afternoon. Whatever came out of the repair shops was to depart for there immediately. I stayed by my Messerschmitt and waited. I helped with the repair work as best I could and hoped that the damage could be repaired very soon. As well as the damaged tire there were now various holes from bomb splinters. I rightly feared every new Russian attack.

Time passed, while my mood alternated between hope and despair. Finally evening was approaching. My Bf 109 was ready! I was about to take off when Russian artillery suddenly began pounding the dispersal. Before I knew it, the left wing of my aircraft had been holed. With that my last hope of getting away from the Crimea in an aircraft disappeared. I was desperate like seldom before.

It was standard procedure that every departing fighter aircraft had to take one or two members of the technical personnel to the mainland stowed in the fuselage or cockpit. The Bf 109 was designed for one man and it was well known how difficult it was to accommodate another person. But situations such as this showed often enough that the "*Beule*" was quite capable of flying with two men. It simply had to be done! This was of course only possible if small people were involved, as these had to fit in the narrow, short cockpit.

My discussion with the *Kommandeur* ended with him ordering me to fly in the baggage compartment of the aircraft belonging to the adjutant, Lt. Van de Kamp. I was by far the more experienced pilot, but Van de Kamp would never have fit into the narrow space. We stowed the most vital things in the fuselage of the Messerschmitt and I squashed myself into the cockpit as best I could.

Then the *Leutnant* took off and for once the Russians left us in peace. What should Van de Kamp, with his twenty combat missions, have done had this not been the case?

I lay in the cockpit with my legs bent as much as the narrow fuselage allowed. In spite of this my upper body still projected some way into the actual cockpit and Van de Kamp had to lean forward so that I could at least rest my head on his shoulder. The takeoff was successful and I was overjoyed when the machine lifted off. Now we had to hope that no enemy aircraft spotted us and that the machine would survive everything.

We hurried toward our destination at full throttle, staying low, close to the surface of the water. When we could no longer see the Crimea, Van de Kamp began to climb.

My limbs hurt so that I had to turn for the first time. It really was an acrobatic feat and I congratulated myself on formerly having played so much sports and on being so supple. My face now lay against the *Leutnant*'s cheek. For his part he sat there with clenched teeth and tried to hold the machine on course and he was visibly having trouble. The machine was completely out of trim and because of the unusual load had become rather nose-heavy, so that Van de Kamp could only keep it straight and level by pulling the stick back and to the right.

After five minutes it was time to turn again. I simply couldn't stay in one position any longer. Finally, finally, 45 minutes had passed and from 4,000 meters the land was visible as a gray something in the distance. Not much more could happen to us now. We were almost saved.

We crossed the coast not far from Mamaia airfield. They fired a green flare, the signal that we could land. Van de Kamp tried to make his approach without regard to the wind direction. In doing so he took the wind sock off the flight control building with one wingtip, and what was more came in far too wide and was forced to pull up and go around. I lay beside him, unable to help. Once again he had to go around. On the third try I realized that we were much too high, but the *Leutnant* couldn't or didn't want to make another approach and forced the machine toward the ground still going quite fast. We touched down far beyond the landing cross and raced over the ground. Braking was useless and we hurtled toward a pile of fuel drums which had been placed on the landing field. Van de Lamp did the only correct thing. He stepped so hard on the left rudder pedal and brake that the Bf 109 abruptly swerved to the left and sheared off the right landing gear leg. We slid along the ground and the machine came to a stop just short of the fuel drums.

Although we were in the last machine to come from the Crimea to Mamaia, some other pilots did not get off so easily as we. Proof of this lay in the many crashed and overturned aircraft on the field. Luckily the hasty flight had not cost any lives from among the pilots. There were no injuries apart from scrapes and bumps.

I then celebrated a very moving and happy reunion with my friend Heino Sachsenberg. He too had made it, but his trip to Mamaia had been significantly more difficult.

# CHAPTER VI
# Romanian Summer

There was practically no flying in Romania because almost all of *Jagdgeschwader* 52 was non-operational at first. We all needed rest to heal our wounds, both physical and emotional. And rest is what we got.

In the following days the personnel of our *Gruppe* and the *Geschwaderstab*, but no aircraft, transferred to Zarnesti, a small mountain town northwest of Buzeau. There was plenty of wine, with which we repeatedly celebrated our survival. Most of the officers and *Staffelkapitäne* lived with their pilots in a so-called mess. I had private quarters and very soon made friends with my hosts, which contributed significantly to my recovery.

But even good days can become hard to bear in the long run. We pilots had soon overcome or forgotten all the horrors of the Crimea and felt it was time to get back to the job for which we had been trained. We wanted to fly, we wanted new aircraft.

On May 24, 1944 I climbed into a Messerschmitt again for the first time since the Crimean tragedy. At first I was only allowed to make five practice flights. Four days later an order reached the *Gruppe*, according to which a *Staffel* was to be detached to the Reich Defense. We knew all too well that it was a virtual death sentence for anyone who had to move to the Reich. But none of us thought of refusing. 6 *Staffel* had the most pilots and it seemed likely that it would be chosen for this reason alone.

The *Kapitäne* of 4 and 5 *Staffeln*, Lt. Waldmann and Oblt. Batz, came by to "congratulate" me on my luck. But the *Gruppenkommandeur* arrived at the same time and informed us that 4 *Staffel* had been chosen for the Reich Defense.

I must admit that the news took a load off my heart. Naturally I would have flown against the heavy bombers and Mustangs and would probably have shot some down. But the outcome of this affair was predictable. Everyone who flew in the Reich was "burned" sooner or later. The same thing could happen any day against the Russians, but here there was a much better chance or getting home again in one piece. Lt. Waldmann, who was later transferred to JG 3 and then JG 7, was in fact killed in March 1945. After a total of 134 kills he died in a crash following a collision with an Me 262 in Holland.

The two *Staffeln* of our *Gruppe* transferred to Husi on the Prut River on May 27. From there we resumed combat flying. Also based at Husi was *Major* Rudel and his Stukas. We fighter pilots were given the job of providing escort for the bombers when they flew up to Jassy. In the period which began on May 31, 1944, I shot down a total of nine enemy aircraft while on escort duties.

We soon learned that there were Russians in this combat zone who could fly as well as we.

My wingman and I approached the front slowly at 2,500 meters, looking to all sides because a number of Il-2s had been reported. Then we sighted them, about 1,000 meters below us. As a precaution I looked around one more time before attacking and spotted two enemy machines with red noses coming at us from out of the sun. I quickly instructed my wingman to stay close, but waited and acted as if I hadn't noticed the attackers. When the Russians were in firing range we hauled our machines around into a tight turn. The two Airacobras shot past as they were unable to turn with us due to their greater speed. They didn't give up, however. The two fighters pulled up and came down at us again. They made one attack after another and forced us ever lower.

The two enemy aircraft became four. Now we had to face constantly alternating attacks and never got an opportunity to fire. My wingman was even hit several times.

Then I rammed the throttle forward, pulled the stick back into my stomach and spun down from 1,000 meters almost to ground level. I pulled out and raced away just above the ground toward the southwest. I saw an aircraft at my seven o'clock position and with relief recognized my wingman's "109." He had stayed rigidly behind me and had even emulated my spin.

I wasn't about to let the Russians catch us so easily a second time, so we climbed quickly to 4,500 meters. But even at that altitude several Airacobras jumped us from above and gave us such a scare that it was not until the flight home that I really recovered my senses. On the third sortie we climbed to 6,000 meters; I had never encountered Russian aircraft at a higher altitude. But once again we didn't even reach the front. All I saw was Airacobras above. Once again they forced us to flee. Now I had really had enough, and following a steep Split-S I made my home with my wingman as fast as I could. I was furious when I landed. Never before had the Russians simply not allowed me to get into attack position.

The next day I ran into the "fighter school" which Heino Sachsenberg had described. I arrived at the front at 5,000 meters and saw a good dozen aircraft about 20 kilometers inside Russian territory, beautifully spaced laterally and vertically and likewise approaching the front. They may have been 1,500 meters lower. At first I ignored them. I let them fly past below me in peace, then took up position in the sun with my wingman and followed them in the direction of our lines.

Let them fly on, I thought, as long as they're heading west it's in our favor. The enemy aircraft would soon have to turn for home. And they did. We fell on them while the Russians were concentrating on turning in the best possible order and avoiding one another. I left the last two machines to Brandecker, my wingman. I moved in on the third Russian and, flying at the same height as the last enemy aircraft, fired from the left and below into his wings and fuselage. The aircraft immediately began emitting smoke and pitched downward.

I watched him as I climbed away. To my disappointment the Ivan recovered at about 1,000 meters and tried to escape toward the east. I hadn't thought it possible, because I had scored quite a few hits from close range. So I dove after him. The pilot didn't see me coming and it was all over in seconds. After a few bursts he blew up and plunged toward the earth.

I wanted to get back to the "school" after my kill but it had taken to its heels. Instead I ran into a lone Yak-7. Its pilot was so audacious that he approached us head on and opened fire. I had seen this coming. I gained speed, and before the Russian had completed his reversal I was above him. He probably hadn't expected me to move so fast. I hit him several times but it wasn't enough for a kill.

The Yak immediately straightened out and tried to dive away. That was a big mistake. He went down after a few bursts and crashed at 0805, exactly three minutes after his predecessor.

I scored another double the same day. Again Uffz. Brandecker was my wingman. This time he got involved, shooting down a Pe-2. We took off from Husi shortly after eleven o'clock and climbed to 3,000 meters. By chance I spotted a large number of small flak bursts beneath me over friendly territory, which meant that there must be Russian aircraft below.

We hauled our machines around and dove toward the flak bursts. Then I saw what the fuss was about. Flying at the lowest altitude were about twelve large aircraft, so big that they couldn't be missed, and above them a swarm of escort fighters. As I dove, one startled Russian flew right in front of me. I immediately shot off half of his right wing without having to alter course. He went down like a stone, spun a little and then smashed into the ground.

Brandecker and I had meanwhile pulled up and now approached the formation from beneath. Again I hit an enemy aircraft, which fled away beneath the others trailing a banner of white-gray smoke. We swooped down again. The Russians scattered, with each trying to get to safety.

But we ignored the fighters and plunged on toward the bombers. These fired away at us and plenty of tracer flashed past our ears. "Take the rearmost bomber, I'll attack the one in front of it," I called to Brandecker. "And don't fire until I say so!"

Our pursuers, the Russian fighters, were still far from being in good firing position. The dance could begin. "Now, Brandecker!"

I glanced briefly to the side and saw flames spitting from the guns of the Messerschmitt behind and to my left. Pieces flew off the bomber flying to my left. Then it was time for me to fire. I aimed carefully, while the bomber in front of me quickly grew larger. I wanted to hit the right engine. That wasn't too difficult, because the enemy machine was flying straight and level. There were flashes as I hit the Ivan and soon the engine was blazing fiercely.

I moved over through the fire from the rear gunner to hit the left engine, but the machine in front of me suddenly came to life. It bucked, weaved and danced so violently that it was difficult for me to aim properly. I was concerned to see the fighters markedly closer behind us, and if I didn't finish off the bomber in the next few seconds it would be my turn. I dropped below the bomber, hoping it would settle down again. And in fact the Russian reacted as I had hoped. He had become separated from his companions and now tried to rejoin formation quickly. However that was his undoing. I pulled up and let him have it with everything my guns could put out in half a second.

The bomber's left engine was now also in flames, while behind me the one shot down by Brandecker fell burning to earth. It was high time for us to dive away, because the fighters were now behind us and firing wildly. We danced the waltz of our lives and turned into the valleys southwest of Jassy in the direction of Husi. During this flight I was hit three times in the wings and Brandecker eight, but in return I had four kills on the day.

The *Gruppe* soon transferred to Manzar in the southeast part of Romania. All in all we spent a quiet time there, nestled in private quarters.

After a longer period of quiet the so-called "Star Flights" began. These were sorties against American four-engined bombers. At first, however, such "Star Flights" were made for test purposes.

Things got serious on June 11, 1944. A large number of American machines flew into the Ploesti area to attack the oil refineries there. We flew to Zilistea with 16 aircraft, refuelled and took off again. Thanks to excellent work by the ground controllers we were vectored right to the formation and immediately made contact with the "Fat Autos."[1] It was quite different from flying against the Russians. The number of aircraft was amazing.

Behind the huge formations were long, thick condensation trails; one simply couldn't miss them. Above the bombers, probably up to 10,000 meters, the sky swarmed with fighters. There were so many I

[1] Auto. Radio code word for enemy twin-engined aircraft. Fat Auto (*dicke Auto*) denotes a heavy bomber.

didn't dare look up. What could we possibly do against such overwhelming numbers?

As long as we stayed away from the bombers we didn't cause much of a stir. We turned and climbed ever closer to the bomber stream. At 5,500 meters the Liberators were still above us. As we climbed we flew through a swarm of American fighters, which totally ignored us! Did they think we were some of theirs?

On reaching 6,500 meters I spotted a lone Fortress several hundred meters below. Sachsenberg had seen it too. He came with me. I concentrated on the four-engined bomber. It was some piece of work! The closer I got, the larger the ship became. But now it was time to fire.

The American bomber made no move to defend itself; perhaps, like the fighters, it thought I was one of its own. The barge in front of me more than filled my gunsight; I opened fire and saw my tracer disappear into its fuselage. I concentrated on the right, outer engine. The Fortress was flying straight and level and my aim was good. Soon the second engine was also burning. In that very instant, to my horror, I saw a dense stream of tracer flash over my canopy. I pulled up. But it wasn't the Americans who had frightened me so badly, instead it was my friend Sachsenberg. Flying inverted, I was able to watch closely as he set the other two engines on fire and then hung on until the mighty machine was completely in flames. Afterward the Fortress broke apart and five parachutes hung in the air.

But now the enemy fighters dove on us, almost 50 machines. There was only one thing to do: throttle forward, stick back and full left rudder. Everything else was up to my brave Messerschmitt. I slow rolled from 6,000 meters down to ground level, then levelled off and raced away. I wasn't about to allow myself to be had that easily. And no American had ever shot me down, something the Russians had done five times.

Finally I saw the Danube below me, and I was thus able to figure out my approximate position and find my way to Zilistea. Four Messerschmitts had already landed there, one of them with eight bullet holes. All but three of our pilots returned.

That evening we gathered in the mess and celebrated our first encounter with the Americans – and our safe return as well. We had learned a great deal from this first contact with the new enemy. We all felt that it was a damned dangerous thing to tackle such superior numbers. Unfortunately none of us had been able to learn anything about the fighting qualities of the Mustang as there had not been sufficient time. In any event this type of attack was risky enough, three of our pilots had been killed. We weren't concerned about the bombers. In future we would have to try and avoid the many fighters as long as possible.

The next "Star Flight" was a false alarm, as the Americans did not fly into our area, and so we flew empty handed back to Manzar. The next operational orders came after a pause of 13 days. As we had lost three pilots on our last mission, we took off with rather mixed feelings. There was not a cloud in the sky when about 300 heavy bombers were reported. This news made us even more quiet.

I assigned the pilots, and everyone put on a cheerful face for the others. We took off from Zilistea again in our last nine aircraft, scarcely taking enough time to refuel. I had worked out a plan. In no case would I again attack a lone bomber, because I had learned that such machines often turned out to be so-called "flak cruisers," which carried a greatly strengthened defensive armament instead of bombs. Such aircraft flew alone to attract German fighters.

Once again the ground control was outstanding and we were the first formation to sight the enemy. As we climbed I saw three large formations of about 40 aircraft each passing high above us. The escorting fighters were even higher. There were so many aircraft flashing in the sun above me that I was compelled to keep looking at them, as if spellbound.

Slowly we approached the gleaming silver birds. The three formations were arranged with the first ahead and somewhat higher, the second in the middle and below, and the third at the same height as the first. Apparently the two higher formations would cover the lower with their defensive weapons. A defense from 120 machines, that could be quite a fireworks display! And that was to say nothing of the many fighters which would soon be on our backs. "Don't despair, oh tiny band." The sentiment was really appropriate in this case.

We overtook the lower group of Americans in closed formation. I had decided to make the first attack from the front. Far ahead of the heavy bombers I said: "Attention, we're going to reverse course and make a frontal attack. Everyone stay close and don't fire until I do!"

Reversing course and rejoining formation took only a matter of a few seconds. In fact my pilots performed as if taking part in an exercise, which would have pure joy had the circumstances been different. I was in the lead and the enemy now appeared to have noticed what was coming. Perhaps they hadn't believed that a few 109s would dare to attack them. They tried to evade our attack by altering course but it was too late, we were too close.

We closed at terrific speed. The higher formation opened fire at us. "Don't shoot yet, don't shoot yet," I called to my men. Then it was time, and we could return fire. All hell appeared to have broken loose. I saw little of what was going on around me, rather I aimed carefully at the approaching aircraft. There were flashes all over the bomber and then I had to pull up to avoid flying into the enemy aircraft.

I flew close over the formation, then dove away immediately and began looking around for the American fighters. Of these there was nothing to be seen. Six other Messerschmitts flew beside me at about the same altitude, several were missing. I reassembled my small band and immediately began turning around in preparation for an attack on the Americans from behind.

While we were turning a voice rang out over the frequency: "Where is enemy contact?" Now if our people could overlook this demonstration, then they were beyond help. So I gave no answer and instead devoted my attention to the coming attack. We had meanwhile rejoined formation and were slowly approaching the heavy bombers. The Americans opened fire long before we did. We roared through the whole formation, firing all the while, and once we were a safe distance in front turned around again. This time the bombers frustrated our attack by altering their direction of flight. As a result we were only able to fire on the machines at the back of the formation from ahead and to the side. After this attack I saw my wingman, the young Uffz. Tamen, flying beside me. But where were the others?

I had lost all my enthusiasm for another pass at the "fat ones." Two machines against about 100 was just too much. I didn't spend much time calling to the other pilots, instead I ordered Tamen to stay close and together we attacked several stragglers flying behind the main formation. There were at least eight and all were emitting a lot of smoke. We picked out one of the damaged aircraft for our attack.

When I made the first pass the American was still fighting back spiritedly. I set one of his port engines on fire. Tamen, who came in right behind me, also shot well. After checking for enemy fighters I slowed down to match the bomber's speed and fired into its fuselage until it literally blew apart. This all happened so quickly that none of the crew had time to get out.

A little farther ahead wallowed a second Liberator. We attacked this one too, ignoring the defensive fire. Each of us made two attacks and the aircraft was already burning when Tamen ran out of ammunition. I positioned myself behind the bomber and stayed there until it, too, exploded. I saw two men bail out before the Liberator blew up.

Altogether German fighters scored nine victories, two of these by our *Gruppe* – one by Tamen and the other by me.

Together with Uffz. Tamen, I landed at Buzeau. We climbed out of our aircraft, hugged each other and celebrated our victories – and our safe return. We had good reason to celebrate. We were the only ones to return to base safe and sound. Five of our fellow pilots had been shot down by the Americans and two of these had been killed. Lt. Ewald managed to get out of his burning aircraft at the last moment. In the process he sustained such serious burns that his survival was in doubt for some time. Two machines were forced to make belly landings due to damage received in combat.

The tally after these "Star Flights" was devastating. There were only two combat-ready aircraft from the two *Staffeln* which up until that time had proudly called themselves a *Gruppe*. Without the necessary machines the eleven pilots still available were, so to speak, worthless. But more than the shortage of aircraft, it was the impression of the battle with the heavy bombers and the numerically superior enemy which hit us the hardest. The pilots weren't of much use at the moment. The *Kommodore* must have realized this too, because afterward he got onto *Fliegerkorps* and arranged our transfer to Poland.

There was little flying in the period from June 24, 1944, when we had been so badly knocked about, and our transfer to Zamosc in Poland. On June 27 I succeeded in shooting down an Il-2 over Russian territory. It was kill number 129.

Then in command of I *Fliegerkorps* was *Generalmajor* Deichmann. The *Gruppe* and I were frequently placed under his direct control. He did all that was within his power to make life at the front easier, and we showed him our gratitude by doing everything he asked of us. Deichmann was often heard to declare emphatically, "II./JG 52 is my pride." During the time we were without aircraft at Manzar I could not help feeling that the medical officers and several officers of the IV A Department had done a great deal of talking to our superiors, as a result of which we obtained something of a bad reputation. They claimed that our physical condition had sunk below the zero point primarily through the excessive consumption of alcohol.

I therefore decided to put on a sports-day with the pilots of the two *Staffeln*. We wanted to use the occasion to show *Generalmajor* Deichmann what we were made of. So every evening we trained in the long jump, high jump and the 1,000-meter run and were soon achieving respectable results. We also invited several competitors from the surrounding units to take part in our sports-day, which was to take place on a Saturday. Deichmann arrived too, but we had to cut short our meet soon afterward, as he brought with him our transfer orders for Poland. But he did see several events, and said repeatedly: "Very good, Lipfert, very good."

Our transfer came so suddenly that some of the pilots, who had all received new aircraft in the meantime, were unable to find the right maps for the flight to Poland. Even I, the acting *Gruppenkommandeur* – Barkhorn was in hospital after being wounded – had only a very primitive map. Before takeoff I was told that I had to fly north-northwest about 400 kilometers along the edge of the Carpathians. At some time or other my pilots and I would come to Lvov.

As a precaution, especially against losing our way, we had long-range tanks hung under the bellies of our Messerschmitts. These would give us adequate fuel to find an airfield in the vicinity of Lvov. All aircraft got off safely and, after flying a farewell circuit of the airfield, we set course for Lvov. At first things went pretty much according to plan, and I had no difficulty pinpointing our position on the map, but as we went on this became increasingly difficult. Soon I had no idea where we were. Then I heard Sachsenberg's voice over the radio: "Radetzki from six one, what's our position?" I replied: "Heino, I can't say at the moment, but we're heading in the right direction in any case."

After a few seconds of silence Sachsenberg replied in a disguised voice, which I remembered well from the sports-day: "Very good, Lipfert, very good!"

In spite of our map shortcomings we reached Lvov safely and from there flew on to Zamosc-Mokre, our new base, about 150 kilometers north of Lvov. That was July 12, 1944. Two days later I shot down an Airacobra. There was plenty going on up there, with scarcely a day that did not bring us into contact with the enemy. Within a week I had scored 10 kills flying from this airfield, including three in one sortie.

Then we were required for action farther south and on July 21 we transferred to Lvov. In the course of this move I once again came within a hair of not coming back. Actually the event was not so unexpected, because for days I had the feeling that another test was coming. And it came.

I was flying at the time with a new wingman, Uffz. Dalecki. We had been instructed to fly to the front again and then land at Lvov. Flying a combat mission as part of a transfer flight and possibly becoming involved in combat was not popular with the older fighter pilots. One didn't know the new airfield and had stowed all his meager belongings in the machine's fuselage and baggage compartment. Instead of a seat parachute I had the tarpaulin in my cockpit, as there was no more room for it in the baggage compartment.

I told my wingman that we would have a quick look at the front and then immediately set course for home. And finally, for the first and last time, I did not have my flying helmet on with its built-in headset, but instead flew in my coat and peaked cap. My wingman was close beside me so that we could communicate using hand signals. Under these circumstances we headed for the front.

I spotted two Russians circling, although they were quite some distance away. They appeared to be chasing one another around a cloud and were playing the game with considerable skill.

We were 50 kilometers from Lvov, about 30 kilometers inside enemy territory. The sky was clear of other aircraft, so I could have a go. I needed no particular attack position, because the two Ivans were quite busy with themselves and not suspecting trouble. Just as I dove, the first Russian ducked back into a cumulus cloud and the other climbed slightly and hung above it so that he could see his comrade when he emerged.

The Russian was about to descend in a gentle left turn, when I arrived behind him and hit him with everything I had. The pilot immediately jettisoned his canopy and bailed out. His parachute opened soon afterward. I pulled up to look for the other one, but I sensed instinctively that something was wrong. Some sort of danger seemed to be approaching.

To be sure I saw the Russian turning around his cloud looking for his comrade, but I climbed higher until was back with my wingman. I checked all the instruments again, scanned the surrounding airspace and prepared to attack again.

But the Russian also appeared to have noticed that something was up, because he suddenly dove away toward the northeast. I dove after him for some distance and could definitely have caught him had not the feeling of uncertainty suddenly returned.

Heeding my premonition, I pulled up at 2,500 meters and turned in the direction of home. My wingman followed from above. We were still perhaps 20 kilometers inside enemy territory when there was a loud bang. The next thing I knew my propeller was stationary. When that familiar odor reached my nose, I started calculating: if the machine doesn't catch fire and no Russian shoots me down, then I can glide about 20 kilometers. That might be enough to reach our lines.

I had to stay with the aircraft in any event, as I had no parachute. I calmly placed the propeller in the gliding position, lowered the flaps slightly and wobbled along at 270 kph. I intended to fly on toward the west as long as the aircraft still had altitude. It would come down to earth somewhere on its own and then I could decide whether the territory I was over was held by the Russians, Polish partisans or Germans. It was at least reassuring to have my wingman escorting me.

I lost height steadily. It was time to start worrying about the terrain. But wherever I looked there was only forest. Had not a pilot recently said that it was possible to land a "109" in the treetops? I had no other choice. "Approach very near, half-stall the machine and then set down softly on the treetops." Still, the Messerschmitt, with its three tonne weight, would still roar into the forest at 160 kph. It would be disastrous.

50 meters, 30, 10 meters. Just as I was about to begin the landing I saw a small clearing to the left in front of me. A road cut through the clearing. Although I knew that a low-speed turn probably meant a crash,

I risked it. I nursed my mule into the clear area, set it down on its belly, bounced over the road and came to a stop just short of the forest on the other side. Before the Messerschmitt came to a stop I had released my straps and opened the canopy hood. I saw field-gray uniforms running toward me as I jumped down from the wing. I was saved.

I learned from the soldiers that we were only three kilometers from the front and that it would be advisable to prepare the machine for demolition. While we conversed my faithful wingman flew overhead. Satisfied that I had landed in friendly territory, he roared away toward the west. An infantry *Leutnant* gave me a stiff drink, which I needed, and then prepared my machine for demolition.

A *Storch* arrived at about noon to pick me up, but it nosed over on landing, shattering the propeller. Now there were two wrecks in the small clearing. Finally a borrowed car took me to Lvov, and I immediately dispatched another *Storch* with several technical personnel. They were able to repair the first *Storch*, which took off again, but my Messerschmitt was lost. It was blown up that evening, just before the Russians arrived.

Our stay at Lvov, too, was brief. The next day we moved to Stry, and once again I shot down an enemy aircraft, a Boston, during the transfer flight. My wingman also downed a Russian. I saw his kill, but he did not see the machine shot down by me, so that the Boston was not confirmed.

One day the aircraft reporting service failed to do its job and without warning large formations of Russians appeared very near our base. When I saw what was coming I got into my machine so quickly that I almost got off the ground ahead of the alert *Rotte*. I held my Messerschmitt close to the ground, kept clear of the Russians' flight path and then climbed. The Russians had completed their bombing attack on our airfield before I reached the higher altitude necessary for a promising attack and the aircraft turned away toward the northeast. But another formation was already approaching.

In an effort to upset their aim, I flew into the approaching parade of 20 to 30 machines from ahead. Meeting heavy return fire, I pulled up to look for a straggler from behind. But the Russians stayed in formation, so I flew toward them again spraying fire among the aircraft from long range. This had the desired effect of unsettling the Russians. The Il-2s tried to drop their loads quickly and none of the bombs hit the airfield.

Then the Ivans made their familiar reversal and turned away in the direction of home. But there must have been a beginner among them. I recognized this because he apparently didn't yet know the rules of the game. While the others completed their turns and disappeared at full throttle as fast as they could, this one turned to the right from the standard left turn, left the formation and looked over a fuel tank burning on our airfield. The whole thing was played out at about 600 meters and in full view of those on the ground.

These few seconds were enough for him to become separated from his companions and to allow me to approach. I rammed the throttle forward and descended so as to position myself directly behind him. The Russian saw what was coming and my first attack failed. I scored no hits as the enemy pilot turned immediately. I stood my machine on one wingtip and turned with him. I reduced speed slowly, positioned myself as close behind him as possible and waited for his next move. I had time, because he had a long way to fly to get home.

I instructed a second Messerschmitt which showed up – it was Uffz. Buchheit – to provide top cover 500 meters above us. Meanwhile the Ivan turned for his life. He pulled so hard on the stick that the machine shuddered and several times vapor trails formed behind both wingtips. He tried to straighten out his Yak and I opened fire at once. He was forced to resume turning, but there were a few flashes from hits on his aircraft. Then the Russian made a Split-S from 600 meters which I could not follow. I dove after him, but the enemy had already gained several kilometers. I soon caught up however and he had to start turning again. I scored more hits when the Russian attempted to straighten out again.

My bullets must have damaged his controls, because he remained in a shallow left turn and I closed in behind him. For a fraction of a second all my shells wandered into the fuselage of the Yak. I broke away and flew past the aircraft very close. Just then it exploded. Pieces fell burning to earth and I felt the force of the explosion in my "109."

That was my last kill from Stry, because on July 25 we moved to Milek and three days later to Krakow. This marked the beginning of another dry spell. There was little contact with the enemy and what was more it was about 100 kilometers to the front. No one could confirm the only kill I made, which came finally on August 2, 1944, and so it was considered an "also ran."

One notable event occurred at Krakow: I was married between two sorties. But more about the attendant circumstances later. One thing should be mentioned though. At that time Sachsenberg returned from leave. At the guard post he asked the sentry: "Is II./JG 52 based here? Is *Leutnant* Lipfert here?" The sentry answered that the unit in question was present, but that there was no *Leutnant* Lipfert. There was a *Hauptmann* Lipfert, who had been married the day before. Friend Heino was thunderstruck. "*Hauptmann* Lipfert and married? – No that can't be him, he was generally quite normal."

During the three months Sachsenberg was in hospital recovering from his "nervous breakdown" I had been promoted to *Hauptmann* and had received the Knight's Cross.

From Krakow we went to Radom, from there to Mzurawo and back to Krakow again. On August 21 we took off for the long trip across Hungary to Romania, to an area near Manzar, which was well known to us. In the meantime I had scored two more victories and when I returned to our former combat zone I had 143 kills. But again we couldn't stay long, as Russian tanks were already approaching our airfield. Since all contact with corps had been lost, I had to take matters into my own hands. Under no circumstances did I want to be accused of cowardice, but abandoning a position without orders was a risky affair. I sent a Bf 109 back to corps, but the first T-34s had already rolled past the airfield before it returned. It was a damned ticklish situation in which I now found myself. If I stayed at the base with my half *Gruppe* we would certainly be overrun by the Russians and the machines and pilots would be lost. There were 18 or 19 machines on the airfield but I had only 12 pilots! If I began evacuating the field and the Russians were halted again, then a court martial against me was almost certain.

When I still was unable to make contact with corps I began the evacuation on my own. The available Ju 52s were loaded with the most vital equipment and on their return they had to bring back pilots from a reconnaissance *Staffel* so that we could bring out all of our machines.

The first Junkers approached the airfield very low and landed safely. The second transport was fired on but likewise got down safely. The Russians arrived as we were taking off with the last transports for the second time. The Ju 52 which had just taken off with some of the technical personnel on board had to fly through a rather heavy curtain of flak. When the last transport aircraft got airborne, Russian fighters and bombers were already over the airfield.

We let them drop their bombs undisturbed, but they failed to inflict any further damage on the airfield. Then we climbed and attacked. Every pilot did the same without regard to position and without worrying whether or not his kills were seen and confirmed. In the melee I shot down a Yak which was about to shoot down Heino Sachsenberg. The kill was not confirmed but I had saved the life of my friend.

Halfway to Galatz, while flying alone, I encountered the enemy again. The aircraft I was flying was a real dog and definitely ready for the repair shop. I therefore wanted to avoid combat and flew at low level, but the situation that was presented me was too good to pass up. Nevertheless it nearly ended badly for me. Suddenly there were two Il-2s in front of me. They were firing on German troops marching toward the southwest. I rammed the throttle forward and open fire. Pieces flew off both machines.

Both Il-2s took hit after hit. I was so engrossed that I sat up in shock when a burst of tracer shot over the wing of my Me. Quick as lightning I dove away and in the same instant saw a Yak about 100 meters behind me.

He followed as I passed beneath the Il-2s, both of which were still firing, and I realized that the pilot behind me knew what he was doing. I called on all my skill as I fought for my life. But the lad stayed rigidly behind me and was able to score repeated hits on my Messerschmitt. I dared not turn in this machine, but I couldn't climb either, as waiting there were the Il-2s and a large number of fighters. So I had to stay close to the ground and let the other fellow put his gunnery skills to the test. It required all my attention just to avoid flying into the ground. Even though I didn't fly straight and level for an instant the Russian continued to score hits.

Finally my aircraft had built up enough speed so that I slowly but surely began to pull away. Then I climbed a little higher and made my way to Galatz as quickly as possible.

All the other members of the *Gruppe* had already gathered there and were waiting for me. They marvelled at my shot-up "*Beule*"[2] and many

[2]*Beule*. Nickname given later versions of the Bf 109 G series. Meaning "bump" or "bulge," it refers to the external fairings and protrusions which distinguished the aircraft from its predecessors.

*The senior NCO of 6 Staffel, Hauptfeldwebel Bolinski. The senior NCO was an indispensable part of a fighter unit.*

*Ofw. Tobaben, chief mechanic of 6 Staffel, was responsible for the combat readiness of all the Staffel's aircraft.*

*Hptm. Lipfert's crew chief, Uffz. Schmid. Without him there would have been no success.*

*Messerschmitt Bf 109 Gs on the production line . . .*

*. . . and in action. JG 52 flew the Bf 109 exclusively.*

*Hauptmann Lipfert and the personnel of 6./JG 52, photographed at Csor, Hungary in December 1944.*

*"Shape up" 1944. Staffelkapitän Lipfert believed that a good fighter pilot needed physical strength . . .*

*. . . and exercised just like his pilots.*

*Hptm. Erich Hartmann and Hptm. Helmut Lipfert at Csor, December 1944.*

*December 24, 1944. Hptm. Lipfert prepares for his 610th combat mission at Vesprem. Helping him get strapped in is Uffz. Schmid.*

*Lipfert's 610th combat mission resulted in his 164th victory. At 1425 on December 24, Lipfert shot down an Il-2 two kilometers north of Seregelyes. The photograph shows Hptm. Lipfert leaving the cockpit of his aircraft soon after landing.*

*Major Hermann Graf led Jagdgeschwader 52 from the beginning of October 1944 until the end of the war.*

*Oblt. Friederich Obleser, one of the successful pilots of III./JG 52, led 8 Staffel until wounded in late December 1944.*

*Lt. Friederich Haas took over command of 5./JG 52 in December 1944. On April 9, 1945 he was shot down over Vienna by Russian fighters. Due to the low altitude at which the combat took place there was no time for his parachute to open. Lt. Haas was awarded the Knight's Cross following his death.*

*Another shot of "Bubi" Hartmann and Helmut Lipfert at Csor. Hartmann wears a rather skeptical expression as he listens to what Lipfert has to say.*

*Christmas 1944: From left to right: Uffz. Welz, Fw. Reichstein, Lt. Steins (in tent), Hptm. Lipfert, unidentified. Steins, who later became Kapitän of 6./JG 52, was posted missing after an air battle on January 22, 1945.*

*December 1944. A Hungarian general presents decorations to German and Hungarian fighter pilots. Hauptmann Lipfert was probably the only German to receive the "Hungarian Officers Golden Medal for Bravery," which was awarded only eleven times.*

*Vesprem, Hungary December 1944. Hptm. Hartmann, Major Barkhorn, Hptm. Lipfert (2nd from right) and Hptm. Sturm with Hungarian pilots. At the time the photograph was taken the three German pilots had accounted for about 790 enemy aircraft.*

*Hptm. Lipfert scored his 172nd kill the same day Major Barkhorn got his 300th. Nagyigmand, Hungary, January 4, 1945.*

*Fighter aces of II./JG 52. Left front is Major Batz, behind him Lt. Düttmann, sitting on the radiator Lt. Sachsenberg, and in front of him Hptm. Lipfert with Lt. Ewald, looking somewhat skeptically into the lens. Probably at Vesprem airfield, February 1945.*

Hptm. Lipfert scored his last two dozen kills as Kommandeur of I./JG 53. Here are the victory and witness reports for Lipfert's 200th kill, which came on April 8, 1945 near Hainburg, west of Bratislava.

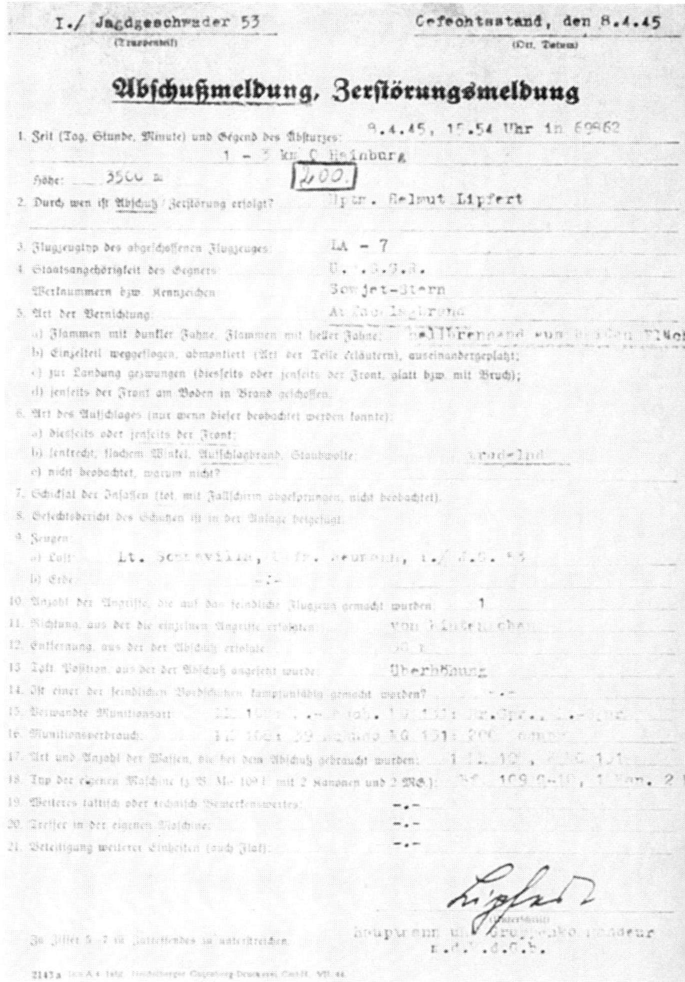

I./ Jagdgeschwader 53 (Truppenteil) — Gefechtsstand, den 8.4.45 (Ort, Datum)

**Abschußmeldung, Zerstörungsmeldung**

1. Zeit (Tag, Stunde, Minute) und Gegend des Absturzes: 8.4.45, 15.54 Uhr in 69862 1 - 3 km O Hainburg
Höhe: 3500 m [200.]
2. Durch wen ist Abschuß / Zerstörung erfolgt? Hptm. Helmut Lipfert
3. Flugzeugtyp des abgeschossenen Flugzeuges: LA - 7
4. Staatsangehörigkeit des Gegners: U.d.S.S.R.
Werknummern bzw. Kennzeichen: Sowjet-Stern
5. Art der Vernichtung: Aufschlagbrand
a) Flammen mit dunkler Fahne, Flammen mit heller Fahne: hellbrennend aus beiden Fläch[en]
b) Einzelteil weggeflogen, abmontiert (Art der Teile erläutern), auseinandergeplatzt;
c) zur Landung gezwungen (diesseits oder jenseits der Front, glatt bzw. mit Bruch);
d) jenseits der Front am Boden in Brand geschossen.
6. Art des Aufschlages (nur wenn dieser beobachtet werden konnte):
a) diesseits oder jenseits der Front;
b) senkrecht, flachem Winkel, Aufschlagbrand, Staubwolke: trudelnd
c) nicht beobachtet, warum nicht?
7. Schicksal der Insassen (tot, mit Fallschirm abgesprungen, nicht beobachtet).
8. Gefechtsbericht des Schützen ist in der Anlage beigefügt.
9. Zeugen:
a) Luft: Lt. [illegible], [illegible], I./J.G. 53
b) Erde: -.-
10. Anzahl der Angriffe, die auf das feindliche Flugzeug gemacht wurden: 1
11. Richtung, aus der die einzelnen Angriffe erfolgten: von hinten oben
12. Entfernung, aus der der Abschuß erfolgte: 50 m
13. Takt. Position, aus der der Abschuß angesetzt wurde: Überhöhung
14. Ist einer der feindlichen Bordschützen kampfunfähig gemacht worden? -.-
15. Verwandte Munitionsart: [illegible]
16. Munitionsverbrauch: [illegible]
17. Art und Anzahl der Waffen, die bei dem Abschuß gebraucht wurden: [illegible]
18. Typ der eigenen Maschine (z. B. Me 109 F mit 2 Kanonen und 2 MG): Bf 109 G-10, 1 Kan. 2 [illegible]
19. Weiteres taktisch oder technisch Bemerkenswertes: -.-
20. Treffer in der eigenen Maschine: -.-
21. Beteiligung weiterer Einheiten (auch Flak): -.-

Lipfert (Unterschrift)
Hauptmann und Gruppenkommandeur
m.d.F.d.G.b.

Zu Ziffer 5-7 ist Zutreffendes zu unterstreichen.

2143a [illegible] Heidelberger Gutenberg-Druckerei GmbH. VII.44.

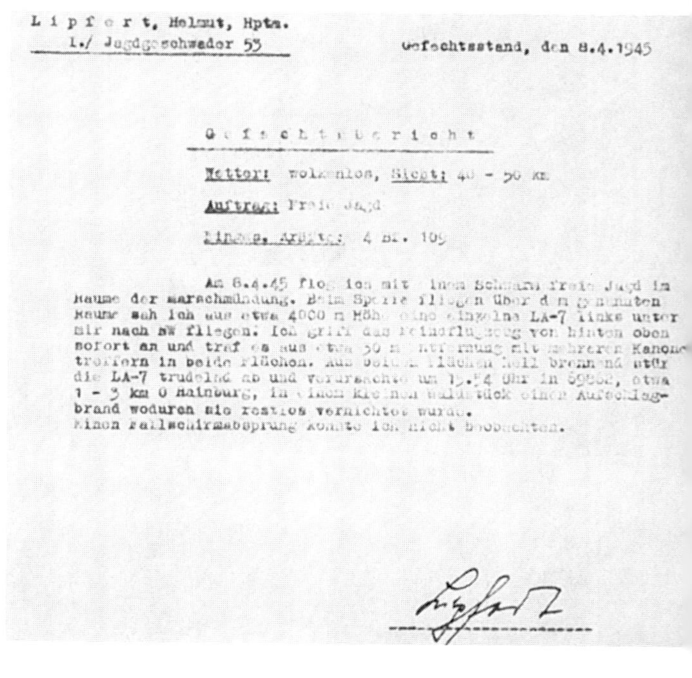

Lipfert, Helmut, Hptm.
I./ Jagdgeschwader 53 — Gefechtsstand, den 8.4.1945

Gefechtsbericht

Wetter: wolkenlos, Sicht: 40 - 50 km.

Auftrag: Freie Jagd

Einsatz. Anzahl: 4 Bf. 109

Am 8.4.45 flog ich mit einem Schwarm freie Jagd im Raume der Marchmündung. Beim Sperre fliegen über dem genannten Raum sah ich aus etwa 4000 m Höhe eine einzelne LA-7 links unter mir nach SW fliegen. Ich griff das Feindflugzeug von hinten oben sofort an und traf es aus etwa 50 m Entfernung mit mehreren Kanonentreffern in beide Flächen. Aus beiden Flächen hell brennend stürzte die LA-7 trudelnd ab und verursachte um 15.54 Uhr in 69862, etwa 1 - 3 km O Hainburg, in einem kleinen Waldstück einen Aufschlagbrand wodurch sie restlos vernichtet wurde.
Einen Fallschirmabsprung konnte ich nicht beobachten.

Lipfert

Sommavilla, Erich, Lt. 8. April 1945

I./ Jagdgeschwader 53

**Luftkampfzeugenbericht**

Am 8.4.45 flog ich im Schwarm von Hptm. Lipfert zur freien Jagd im Raume der Marschmündung . Dort bekamen wir Luftkampf mit einer einzelnen LA-7 die Kurs NW flog. Ich sah, wie Hptm. Lipfert das Feindflugzeug von hinten oben angriff und Treffer in beiden Flächen erzielte. Die LA-7 brannte sofort aus beiden Flächen und stürzte trudelnd ab. Durch Aufschlagbrand in einem kleinen Wald wurde das Feindflugzeug um 15.54 Uhr, etwa 1-3 km O Hainburg, restlos vernichtet. Einen Fallschirmabsprung habe ich **nicht** beobachtet.

........Sommavilla........

N e u m a n n, Fried.-Wilh., Uffz. 8. April 1945

I./ Jagdgeschwader 53

**Luftkampfzeugenbericht.**

Am 8.4.45 startete ich im Schwarm von Hptm. Lipfert zur freien Jagd. Im Raume der Marschmündung sichteten wir eine einzelne LA-7 die in Richtung NW abflog. Hptm. Lipfert griff das Feindflugzeug sofort an . Die Treffer lagen in beiden Flächen . Aus den Flächen hellbrennend stürzte nach Beschuss die LA-7 trudelnd ab und wurde um 15.54 Uhr im Pl.Qu. 69862 durch Aufschlagbrand restlos vernichtet.

Einen Fallschirmabsprung beobachtete ich nicht.

...Neumann......

*High-ranking visitor at Pistyan, February 1945. Generaloberst Dessloch, commander in chief Luftflotte 4, inspects fighter units on the Eastern Front.*

*Hörsching, Austria, April 20, 1945. The Oak Leaves for Hptm. Lipfert and the Knight's Cross for Lt. Ewald. From left to right: Lt. Ewald, Hptm. Lipfert, Lt. Düttmann.*

may well have said, shaking their heads: "That such a thing should happen to old Lipfert!"

Galatz was a terrific airfield. It was just too bad that we weren't there alone. Close-support, reconnaissance and other units swarmed about. The Russians couldn't ignore such a target. We had visitors every night, which was hard on our nerves, especially since our quarters and the command post were quite close to the landing field.

Together with Kannstein, our man from the IV A Department, I made my way to Galatz one day when there was no action to organize some nice things for us. The front was drawing ever closer and we wanted to at least live well again. There was now beef and pork, good wine, yes even beer and – fresh strawberries!

At that time we were joined from the Mediterranean front by the badly-battered III./JG 77. They brought several new Bf 109s armed with three cannon. Naturally these mules had to be tried out! Heino pointed one of them away from the city and pressed the firing buttons. One could actually see the large shells from the 30mm cannon flying through the air and then the impacts in a facing vineyard! It looked as if a small mortar was being used. With this we'd finally be able to teach even the heavily-armored Il-2 some respect.

In spite of the retreat our morale was still relatively good. But the "damper" came promptly. Heino and I had taken off on a sortie with two other aircraft and chased after the incoming Russians.

After several dogfights I shot down one of the enemy aircraft, while farther behind Heino chased after the others, which had reached friendly territory in the meantime. It was a gray, stormy day and the Russians flew very skillfully. They stayed mostly in the clouds and came out only now and then. But we wanted nothing to do with that. Heino had soon had enough and turned for home.

Heino was not exactly sure what happened next. In any case there were flashes all over his aircraft and he knew at once that he had been hit. When his aircraft began to smoke he sought safety in flight. The Russians stayed on his tail. They were just as fast as he was and hit him repeatedly. Heino defended himself as best he could, even shaving off several treetops as he hugged the ground. But it was all to no avail, the Russians hung on and hit his aircraft again and again.

Finally Sachsenberg crash-landed his machine. Bleeding from

several wounds, he lost consciousness just before touching down. However this proved to be a blessing in disguise. According to an eyewitness report his Me bounced several times and then slid to a stop in the mud and gravel right beside a field hospital. Staff hurried over to the aircraft and recovered the unconscious pilot. But he was alive!

The Russians were over our base again at about 2300 that same day. This time they came not with the usual "sewing machines," but with larger machines. We were repeatedly startled by exploding bombs. The Russians approached singly and dropped their bombs across the airfield. It was impossible for them to miss as several aircraft were already burning. Then a bomb went off with a huge explosion right beside the command post and caused the house where my field cot lay to collapse. Luckily no one was buried, as the sturdy roof beams fell at an angle and were able to hold up some of the masonry. I got off relatively lightly, but was bleeding slightly from the face. I dug myself out of the rubble and sought the protection of the trench as quickly as possible.

The Russians gave us no pause and forced us to stay in the trenches until long past midnight. We could count five burning machines around the landing field, and they provided a real festive illumination with their exploding ammunition. There wasn't much left to be saved. Three Messerschmitts were completely burnt out, including one from our *Gruppe*. Two others were damaged beyond repair.

Following this night of bombing we left Galatz, as the Russians were already close to the airfield. While transferring to our new base we were supposed to strafe retreating Romanian troops, because that same morning Romania had renounced its pact with Germany. We carried out this order from *Fliegerkorps*. Together with my wingman I was able to set two trucks on fire, but then I was horrified to see that there were German soldiers retreating with the Romanians. I called off the strafing attacks immediately.

Now we had to land at an airfield which was full of Romanian aircraft and soldiers. As our advance detachment did not seem to be there below, I ordered the other *Rotte* to land while I stayed in the air with my wingman to see what they would do down there. My pilots taxied their aircraft to an empty corner of the airfield and waved to me. But I stayed above until my fuel was running low, not landing until the other two aircraft had taken off on my order and were in the air. Our technical personnel arrived soon after I landed.

We pitched our tents. I then went over to the Romanians with another officer to check out the situation. But the Romanian colonel treated us coolly, pointed to his two machine-guns and let me know through his interpreter that the aircraft which had landed were not to take off again without his permission. I went back to where our aircraft were parked. I had four machine-guns moved into position and saw to it that there were always two Messerschmitts in the air over the base.

In those days most of the Romanians made an about-face and made common cause with their former enemies. They barricaded all the passes leading from Romania to Hungary, cutting off everything still on the near side of the Carpathians. The pass leading north from Buzeau was reopened by the army, however, and was used by our ground elements, although with a great deal of interference.

The pitiful remains of the *Gruppe* took off from Buzeau for Sächsisch Regen in Hungary at 0910 on August 28, 1944. On the 29th we moved out to make room for the Stukas and the other *Gruppen* of the *Fliegerkorps*, flying to a secondary airfield about 25 kilometers to the west. At first we were hopping mad that we once again had to make way for the others, unaware that we had, in fact, drawn the lucky card. The next day Sächsisch Regen was attacked by about 50 Mustangs, which destroyed or damaged some 70 of the corps' aircraft. The Mustangs had an easy time of it. The airfield had absolutely no anti-aircraft defenses and the aircraft were parked so close together that the Americans could scarcely miss. The Amis used this opportunity to chase *Oberst* Rudel here and there beneath his machine for several minutes. He related this to me later, half laughing and half cursing. We in Budak didn't learn of the attack until the next day.

That morning we received a report that the Russians had flown into our area with numerous Il-2s. A *Schwarm* and a *Rotte*, or a total of six aircraft from my *Gruppe*, took off immediately. The *Schwarm* was led by the experienced and very capable Lt. Fönnekold, who had achieved 136 victories and was one of the *Gruppe*'s best pilots. I led the *Rotte*, with *Gefreiter* Günter Ständer as my wingman.

While the *Schwarm* flew in a rather loose formation, we stayed close together about 200 meters higher. We had just passed 1,000 meters, when I saw a large swarm of aircraft in front of me and somewhat lower.

They were flying in a huge circle, repeatedly diving earthward and firing at the aircraft parked there. Aha, I thought, the Il-2s. I called to Fönnekold: "In front of us at *Hanni* 500, the Il-2s. They're attacking Löver airfield. I'm going to attack immediately. – Ständer, attack with me. Fire at anything that comes in front of your guns!"

But what a grave mistake I had made! First I thought: now then, is that a new type of Il-2? When I roared at full speed into the circle of machines flying in front of me I recognized them – Mustangs!

"Attention. – Damn it, they're Mustangs!"

"Fine Il-2s," I heard Fönnekold mutter. Looking back, I saw him following with his *Schwarm* in line astern. My speed was high and luckily I came from directly below right between two Americans. The one in front of me held his course until I opened fire. Before I was very close to him his Mustang pitched forward abruptly and fell away trailing a dense, white smoke trail. I climbed back up without being fired on and observed how my wingman fired into the Americans like an old hand. As he broke away he called: "Congratulations six one, I saw your kill!"

"Come with me, we'll attack again. Each man for himself!" Again I got behind a Mustang, but unfortunately only one machine-gun would fire. I blazed away with the one gun, then closed in to where I couldn't miss. As was my custom, I took one last look around and saw to my horror that another Mustang was on my tail. He hadn't opened fire yet, however.

I quickly rammed the throttle forward and dove away to the right from my left-hand turn. But the Ami knew what was going on. I saw black smoke pouring from his exhausts and he began the pursuit. Four or five other machines followed.

Things were becoming dangerous. Although the American was soon in firing range he limited himself to chasing me. I began to sweat when I noticed that the others had dropped down to my altitude and appeared to be gaining slowly.

It was a misty day and the visibility was not particularly good. While trying to get away I flew as close to the ground as I could justify and roared along at 500 kph. The wild pursuit led us over a forest. I pushed my machine even lower and seconds later I was over a small valley. Acting on a sudden inspiration, I hauled my Messerschmitt around through 90 degrees and followed the valley. For some time I had no chance to look around, but when I did seconds later my pursuers were nowhere to be seen. I flew on toward the south at low altitude for a while and then put my "109" into a steep climb. At 1,000 meters I quickly scanned the sky. When I saw nothing I cautiously continued climbing and arrived over Löver at 4,500 meters. In fact the Americans were still there. They were prowling around at their original altitude of about 600 meters but had broken up their circle. Occasionally a few aircraft would peel off and attack the small airfield.

I carefully scanned the sky around and especially above me, then dove at terrific speed, pulled up far below and approached four Mustangs from behind. None of the four pilots looked around. I selected the trailing machine, aimed carefully and, when I couldn't miss, pressed the triggers. Again only one gun fired, but all my bullets were on target. The Ami began pouring black smoke, but I had to break away and was unable to watch him any further.

As I was still travelling at more than 600 kilometers per hour I immediately moved in on the next trio. Again I hit the trailing aircraft, but unfortunately I couldn't stay behind him long enough as tracer was now flashing about my ears. I pulled up and saw that a Mustang had got on my tail in an effort to drive me away from my intended victim, which he in fact did.

However my speed was still such that I was able to escape the danger zone in seconds. At 1,000 meters I looked over the situation again, well aware that I was above everyone. Then I attacked for a third time.

As I approached I rolled the Messerschmitt onto its back, jockeyed the controls and cocked the weapons again. If at least the two machine-guns would fire! Again I approached the Americans at high speed, but the element leader spotted me and peeled away. The second aircraft also dove to safety. The last dropped the left wing of his Mustang to begin a turn, but I was 200 meters behind him and opened fire. And wonder of wonders, all weapons fired! The tracer wandered over and there were numerous flashes as it disappeared, mostly into the fuselage of the enemy aircraft. A dense, black-gray banner of smoke showed that I had hit him well.

I now abandoned caution and followed the feebly-turning machine. It stayed in a shallow turn and that was its undoing. Although my faithful "109" shook and shuddered, I turned even tighter, aimed in front of the

Mustang's nose and fired. The American fighter flew right through the stream of bullets and took the full burst. I had allowed so much deflection that I could no longer see the Mustang. When It appeared from beneath my nose I was shocked at how close I was. I had almost rammed the fellow!

The Mustang's fuselage was riddled and the cockpit wrecked. As well the machine was burning; it rolled over to the left and fell away in a spin. The Mustang crashed beside the road to Sächsisch Regen.

Meanwhile the other two Mustangs had seen their chance and had turned in behind me. They opened fire. This time I did not make the mistake of diving, instead I climbed away in a pirouette. I must have been in their sights for a while, but I was unable to observe their actions.

Then I was out of their zone of fire and flew away toward the west in the direction of "Garden Fence," which I reached in a few minutes. From above the airfield appeared deserted. A single Me sat alone and abandoned in the middle of the landing field. I landed and taxied in. I hadn't yet reached the dispersal when my crew chief swung himself onto the wing. I could see by his face that something was wrong. I stopped the machine, opened the canopy and asked: "Where are the others, what's up with the aircraft on the field?"

"It's Fönnekold's machine. He's dead. None of the others have come back yet!"

I couldn't believe what I was hearing and asked again, but I received the same answer. I shut down the engine and climbed out with shaking knees. I sat on the wing and listened to my mechanic's account, according to which two aircraft had suddenly appeared over the airfield. "We thought they were two of ours returning early with engine trouble, especially since one machine was smoking heavily. But then we realized that the second machine was a Mustang. We were surprised to see the Me begin its landing approach with the Mustang about 30 meters behind it. The only burst the American fired was on target. The Mustang broke away and the Bf 109 landed smoothly. It rolled to a stop. We hurried over and lifted Fönnekold out. He was dead. A single bullet had gone through the fuselage, pierced the armor plate and struck Fönnekold right in the heart."

Weary, I climbed down from the wing and walked the few steps across the grass to the end of the landing field. Fönnekold, one of the best pilots in the *Gruppe*, was dead and had lost his life in such a tragic fashion. And none of the others were back. I sat down and took my head in my hands, and the tears ran through my fingers.

A short time later the *Kommodore* landed at our airfield at Budak. Normally I would have been the first to go to him and report. But that day I slipped away quietly. I had to be alone for a while to regain my composure. Slowly I became convinced that I was all in, completely flown out and, as they say, shot. The difficult sorties and the profound events of the past weeks and months now made themselves dramatically noticeable. I asked the *Kommodore* for leave, which he promised for the coming days. I flew three more missions then I ferried a machine to Budapest and from there to Germany.

Two days before going on leave I led a *Schwarm* in a strafing attack on a Rumanian airfield. I was especially unhappy about this assignment, which was quite difficult. Now that Fönnekold was dead, there was only one other officer in the *Gruppe* besides me. That was Hptm. Sturm, with whom I had flown – how long ago was it – my first combat mission.

I gathered my three pilots around me and gave them some last-minute advice. The way they stood there, in particular *Gefreiter* Tamen, their eyes shining and visibly filled with a desire for action and satisfaction that their *Kommandeur* was flying with them, again buoyed my spirits somewhat.

We took off and climbed into the clear, blue sky. There was no contact with the enemy and it seemed as if we were totally alone in the air. We passed the border and flew into Romania. Far below I saw a train steaming along the line to Kronstadt. I ordered the other three to stay above and descended alone to investigate. The train had two locomotives. I immediately attacked the front one and hit it so well on my first pass that it began spraying steam. I roared low over the train and was about to attack the other locomotive from behind when a thought struck me. Here was a chance to let the others fire their guns.

"All of you come down, I'll tell you how you are to attack!"

I heard an enthusiastic "*Viktor*, *Viktor*!" on the frequency.

Instead of stopping, the train made full steam and raced away. It wasn't difficult for a fighter to disable a locomotive. First I instructed Tamen to attack and told him when to shoot. The *Gefreiter* handled himself very well. After two passes I had him climb up to allow the other two to take a turn.

The train was soon shrouded in dense clouds of smoke and steam and then finally ground to a halt. This gunnery practice had allowed the three pilots to pass through their baptism of fire. Hopefully they would be able to keep their nerve as well in future low-level attacks.

The first airfield we approached was abandoned. The Romanians had probably smelled a rat and suspected our coming. Below all was empty, except for several trucks and a few members of the technical personnel, who quickly ran for cover. The next airfield was Medias, about 120 kilometers behind the front. We were luckier there. I had previously given my *Schwarm* precise instructions, and before the Romanians were aware of the danger all four of us were firing into the parked vehicles. Together with my wingman I took the side on which the hangars stood. Tamen and number four curved toward the other side of the field. We dropped down to about 10 meters and simply couldn't miss.

Five machines were burning after the second attack and the base slowly came to life. On the next pass I fired at aircraft – a German Ju 87 which the Romanians had received from us – but sadly once again only one machine-gun was working. In the middle of my fourth attack, on a quadruple flak, this weapon also quit. In return I received five hits in the wings and two in the fuselage, as it later turned out. But at least I had the satisfaction that the anti-aircraft gun was silenced for a time.

For me there was no longer any purpose in diving at the airfield again, as I couldn't fire no matter how much I shook my machine or how many times I cocked the weapons. So I circled overhead at 1,000 meters, observed the surrounding airspace and directed the attacks by the others. By now nine machines were burning down below. In the midst of all the fuss a fuel truck suddenly roared across the airfield and tried to reach the safety of a hangar. Tamen moved in behind it. He hit the truck so well that it exploded as it drove into the hangar. The hangar and all the aircraft inside went up in flames. What a fireworks display!

"Bravo, Tamen, bravo!"

The *Schwarm* reassembled and we headed home at low level, roaring along wingtip to wingtip. In spite of our close proximity to the ground I let go of the stick and waved left and right with both hands. The pilots beamed. From this time on, *Gefreiter* Tamen sat beside me to my left at the mess table.

After landing I learned that my machine had been hit in the ammunition compartment. I was lucky that the Messerschmitt hadn't exploded. Two days later we – the same four pilots – took off on a similar mission. Seven enemy aircraft were destroyed, but I was only able to make one pass as my weapons failed again. It was as if I was cursed. I was hit four more times and my faithful crate had to go into the repair shop.

Finally I got my leave. Hptm. Sturm took over the *Gruppe* while I flew to Germany. I spent seven lovely days there. The world seemed beautiful again and life worth living. I received a mighty impulse and returned to the front with my spirits greatly lifted.

# CHAPTER VII
# In The Land of the Magyars

On my return I found that there had been several changes in the *Gruppe*. It was now stationed in central Hungary and had been reinforced by a further *Gruppe* under *Major* Barkhorn. We felt quite powerful and proudly referred to ourselves as a *Geschwader*. As well there was Erich Hartmann, with his 308 kills by far the best fighter pilot in the world. I had only one thing over this *Hauptmann*: more luck. Up to this point I had scored 145 kills in 572 combat sorties and had not once been wounded. Hartmann, on the other hand, had been put to bed several times. Fortunately he got off fairly well in each case.

We were, as mentioned, quite "strong." *Major* Barkhorn as *Gruppenkommandeur*, Sturm, Hartmann and I as *Staffelkapitäne* and a number of proven *Schwarm* and element leaders. No wonder everyone was in top form. As always, when one believed he was at the peak the end was not far away, and it was just as well that no one knew this in advance.

Four three days we remained at Tisza-Löck on the Theiss River in northern Hungary. But we couldn't fly. It rained heavily and the airfield was softened badly. But then the Russians made a push and we were forced to move. The order had already arrived. Someone would have to risk the first takeoff.

I attempted to taxi out for takeoff, but the wheels sank so deep into the soft ground that it was impossible for the aircraft to get out under its own power. My machine had to be towed to the takeoff point. In the course of this my radiators were splattered with so much mud that they had to be cleaned before I could take off. I began my takeoff roll, but my Me accelerated only slowly during the first 100 meters. The speed had not increased much by the middle of the field. What was more the aircraft was rocking so badly that I feared it might nose over at any moment. If I pushed the stick forward the "109" couldn't get off the ground. I therefore pulled back lightly and then slowly increased the pressure. Finally the 109 lifted off. At the same time, however, the left wing dropped sharply. I applied full opposite rudder and moved the stick all the way to the right, but the aircraft was not answering to the controls. It curved to the left, already almost on its back, and raced toward a group of parked Bf 110s.

I hurtled along, my left wing almost touching the ground, and saw the Bf 110s literally racing toward me. "Off!" I said to myself, and since nothing else seemed to be doing any good, pulled back on the throttle. Then the miracle happened. The machine righted itself and at simultaneously touched down on both wheels. At the same instant I reached the parked Messerschmitts. There were two terrible crashes and I found myself sitting in the open.

Involuntarily I was forced to think of my previous crash when I had roared through the house. As this had happened to me before, I wasn't all that surprised this time that I was still alive. Even before I came to a stop I noticed that my machine had lost its left wing and that the fuselage aft of the cockpit was missing. The parked Hungarian Bf 110s had also suffered considerable damage.

My knees were still shaking when I returned to the dispersal. Several schnapps and my sense of humor helped me get back on my feet. I watched with interest as the others struggled to get into the air from better starting positions. They succeeded. It was easy after Lipfert showed them where not to take off from and how it shouldn't be done.

After a quarter of an hour I was ready and successfully took off in another aircraft. By the time we landed at Takta Kenez I had regained my confidence.

At Takta Kenez taking off, and even more so landing, was an art in itself. The airfield was poorly situated, because opposite it was a tank-like structure surrounded by a broad, water-filled trench. With time, however, we got used to this obstacle. In fact I grew to like this base, not least of all because the Russians never found it with their reconnaissance aircraft or bombers and we had plenty of peace and quiet on the ground. Added to this was the fact that the pilots of 6 *Staffel* and I found lovely quarters in the small village. The doctor who owned the house had fled, but not without leaving us several bottles of real Tokai.

At that time it was customary after a round of drinks for Peter Düttmann, or "Boniface" as he was known, to sit himself down at the piano that was there and do his "poet and yokel" routine. Once we officers made a trip up to Tokai. It was only twelve kilometers. It was well that we took drivers with us. Without them we would never have made it home that day.

At first there wasn't much going on in the air. I had to abort my first takeoff from Takta Kenez due to undercarriage trouble. I shot down a Yak on my second sortie, but I had allowed my wingman to go off on his own and I thus had no witness for the kill. I wasn't too upset about it, as virtually every subsequent sortie resulted in contact with enemy aircraft.

Nevertheless, it wasn't until October 17 that I was able to shoot down an enemy aircraft, in this case a Yak-11, with witnesses. It was kill number 146. And before I got number 147 I downed an Il-2 "without." At this time I received a Bf 109 armed with a 30mm cannon, and I looked forward to my next encounter with the Il-2. A well-placed shot from this weapon should be able to get even the Il-2's attention.

On top of that I had received a young *Oberfänrich* as my new wingman, who shaped up very well as a pilot. We took off at 1455 on October 23, 1944, and turned south toward the front, climbing as we went. We kept up a brisk conversation as we were all alone in the sky. Then suddenly the ground station reported that many enemy bombers were approaching, flying down the Theiss in the Skolnok area. My hunch about flying south had thus been a good one. The Russians were obviously after the bridge over the Theiss to Skolnok. If they managed to knock out the bridge it would be a serious blow to the bridgehead across the river.

We flew in the direction of the reported enemy aircraft at full throttle, black smoke pouring from the exhaust stacks of our machines. There was Skolnok. We descended. As we approached I saw flak bursts and almost simultaneously the Il-2s.

Amazingly we had come upon the Il-2s at 1,000 meters, an altitude at which they scarcely ever flew. Apparently our flak, which was putting up quite a barrage, was the cause. We were coming from the north, the Russians from the east. We thus had to turn only 90 degrees and we were right behind them. In spite of the presence of a fighter escort, I reduced power and opened the radiator flaps to lose speed. This time our flak was on the ball and ceased firing when we got behind the Russian machines.

We approached slowly. We were still lower than the Il-2s, however they must have spotted us by now. I could clearly see the leading Ivan looking around. *Oberfähnrich* Steins, who had hung back somewhat, reported that all was clear behind us. Alright then, let's go!

I climbed up close behind the trailing Il-2. I didn't want to fire from below, because Düttmann had had a bad experience in such a situation a few days before. His Il-2 had unloaded large quantities of fist-sized objects and Düttmann had flown into them. It turned out that they were aerial mines, and one of them damaged the *Leutnant*'s "109" badly.

I therefore climbed and fired in one motion. The range may have been 30 to 50 meters. I couldn't miss and watched as the shells from the new weapon struck home. Up until that time I had never made or even seen an Il-2 shot down like this.

This heavily-armored bomber, which we had named "cement bomber" for this reason, blew apart in the air. It happened so quickly that I had no time for evasive maneuvers. Many small pieces came flying back at me, then four larger ones, probably the engine, wings and tail. The heaviest part, the motor, passed below me, while the wings and other pieces were blown upward by the force of the explosion and passed right over my canopy. Other pieces, some burning, struck my fuselage and wings and dented my machine badly. But I was lucky. In a few seconds I was through the shower of pieces. That could have been the end of me, because I had once seen a wingman of mine fly into a kill. That was Fw. Gleissner, then near Karbadinka in the Caucasus.

Steins was still behind me and the Russian fighters were some distance away, so I made another attack. Since my speed was almost the same as that of the close-support aircraft I didn't want to break way and turn in again. I pulled up to the left behind the other two Russians and rolled my aircraft onto its back so that I ended up right on the tail of the nearest Il-2. Now in level flight again, I opened fire, ignoring the enemy's furious defensive fire. First I saw flashes from the machine-gun bullets and then the 30mm ammunition struck its target.

The rear third of the Il-2's fuselage broke off at once. This time I was better prepared for a surprise and immediately pulled up to the left so that the wreckage passed beneath me. Meanwhile Steins had caught up. He had no 30mm cannon, but fastened himself to the tail of the third Il-2 and fired until it caught fire and began to go down. The Russian pilot was apparently trying for a forced-landing. Meanwhile I covered Steins' rear. We circled over the Russian for a moment until he crashed. Then we headed for home and congratulated one another.

These two kills had come within a minute. I used a total of only 10 rounds from the cannon and 35 rounds of machine-gun ammunition. However my machine had to go in for repairs, as the wreckage from the first Il-2 had inflicted more damage than I at first thought.

During a briefing on the evening of October 27 the *Kommandeur* informed us that next morning we would be flying a strafing mission against Debrecen airfield. Such an attack on a Russian airfield was always a risky business and we would probably lose some more hair before it was over. The base lay more than 150 kilometers beyond the front. A hit in the oil or coolant tank would mean a certain landing in Russian territory. The Bf 109 was more vulnerable there than any other aircraft.

Sitting together that evening were *Major* Barkhorn, Hptm. Sturm, Hptm. Hartmann, Lt. Düttmann, Lt. Ewald and I, as well as a number of good *Schwarm* and element leaders. Together we had a total of far more than 900 kills. To begin with we celebrated our possible departure. Who could say who might not come back?

Early in the morning I woke the *Staffel* and then went with Steins over to our aircraft. The day began dull and rainy. If we could find Debrecen quickly it would be an ideal day for a low-level attack. We were soon in the air and headed southeast in formation. We flew a wide arc to the south and approached the airfield from the east. We were all just beneath the overcast at 2,500 meters, flying in and out of the strands of cloud. Not a word was spoken.

When Debrecen appeared out of the mist in the distance, Barkhorn called: "Stay close, everyone close formation, we're attacking!"

Not far from the field a Russian courier aircraft flew past in front of our noses. However we couldn't and didn't want to bother with it and instead flew toward the target at high speed. I could imagine the shocked faces of the Russians. They had no chance to jump into their aircraft or start the engines, because we were on them before they knew it. We went even lower. I didn't pull out until I was five meters above the ground and had my target, a Yak, in my sights. I opened fire from a range of about 100 meters. Hits sparkled along the enemy aircraft's fuselage and then I was past him. A brief glance behind me was enough to see that the Yak was in flames.

Then I found myself on the other side of the field where the hangars were. Tracer flashed toward me, but I was able to hit another fighter and a hangar. In the next instant the airfield was behind me. I stayed low to avoid the anti-aircraft fire. My *Staffel* and I flew away for perhaps a minute before climbing, turning around and heading back. Racing along beneath the clouds, we returned to the airfield. The flak gave us a lively reception. Nevertheless, we went down a second time and delivered our greetings. Luckily no Russian fighters had got off the ground; we wouldn't have had enough fuel left for an air battle anyway. So we headed back to the "Picnic Ground." I counted the burning machines down below – about twelve – from a respectful distance. Then my wingman and I headed home. A few aircraft had been hit, but miraculously we had suffered no losses.

I took off again at 1125 that day with a *Schwarm* again with Steins as my wingman. Ewald led the other *Rotte*. We prowled around the front, but the Russians apparently had no lust for flying in spite of the now favorable weather. Our fuel began to run low and, disappointed, we turned for home. I was about 20 kilometers from the field when Ewald reported that he was about to land, but he had not finished his transmission when the ground station called: "Six one from Garden Fence, one Furniture Van and two Indians over Picnic Ground at *Hanni* 1,000. Try and shoot the fellows down if you can, they've discovered our base."

If our fuel ran out, then we'd both have to make forced-landings: in no case could the three be permitted to get home, otherwise our peace and quiet here would be gone forever. Then I heard: "The Russians are still over the airfield. Six one, are you coming?" I had no time to answer. I quickly screwed my throttle firmly in the full open position and dove to just above the ground before calling Steins: "Six two, are you with me?" – "*Viktor, Viktor*! I'm sitting almost right beside you!"

There was the airfield. Time to climb! "The Russians have just flown away!" I asked for the heading on which the enemy aircraft had flown away and at the same time spotted the Il-2 in the distance. Then I saw the two escorting fighters about 500 meters above it. We closed quickly. With my superior speed I climbed above them effortlessly. A look at the fuel gauge showed that I had only minutes left for an attack. The red light was already burning. "Steins, do you have fuel left? Can you stay with me?" Steins stayed behind me, he wasn't about to land yet either.

"We must attack the fighters first," I called to him. "Try to get the second Yak. If he should dive away keep going and shoot down the Il-2!" Then I attacked. But the Russians were on the ball. They must have spotted us already. They calmly allowed me to approach and then suddenly, as if on command, they broke left and right. With my extra speed I couldn't turn as tightly and I didn't attempt it. Instead I closed the throttle, lost speed and dove on toward the Il-2, which was trying to dive away to safety.

I reached for the radiator flap control and lost even more speed. Then I chanced a look behind and saw that both Yaks were about to come after me. But I saw Steins above them, his nose pointed toward the two enemy fighters. He was thus doing his job and I had no need to worry.

The Il-2 grew in my sight and then it was time. The rear gunner fired furiously but I paid him no mind. Radiator flaps closed, throttle forward! But there must have been an experienced pilot flying the Il-2, because before I could open fire, the enemy aircraft began dancing all over the sky. It was good that I had reduced speed, otherwise the enemy machine would definitely have escaped me. But I stayed with him and began spraying him with my two machine-guns from a range of 60 meters. This made the Russian visibly uncomfortable. The Il-2 bobbed and weaved so that I had difficulty scoring even a few hits, but at least the fire from the rear gunner had stopped. His machine-gun pointed straight up in the air.

Again I hit him, and then again. Now it was time to use the cannon, because I could scarcely miss. The bird was huge in front of me. I was quietly amazed that there was no tracer yet flying about my ears. It baffled me, but I had no time to look around. I must ram the enemy any second. I pressed the firing button for the cannon. Pieces flew off the Il-2 and whizzed toward me. My Messerschmitt had got into the prop wash of the Il-2 and bucked and heaved so much that I was tossed about the cockpit. I used all my strength to stay behind the Russian, who definitely didn't want to hear any more from me.

I fired again. The Russian continued his defensive maneuvers. I had closed to about ten meters when the Il-2 abruptly tipped forward, and I immediately regained control of my "109." I shoved the stick forward so hard that I banged my head on the cockpit roof. Now it was time to pull around to the left and see where the Yaks were. One of them roared past me to the left, pulled out of his dive and turned in behind me. Before he could overtake me I saw the Il-2 crash into the ground. At almost the same instant two aircraft came down from above. The rear one was Steins' Messerschmitt. He clung to the enemy's tail and fired. The Russian in front of him turned for his life. Nevertheless, he rejoined his comrade and both Ivans used the speed they had built up in the dive to approach me from behind.

Steins had separated himself from his Yak and now hung above me and observed. There was no need for me to direct him, however, because he saw for himself that the two Russians must soon catch me and came down on his own. This happened so unexpectedly that the rearmost Russian didn't realize what was going on until his machine was in flames and going down.

I hauled my machine around and just got out of the way of a long burst from the guns of the Yak behind me. Now the turning contest began. We were about 1,000 meters high. The Russian later defended himself quite desperately, but first it was my turn. I had to employ all my skill to escape the Yak. I soon came to realize that the man behind me was my equal. The contest might have turned out quite differently had it not been for Steins. The latter acted as if the whole affair was of no interest to him. He disengaged and climbed above us, so as to reach a position from which he could attack the Russian from above.

Now the enemy pilot was forced to leave me if he didn't want to be shot down himself, and that gave me the break I needed. I climbed and then came down fast. The Russian had shaken off my wingman and was now attempting to get on his tail. By now we were only at about 100 meters.

On my next attack I didn't fall into the old trap of approaching with too much speed, because the Russian would have turned away from me again. When I reached firing position the Yak whipped around. But I turned as well and stayed rigidly behind him. I wasn't about to let him shake me off. Again he turned, vapor streaming from his fuselage. I saw the Yak shudder and shake. Our altitude was now no more than 40 meters. Again I reached firing position. Then the Ivan hauled back on the stick.

He came out of the turn, but the Yak lost too much speed. The aircraft sagged and nearly stalled. My opponent was forced to fly level for a second. This gave the chance I had been waiting for. I could fire. There were flashes as my shells struck home and almost the entire wing came off the Yak. It crashed into a ditch close to the road.

I was just able to recover and cautiously climbed away. I had already sent Steins home. I saw him only as a small dot in the distance. Now I, too, flew in the direction of our airfield, the engine throttled back to conserve fuel. Would it be enough? Then Steins reported: "Am out of fuel, I'm going to make an emergency landing!" – "Steins, I can't help you. Make it a good one. Good luck!"

Soon afterward I saw him. When I passed over his landing site he was standing beside his Messerschmitt and waved to me. He had thus got down safely. I myself was a little more lucky, because my propeller didn't stop until I was right over the airfield. It was well that I had practiced pinpoint landings with the Bf 109 at Anapa and in Romania, otherwise I never would have made it into this tiny airfield.

As soon as I had landed I sent for a Volkswagen and set out to pick up Steins. I took an engineer with me, who discovered that Steins' aircraft had sustained only 7% damage and could easily be repaired. It was recovered by a tractor the next day and was in fact ready to fly again two days later.

Steins, Platzer, the driver and I drove to the front to inspect our kills. The infantry there repeatedly swore that they had never before witnessed such a terrific air battle, and the officers were in no hurry to let us get away. The last Russian to be shot down must have been an ace. He wore several decorations, including the badge of a "Hero of the Soviet Union." But it was not just his decorations, but the cleanliness of his uniform and his groomed appearance as well that convinced us that we had shot down a very special enemy.

I flew one more sortie with Steins from Takta Kenez, during which I forced a Yak to land undamaged in our territory. The pilot climbed out and waved to us, but I later learned that he managed to elude the German troops who hurried to the scene.

The *Gruppe* then moved to Buda-Örs, southwest of Budapest. From there I achieved a total of seven victories within the next twenty days, including two each on separate sorties on November 16 and 17. Of these kills my 157th was noteworthy, as it showed how it should not be done. Once again I took off with Steins, and after receiving a report from the ground station made contact with a mixed Russian close-support group. Hurrying from the north, I saw the machines drop their bombs in an area which seemed to be rather deep in the German rear and then turn toward the east. I arrived about 2,000 meters above them and dove into the middle of the group without regard to position.

The trailing Russians must have seen me already, because they were wide awake and broke away before I could fire a shot. Steins was also unable to shoot, and it would have been a waste of ammunition to fire blindly into the formation. So we climbed away, especially as we couldn't get through to the Il-2s, and tried again, hoping this time to make a better attack on the escorting Yaks. These naturally used the resulting pause to turn and fly after the bombers – all except one.

This Russian pilot probably couldn't help having his own way. Unlike the others he turned around and looked over where the bombs had fallen. Of course his reckless maneuver separated him from his companions. Then, when he was about to turn, I was on the spot. I had descended below him and now approached unnoticed from behind. I waited until I was at point-blank range and then pressed the triggers, but once again my weapons refused to fire.

A few shots stuttered from one machine-gun, but it wasn't enough to impress my opponent. But while his comrades disappeared into the distance, there was nothing left for him to do but turn. At least he was experienced enough to have mastered and borne in mind this elementary rule of fighter piloting.

I asked Steins to stay behind him and if possible shoot him down while I talked with my weapons and observed the surrounding airspace. Steins so occupied the Russian that he was scarcely able to make any headway toward the east, although he repeatedly tried to "egg" his way along, flying straight and level for as long as possible and turning toward the west only when Steins was about to open fire. In the meantime I got my two machine-guns working. I dropped down behind the Russian just as he was about to fly away toward the east again and scored several hits. Even though he was trailing smoke, the Russian now gave me a battle which couldn't have been more dangerous or interesting. The whole thing was played out at an altitude of about 300 meters.

The Russian wasn't about to go any lower, probably aware that I would out-turn him at ground level. He must have been keeping a close eye on me, because each time he waited until I began to fire then turned and tried to get me to overshoot him by side-slipping and reducing power. This went on for about ten minutes, but we had time. Deep inside friendly territory with a relatively large amount of fuel left, I wasn't about to take any risks and stayed rigidly behind him, letting him do what he liked. Now and then, when he was in an especially favorable position, I pressed the triggers and scored one hit on him after another.

Steins sat above us, keeping a watch to all sides and maintaining a running commentary. He was a perfect wingman. I turned tightly, allowed plenty of deflection and hit the Russian again. This time I damaged him. Resignedly he dove away trailing black smoke and appeared to be about to make a belly landing. I dropped back a bit when I saw that he had reduced power and was preparing to land. But then when he was just above the ground he applied power and tried to reach his own lines. He was a bold fellow, this one! This was not what I had in mind, however. I dove after him and was about to finish him off when he put his aircraft down. It touched the ground and skidded through a tall haystack, which surprisingly stayed in the same place.

The Russian machine raced through a second haystack, stopped a few meters beyond it and immediately began to burn. If he was still alive after all that, the poor fellow must then have been burned to death. We circled over the spot for several minutes but the canopy did not open.

My 159th kill was something of an anniversary victory; I, the old buck, came to grief once again! Steins and I took from Buda-Örs. We had become good comrades by now, knew what to expect of each other and worked well with one another. Steins had made several kills in the meantime and enjoyed flying with me. I had already made up my mind not to fly on the 13th, but this was only the 12th. Events were to prove that bad luck wouldn't let itself be pinned down to a particular day.

We caught up with the Il-2s on their way home. They were already well inside their own airspace when I scored lethal hits on one of them. While Steins worked on another one, I watched my downed Il-2, something I shouldn't have done. One of the Russians must have separated from the others, and before I knew what was happening my left radiator was gone. Naturally I started shouting right away: "Steins, come quickly, this fellow is forcing me to turn, my left radiator is gone. I can only fly for a few more minutes before my coolant drains out!"

The Ivan sat behind me like a leech and prevented me from gaining a meter of ground in the direction of our lines. I was forced to turn and turn and was far worse at it than my opponent of a few days before. He too had to take many hits, but they were nowhere near so dangerous as those I had just taken. Without the faithful Steins I would probably have been a dead man. I have him alone to thank for my salvation.

The Russian had chased me around the circle five times already and had inflicted even more damage as I had lost speed. Finally Steins was behind him. I wiped the seat from my forehead as I turned. Steins fired, but the Russian didn't waver. He was taking punishment, but he kept firing at me as cool as you please. Suddenly he exploded.

But the danger wasn't over. I was in a sick machine at 800 meters and still over enemy territory, as the shells from the enemy flak showed me. To descend would mean a certain belly landing in enemy territory. So there was nothing left for me to do but to try and escape into a cloud, which fortunately was hanging only 200 meters above me. Frightened and trembling, I made it. Then I switched off the ignition, as my oil temperature had long since exceeded the allowable maximum, and began to glide. I sailed through the clouds at about 270 kph with the flaps at 15 degrees, and then I was out the bottom.

What happened next almost took my breath away. Coming out of the clouds I suddenly found myself in the midst of a swarming mass of Yaks and LaGGs, while further below droned many fat Il-2s. My God, I thought, and hauled back on the stick while simultaneously switching on the ignition and ramming the throttle forward. All I could do was climb back into the clouds again.

I made up my mind not to descend below cloud again until the engine was almost finished. When the time came I came out cautiously. Oh what luck! There was nothing to be seen far and wide. Once again things had worked out. But now it was time to shut down the engine and search for a place to land. Smoke wafted through the aircraft and I knew only too well what it meant: the aircraft was about to catch fire. From 800 meters I saw two race courses, one behind the other. I didn't want to bail out, so it was prepare to land in the hippodrome.

The engine was no longer running. I swept toward the first race course, where I wanted to put my aircraft down. As I approached I thought of Liebmann, but I immediately put such thoughts out of my mind. But then I saw that the first race course was far too short for a landing, and when I reached the center of the field at 200 kph in spite of side-slipping and lowering the flaps, I switched on the ignition again. When the engine started I pulled up briefly to clear the poplars which were racing toward me. Then I switched off the ignition again and forced the crate down hard. It was hanging in the air like a fat plum.

Its forward speed almost zero, the aircraft dropped toward the second race course at an angle of about 60 degrees. It struck the ground short of the center of the place, whereby both cannon gondolas and the engine literally plowed up the ground. At that instant I fell a heavy blow in the back. But I remained wide awake and in no time had loosened my straps and jumped out of the crate. Even though my back hurt terribly, I had been spared once again. Then I looked at the landing site. I had been lucky! The two race courses were surrounded by tall poplars and it was unlikely anyone would have dreamed of putting his "109" down there. I had nevertheless accomplished this feat, and with a shot-up machine as well. It was nothing less than a wreck; there was nothing left to salvage. When one bears in mind that it had touched down at 150 kilometers per hour, one can appreciate how sharply it had been braked by tearing up the earth.

It wasn't until after I had removed my parachute that it came to me that I might still be in Russian territory. But then a Volkswagen approached and to my joy an infantry *Leutnant* got out. I told him the whole story and found in him not only a listener, but a keen admirer as well, who had been very impressed by my slick landing. His driver, on the other hand, was more interested in practical things and in no time he had pumped my fuel tank dry using a hose he had brought with him. Afterward we climbed into the car. Two hours later I was back with my unit at Buda-Örs.

Lt. Düttmann had arrived there just ahead of me with his parachute under his arm, black, smeared, but nevertheless, as I saw, happy. Düttmann had shot down an Il-2 and then flown into its bomblets.

We left Buda-Örs in December to transfer farther west. We came to Csor, where a chateau served as our quarters. The airfield was situated on a rise and was unfortunately visited regularly by Il-2s. We did what we could, but the poor weather often hindered our operational activities.

We used the periods of waiting to sharpen our skat skills. I scored two victories while flying from Csor and was once again brought down by an Il-2. I was forced to make a belly landing in the immediate vicinity of the airfield.

I soon learned that my former comrades of the 1st Panzer Division were in action in the Stuhlweissenburg area. I succeeded in shooting down a Russian and serving him up as a present, as it were, in front of the division command post. The next day I took advantage of the bad weather to drive over to the division, where I received a warm welcome. At first the Russian pilot explained that he had been shot down by flak, but I was finally able to convince him that I had brought him down. My former comrades were more than a little amazed that their former *Unteroffizier* had come back as a *Hauptmann* and wearer of the Knight's Cross.

But there was a sad occurrence at Csor. We lost our good friend and comrade Hptm. Sturm. It happened the day I was shot down by the Il-2. Sturm's *Staffel* had achieved a total of 899 victories, two of them by the *Hauptmann* that day. As the *Staffelkapitän* he wanted to get the 900th. So he landed, immediately climbed into another machine and prepared to take off. However his wheels struck the top of a truck which was driving across the landing field. His aircraft was brought back down to the ground and slid to a stop, by now in flames. I rushed over to pull him from the wreckage of his burning machine but it was too late. He had apparently been killed instantly and by now was sitting in fighter pilot heaven, waiting with Fönnekold for me to arrive so we could have our traditional game of skat. We buried his remains at Papa on a gray, cold day.

Soon the *Gruppe* was again forced to move to keep ahead of the pursuing Russians. We arrived at Vesprem, near Lake Balaton. At first there wasn't much going on there, and so it happened that we renewed our acquaintance with the infantry. Everyone, including the pilots, marched, drilled and practiced all the lovely things an infantryman has to know. Several times we marched around the countryside in the snow and cold and on these occasions often sought out objectives which were known and loved for their fine wine. Even the pampered pilots enjoyed such marches and gladly took part in them.

It was at this time, when there were few enemy aircraft about, that I scored a great victory.

Together with my wingman, Uffz. Brandecker, I had been prowling about at the front for nearly an hour without seeing anything. Then, while on the return flight, I spotted a lone aircraft over Lake Balaton at about 5,000 meters. We spiraled up toward it and recognized a Pe-2, a Russian reconnaissance machine. The aircraft was flying leisurely toward the west. The Ivans must nevertheless have been on the lookout, because just as I moved into position from behind and was about to open fire, the Pe-2 swung away in a descending left turn and tried to escape at high speed.

On account of my low speed in the climb, the Russian was at first able to widen the distance between us. Soon, however, we were behind him. No amount of turning or maneuvering could help him now. The rear gunner's efforts were also in vain. Even though tracer whizzed past my ears, I moved in quite close, pressed the firing button for the 30mm cannon and scored two hits. The first would have been enough; the second caused the aircraft to explode.

It was at this point in time that we again became involved with Mustangs; unfortunately, however, the experience we gained was almost all bad. Lt. Ewald and his *Schwarm* ran into eight of these American fighters north of Lake Balaton. Ewald may well have had a score to settle with the Americans because they had fired at him in his parachute over Romania. For whatever reason, he attacked without regard to position. He damaged a Mustang, which dove away trailing black smoke, but in no time the eight had become twenty or thirty. The first group of

American fighters had used their precisely-functioning communications system to summon reinforcements and Ewald and his three Messerschmitts soon found themselves outnumbered ten to one.

The other element leader in Ewald's formation, Fw. Pitzel, shot down a Mustang, but was himself hit almost immediately and just managed to escape by parachute. The two wingmen tried to escape, with the result that both were shot down. Then the pack of hounds set upon the brave Ewald, who defended himself as best he could. By continually turning and firing he managed to work his way back to the vicinity of the airfield. There he suddenly straightened out and roared past the bishop's palace of Vesprem at low level, pursued by three Mustangs. Near the airfield he pulled up into the fire of the German flak. His aircraft was hit several times before he rolled the Messerschmitt onto its back at about 300 meters and bailed out.

While the Messerschmitt crashed to the ground west of the base, Lt. Ewald hung in his parachute and had to endure being fired upon by the SS. Bullets whistled about him, but fate spared his life and he came down safe and sound. Afterward he drove to the SS unit and in less than gentle terms expressed to these people his admiration for their shooting skills.

Several days after Christmas we transferred to Nagymand. The Russians had thrown back all the German forces toward the north and were now trying to break through in the Bakony forest. Nagymand had only a rather small airfield, but we quickly got accustomed to conditions there. On my very first sortie from Nagymand I shot down two enemy aircraft, a LaGG-5 and a Yak.

Then came January 4, 1945. On this notable day I shot down two enemy aircraft on each of two sorties. The first two were Il-2s and the others fighters. I will always remember the last kill, a LaGG-5.

We were on our way back to Nagymand when we made contact with ten Il-2s and ten LaGG-5 fighters. The LaGGs flew so skillfully that I was unable to get at the Il-2s. I was exhausted and thought to myself that I had had enough for today. So Prokoph and I dove away toward German territory. A single LaGG followed me. I wasn't about to stand for that and hauled my aircraft around. Soon the loveliest dogfight was in progress. I very quickly came to the realization that the Russian in his LaGG was my equal in every respect.

At first the Russian clung doggedly to my wingman, who was forced to turn for his life. While instructing him repeatedly not to stop turning, I moved away and then came down behind the Russian machine from above. After a few hits the enemy aircraft turned sharply, trailing black smoke. Now he wanted to get away from us, but as I had much more speed I hit him hard once again. At this the enemy aircraft reared up and climbed straight up into the sky.

In seconds I was behind him again and had my thumb and forefinger on the firing buttons. Suddenly I saw that the right side of the aircraft's fuselage in the area of the cockpit was colored red. At the same time I noticed that the pilot had slid back the hood and was lying in the right corner of the cockpit. I pulled my fingers back and moved in close, whereupon I saw that the Russian must be dead. The red streaming along the fuselage was blood; it had already reached the tail surfaces. I was horrified and at that moment would have given anything if I could have undone this kill.

The events of the following day illustrated how preoccupied I was with the death of this enemy pilot. I was unable to shoot down any enemy aircraft. Not until I was badly frightened again by the Russians did I slowly overcome my inhibitions.

I was flying with Prokoph again and had lost sight of him in a dogfight. As well he did not answer my calls. Contrary to my usual practice and every rule of fighter piloting, I stayed in the combat area and tried again against the far superior enemy. Of course it didn't work. When I realized this I dove away from Budapest, where the combat had taken place, in the direction of Nagymand at about 600 kph. I thought to myself that no Russian could fly this fast. Once over friendly territory I felt even more secure. But then I became mistrustful and began looking around now and then. During one such look back I was amazed to see a red nose about 300 meters behind me and to the left. Aha, I thought, 5 *Staffel* is also about to land. The spinners of this unit's aircraft were red. I waggled my wings to prevent any shenanigans by the people behind me, but at the same instant my aircraft was hit. Before I was fully aware of the pain in my left little toe, I had pushed the nose of my machine down so sharply that all the loose odds and ends in the aircraft were hanging from the roof of the canopy. Throttle forward and slow roll downward at full power! No one could stay with that, I thought, and I was right. I pulled out at ground level and congratulated myself for reacting so well. At that point I looked all around, especially to the rear, and then had time to look at the damage I had sustained. But I could see only two hits in the left wing. After landing, however, I saw more bullet holes in the left wing and tail, as well as one in the left side of the engine cowling. It was this bullet which had ripped into my left shoe and struck my toe.

I had probably tangled with a Russian ace. While the aircraft I had spotted 300 meters behind me remained in that position, the other Ivan, who must have been directly behind me, had moved in close. He wanted to have me for certain and shoot me down. Yes the Russians had certainly learned a great deal.

The following day there was low cloud and generally bad weather. The command post was the scene of great excitement, however, as the intercept service had learned that many Boston bombers were forming up over Stuhlweissenburg for a large-scale attack. This was all well and good, but how were we to find the Russians in this weather? I volunteered for the job and took off with Sepp Prokoph. The dreary grayness swallowed us up. The base of the cloud deck was somewhat higher in the direction of the front, so that we were able to whisk across the Bakony forest. The weather was much better on the other side. We flew straight toward Stuhlweissenburg and arrived just in time to see a single bomber flying toward the airfield. It flew low over the Russian fighter dispersal and waggled its wings, which could only mean: take off, we need fighter cover.

In fact engines were already running down there and several Yaks were taxiing out for takeoff. Then the Boston came back, straight toward us. It waggled its wings again, but we were already on top of him. We dove low over the airfield, swung upward and came in behind the bomber. He was waggling his wings again when my bursts hit him. Without having fired a shot the Boston blew apart and showered the edge of the airfield with burning wreckage. The Russians may well have been totally perplexed at that moment, because their anti-aircraft guns didn't fire a shot.

Prokoph shouted for joy, so loudly that my ears rang. But the other Bostons were approaching, while below us the fighters were taking off. We climbed up into the clouds and waited. The waves of aircraft which approached were flying so close together that it would have been far too dangerous to go down after them. Prokoph definitely wanted to go down, but I discouraged him: "Have you gone mad, where do you intend to attack? Let them pass, wait for an opportunity!"

Russian fighters were definitely in the air. It was time to attack. Then I discovered a larger gap between two waves and called. "Move in now! But take one flying on the outside, otherwise you'll be shot down!"

And then we were sitting in the midst of the seemingly endless stream of enemy bombers. In spite of my long time at the front as a fighter pilot I had never before seen so many Russians in the air. And how they defended themselves! I selected a Boston and shot it up as best I could. Unfortunately my cannon had jammed again – how often this happened in such situations! The machine in front of me was capable of absorbing a lot of punishment and I was so excited that my aim was poor. Finally the Russian in front of me began to burn and sheared away from the formation. A little later he went down in flames.

I soon had the next machine in front of me and fired again. This one, too, showed the effects of my fire. Unfortunately I couldn't watch to see what became of it, as one look behind was enough to spot several enemy fighters. They fired wildly. There was only one thing to do: up into the clouds. "Prokoph," I called, "pull up, we're being attacked!" My wingman appeared to hear nothing. "You're supposed to pull up, lad!" Finally he understood, and we both reached the safety of the clouds in time.

"We'll fly to the east," I called over to him, "the Russians won't be looking for us there. In a few minutes we'll drop back down again!" Prokoph moved in very close beside me on the right. Then we turned around and headed back toward Stuhlweissenburg. There was nothing to be seen far and wide. The sky appeared to be empty, but down below we saw three downed aircraft which were still burning fiercely. I had shot down two of them, the third must have been Prokoph's. Finally we flew home, where we received an enthusiastic welcome. Gustav Bolinski, 6 *Staffel*'s senior NCO, had a pig butchered. It was a celebration of which we spoke for a long time.

At this time another so-called "lunatic mission" fell to our lot. In spite of poor weather with visibility of no more than 300 meters, the corps ordered an escort mission. We were to take He 111s to Budapest. They assured us that the weather was fine in the operations area. But what good was that if we couldn't find our way back to base or flew into the mountains while descending through cloud. Our objections were ignored. At the very least one *Schwarm* was to take off. So away we went: Ewald and I and our two wingmen.

My aircraft seemed to balk at this takeoff. Serious ignition trouble caused it to grumble and stutter so that I decided to turn command over to Ewald and land again at once. He found the He 111s and brought them back safely; there was no contact with the enemy. But as we had feared, he was unable to find the airfield again. He flew along with the bombers until his fuel was almost gone. Then all three Messerschmitts landed far to the north on the other side of the Danube. Ewald landed his aircraft in a meadow. The two wingmen made belly landings and were lucky that only their aircraft were heavily damaged.

At about the same time I made the acquaintance of the new Yak. This latest Russian fighter was somewhat superior to us in speed and maneuverability, its armament was equal to ours, and only in the dive did our machines prove to be superior. Our first meeting with the new Yak almost ended badly: Prokoph and I were deep inside friendly territory and suspecting nothing untoward. It was my custom in the air never to fly straight and level. Not only did I continually change direction, but altitude as well. As a result many wingmen didn't like flying with me. But thanks to this constant remaining in motion it was impossible for the enemy to sneak up on me unnoticed. Prokoph was the best wingman of all for this type of flying.

So it was that I noticed a lone Yak approaching from behind. We were low on fuel and therefore didn't want to get involved in combat. The Russian appeared to have other ideas. Although we were flying at maximum speed he drew ever nearer and finally forced us to start turning. We escaped the first attack only by breaking away suddenly. The Ivan pulled up and away and then came down again behind Prokoph. At first I flew around the circle and tried to get on the enemy's tail, but that was out of the question. By now we were turning at full throttle near ground level. The Russian took his time and repeatedly pulled up out of the left turn, dropped down again, allowed for deflection and fired.

When he began to fire I issued corrections to Prokoph, who listened to my words and immediately did as I instructed. My wingman was hit several times, but he followed my instructions precisely and so avoided being shot down. This was too much for me. "Keep turning," I called to Prokoph, "and as tightly as possible! I'm going to climb above the Russian and come down from above to help you!"

Prokoph's aircraft was hit several more times in the tail. If I hadn't been so furious, I would have had to admire the Russian for the way he repeatedly sheared upward, dropped down into the circle from above and only fired when he had allowed adequate deflection. Prokoph didn't whine and cry for help, rather he turned for his life. Then I was in position to come down from above. "Straighten out, Prokoph!"

The Russian machine straightened out almost simultaneously and I fired a fraction of a second before the enemy pilot. My full burst hit him just as he opened fire, causing him to break away and turn around. I had hit him well, but he had nevertheless scored several more hits on Prokoph. I now moved in behind the Russian, who swung gently back and forth in front of me so that all I could do was spray bullets instead of aiming precisely. In spite of his black smoke trail he pulled away and steadily increased the range between us. I might still have been able to catch him, but our fuel was must gone. I had no choice but to turn away.

There was no denying that I was impressed with this Russian type. The new Yak appeared to me to be far more dangerous than the Mustang.

Prokoph, whom I had immediately sent home, had already landed when I returned. "Now then, *Herr Hauptmann*," he greeted me, "we'll want to get our own back for that!"

Our chance was not long in coming. There now seemed to be nothing but these new Yaks – which we designated the Yak-3 – over the Gran bridgehead. It was well that we had met them before. Most of our comrades didn't want to believe our reports and had to learn the hard way. Many were shot down and others escaped with their lives only because of their flying experience. We had a running series of bail-outs.

Together with Prokoph I tried the following tactic at the Gran. We flew very high, if possible just in the bottoms of the clouds, let the Yaks alone at first and waited until they prepared for the return flight. If they then steamed away in an easterly direction I came down from above, dove below them and came up behind the last one. In most cases this

Russian didn't notice what was happening until it was time for him to take to his parachute. The other enemy aircraft would try to come after us, but we always had enough speed to climb away from them. I could never have thought up such a trick at the beginning of my career. Back then I would dive into the middle of the milling crowd, take a number of hits – much to the dismay of the mechanic – and would have to head home without shooting down any enemy aircraft. Now, with my 175 kills I had become a "tactician" and achieved a kill on almost every sortie without being hit myself.

Ewald and I flew very well together. He saved my life several times. In other cases I was able to return the favor by getting him out of trouble. On one occasion we were flying together in a *Schwarm* over the Gran bridgehead. This time there were LaGG-5s there, patrolling well inside Russian territory. We did the same on our side. It was thus a nice game. Soon I had thought up a plan. At first we flew away to the west. Ewald and his wingman disappeared into the clouds and my wingman and I stayed about one kilometer below them. Then I flew right beneath the Russians, calmly and apparently suspecting nothing. This they couldn't pass up. I said to Ewald: "They'll be coming any minute!" Then the Russians made their move.

All of the LaGGs came diving at the two of us in line astern, but right behind them was Ewald's *Rotte*. I naturally had enough "steam up" and together with my wingman made a tight left turn back toward them so that the Russians roared past about 300 meters beside and below me. One had even opened fire, but his bullets hit only empty air.

Ewald latched onto the last one and opened fire. There were flashes all over the enemy aircraft, and as it dove away he lined up on the next Russian fighter. The Russians now pulled up into the safety of the clouds and were not seen again. I kept looking, because I hoped that they would come out again somewhere. All at once a lone LaGG-5 appeared from below right in front of my nose. It kept climbing and then began a turn. I was behind it and about to fire when I heard a voice saying: "Come now, Helmut, you're not going to prove your shooting skills on a pilotless ship are you? There's no one in it, the pilot jumped out from fright during my attack!" Naturally I immediately left the machine alone, especially since I saw a parachute swinging far below. The LaGG now flew past just above me and I was able to convince myself that

Ewald wasn't lying. There was no pilot in the cockpit. The aircraft righted itself again and made two proper right-hand turns before it fell to earth and exploded. It was remarkable the things one saw while piloting a fighter aircraft. One should be careful not to credit the practice of bailing out in the nick of time just to the Russians. I am convinced that many pilots resorted to this before the Russian – and afterward as well.

In the meantime I had been recommended for the Oak Leaves to the Knight's Cross and about three months later I was informed that 165 kills were now the required for this decoration. Perhaps the gentlemen up above thought, Lipfert will have retired and he will never get the Oak Leaves. However, by the time I received this information I already had 177 kills.

Later, after another transfer to Vesprem, I was forced to leave II./JG 52 and all my comrades, because from then on I led I./JG 53 as *Gruppenkommandeur*. With me went Oblt. Handschug, who became my adjutant, and my faithful *Oberfähnrich* Prokoph, who was to remain my wingman. My beginning with the new *Gruppe* was not the best and I had a very difficult time acclimatizing myself there. At least the *Gruppe* was very well off when it came to vehicles and equipment.

I got along best with the young pilots who had just arrived at the front. It was they with whom I had the most contact, and I therefore flew exclusively with them. Among these pilots who accompanied me on my combat sorties was *Oberfähnrich* Sommavilla, who proved himself to be a true friend and comrade in arms. But all this was still in the future, as I was still with II./JG 52.

At that time we flew mostly in the area east of Lake Balaton, where Russian fighters maintained a screen over their armored spearheads at 3,500 meters. We always approached at 5,000 meters and saw them, usually eight machines, patrolling below us. In such cases I gave precise instructions to my pilots and explained to them how to pick out one without endangering oneself and risking being hit. To this end I first watched to determine where the Russians had set up their turning point. These machines almost always watched over a specified area and had to fly the same route in a fixed rotation. I lurked above them until they began to turn around. When the leader began his left turn the others had their hands full staying in position and had to take care not to collide with one another. This was the most favorable moment.

When the first machine began his turn I was already on my way down, and before the last Ivan had brought his mill into the proper position I was behind him and opened fire from point-blank range. I was so well-drilled in this that I could still shoot down the enemy even if my cannon failed and I was left with only the two machine-guns. When the 30mm cannon did fire, the enemy aircraft blew apart. If only the machine-guns functioned, the aircraft usually began to burn right away, often allowing the pilot to take to his parachute.

But often the Russians noticed that something wasn't right. In that case they rolled onto their backs, pulled through and carried out a Split-S. Only the one I had chosen flew straight ahead and had little chance to escape. Naturally my pilots tried to emulate my tactics, but they almost always opened fire too soon.

A new period began with a run of bad luck. My weapons failed repeatedly. There was a continuous series of engine failures and then I began having stomach problems. I had probably been flying too long without a rest. The most I could consume was a piece of dry bread, a cucumber or a schnapps. Just then II./JG 52 was experiencing a serious officer shortage. There was Sachsenberg and me. The younger officers had almost all been shot down and the others were once again in the "repair shops." Nevertheless *Major* Barkhorn couldn't overlook that I was in rather poor shape. He sent me to the aircrew examination center in Vienna for ten days. These ten days made me almost completely well. At least I was able to remain at the front until the end of the war.

# CHAPTER VIII
# End of the Chase

From February 15, 1945, the day I took over I./JG 53, almost nothing went right. The good Handschug was usually waiting to try and console me when I returned from a sortie, because my weapons failed repeatedly and no one could explain why.

At this time we received orders to transfer to Pistian, on the Waag River in Slovakia. This seemed to snap the jinx. There was an air battle our first day flying from Pistian and I shot down a LaGG and a Yak. On my fourth sortie I downed my 182nd enemy aircraft. Several times we had to fly escort for the close-support unit also operating from Pistian. In the process I made the interesting discovery that the ground attack pilots in their Fw 190s were faster at low level than we were. On the way home I waved over one of the Focke Wulfs and gestured to the pilot that I wanted to race.

We started out at the same speed, then opened the throttles simultaneously and slowly but surely the "190" pulled ahead. I couldn't keep up, even though the aircraft I was flying certainly wasn't a poor one. But this was no fighter which left me behind, but a close-support aircraft for which we "faster" fighters were supposed to be flying escort. But it was not only in level speed that this bird was superior to us. Its main strength lay in its enormous firepower and diving speed. I discussed my experience with the *Kommandeur* of the close-support *Gruppe*, Hptm. Mrkva, and as a result he dispensed with our fighter escort in future.

After that we flew *freie Jagd* in the Altsohl area. Flying and navigating through the mountains when the ceiling was low did not prove to be easy. We always found the city of Altsohl, but the return flight was quite difficult.

We had taken off once again for Altsohl, which was forced to endure incessant bombing attacks. The infantry informed us that the last attacks had been flown by German aircraft which we had supplied to the Rumanians: Ju 88s, He 111s and Bf 109s.

I intercepted one such raid on February 24 at about 1400. The enemy aircraft were flying just beneath the clouds and had not yet reached their target when I approached from below with my *Schwarm*. Each of us fired as best we could. Still plagued by bad luck, only one of my machine-guns functioned. I was able to disable one of the rear gunners and hit the aircraft's left engine several times, but then the smoking machine disappeared into cloud. Two Messerschmitts were coming toward me from the side, their guns blazing, so I, too, climbed up into the clouds. Before entering cloud I recognized their Romanian markings. Perhaps the pilots were two of the Romanians I had instructed at Tiraspol. A unique situation!

I wanted to see what they had learned. Coming out of the clouds, I descended to just above the ground. I saw two machines above and to my right and approached them from behind and below. However they had already seen me and turned toward me before I was in firing range. With my speed I shot past them in the climb and once again noticed their Romanian markings. When we began turning I concluded to my relief that these two definitely couldn't have been at Tiraspol, as they appeared to be very inexperienced. The enemy pilots seemed to be afraid to fly their aircraft to the limit and therefore made only rather gentle turns. Their aircraft also seemed to be rather slow, as I was able to get behind them on my first pass.

After the first shots at the trailing Romanian he immediately tried to dive away in the direction of the enemy lines. But I sat on his tail, blazing away with my one machine-gun. He took no evasive action, seeking safety in flight instead. I was low over enemy territory with no wingman, but I didn't want to let this machine get away so easily. The other Romanian separated from his companion but did not come to his aid. Afterward I maintained an especially close watch behind and continued firing at the Me in front of me. It was already smoking heavily and then suddenly it crashed into a hill. There was no fire.

I regretted the outcome of this combat a little, because a proper dogfight with a Bf 109 flown by a pilot of equal ability would have been something. What was more there were no witnesses. I turned around and flew leisurely in the direction of Altsohl. I found the city, which was usually easy to locate, only by chance. I circled overhead several times and while doing so noticed that my compass had failed. Without the sun I might have flown off in the wrong direction. But with its help I was able to orientate myself and then flew home. I immediately sent my machine into the repair shops. The weather then turned very poor.

Two days later the rain-swollen Waag overflowed its banks and we were forced to hastily evacuate the airfield. I took off at 1606 with *Oberfähnrich* Elle. We were not in radio contact with one another. By chance I looked at my compass several minutes after takeoff and realized that it still wasn't working properly. The sun was hidden, what was I to do now? Strictly speaking, we were supposed to fly to Raab. My wingman and I reached the Danube somewhere but were unable to find the city. After searching desperately we finally arrived at Vienna-Aspern.

Back at Vesprem I learned that we had nearly been placed on the casualty list. They had called every neighboring unit, but no one could remember seeing the crash of two Messerschmitts.

At Vesprem I called upon several mechanics of II./JG 52 for help, and they restored my weapons and compass to working order.

In the following days I./JG 53 achieved seven kills, six of which were credited to me. I made the last two during a mission over the 1st Panzer Division's sector.

Then there was a fateful blow: my faithful and brave Prokoph's last mission!

We took off on March 19, 1945 at 0858 and once over the front immediately made contact with about ten Il-2s and several Yaks.

As we dove on the Il-2s Prokoph reported two Russians behind and above us. I broke off my attack on the close-support aircraft and moved toward the attackers. As we had sufficient speed, we were able to climb above them. A dogfight started, but we were unable to get into firing position. After several circles I saw more Yaks approaching just beneath the clouds. Two of them separated from the others and dove toward us. They were still too far away to fire. Even when they got behind us they were unable to cause us any harm as we turned very tightly. 200 meters in front of me were two Yaks, behind me Prokoph, and 200 meters behind him the other two Russians, who were closing in slowly in a steep left turn. Still no one was able to do anything to the other. "Stay very close Prokoph, things are becoming dangerous!"

At the same moment what I feared most happened. The other Yaks came down to help their comrades. "Let's get out of here, Prokoph!" I roared, and did what seemed the safest. I pulled up steeply until my aircraft was about to stall, then tramped on the left rudder pedal while pushing the stick to the left. The machine reared up and I dove away vertically, slow-rolling as I flew right through the middle of the Yaks.

It was during this maneuver that I noticed that Prokoph was no longer behind me. I saw him turning with four Yaks. Again I yelled "get out of there, get out of there!" But Prokoph kept turning.

Three of the Yaks didn't seem to believe that I had been hit and shot down. While the others turned away, these three came after me and tried to inflict more damage. The battle had taken place at perhaps 2,500 meters. At 1,000 meters I was going so fast that the Russians didn't dare stay with me. Carefully I pulled out of the dive – I had more than 700 kph on the clock – and dropped down to just above the ground. When I levelled off I realized that I was heading east and thus deeper into enemy territory. While many Ivans continued circling above me, I cautiously made my way toward the west, staying close to the ground at full throttle. I did this on the one hand to give the Russian anti-aircraft guns only a fleeting target, and on the other to remain as invisible as possible to the enemy fighters by staying in the dense ground mist.

I had every reason to do so, because while fleeing toward the east I had come upon an enemy anti-tank gun, which must have seen me in combat with the Russian fighters. I saw a flash, felt a sharp jolt and saw a hole in my left wing of approximately 30 by 30 centimeters. There was no way I wanted to climb back up to where the Russians were with this handicap.

Near the German lines I saw an aircraft going down to my right. It crashed barely 300 meters away from me. It was a 109. At the same time I saw the parachute. Prokoph!

There were still several Russians above me. I had to steal away quietly and furtively if I didn't want to be shot down myself. I had to leave my loyal comrade to the Russians. I could have found fault with myself for not breaking off the engagement sooner, but what good would it have done? Prokoph was forced to take the hard road into captivity and it wasn't until 1949 that he returned to Munich.

Sometimes one event seems to lead to another. Scarcely had one been wounded by one blow when he was forced to endure another. Ewald had been the first to come to grips with Mustangs while flying from Vesprem. Now it was my turn again. I had just taken off with a *Schwarm* when the ground station reported a large number of Mustangs. Naturally I became wide awake. Soon I saw a single aircraft flying above me just beneath the clouds which I immediately recognized as a Mustang. As I had plenty of speed in hand I tried to climb after it, but unfortunately I was only able to fire from long range as it slipped into the clouds. I then assembled my *Schwarm* and remained over Vesprem at 2,000 meters. Then the ground station called again: "Mustangs in the vicinity of the airfield." "From six one: back to the Picnic Ground!"

Before my number four had regained position there was suddenly a Mustang on his tail. I shouted to him, but to no avail.

*Oberfähnrich* Elle, who was flying 6/4, did not try to turn, instead he tried to reach the airfield by diving. I hauled my aircraft around at once and flew over the other two aircraft after the Mustang. The American fighter was sitting calmly behind the number four man of my *Schwarm*. At first the enemy pilot only sprayed him with bullets, but he kept closing and by the time they were over the airfield perimeter he was in a good position to fire at Elle.

By now, however, I had moved right in behind the Mustang. Just as I was about to open fire the flak put up a wall of fire between me and the enemy aircraft. As I assumed that I was being shot at, I rolled my aircraft onto its back at a height of 300 meters and climbed slightly. The advantage of this was that it allowed the anti-aircraft gunners to identify me as one of their own – the underside of my aircraft were probably covered with muck – and at the same enabled me to keep an eye on the Mustang. The flak ceased firing immediately.

Before I could intervene, however, the Mustang hit my number four and sent the 109 down in flames. Then the enemy pilot made a sharp right turn, which gave me the chance to cut him off. I was on his tail immediately. I pressed both triggers, but once again only one machine-gun would fire. The American took evasive action, but his efforts were so lame that I couldn't miss. The Mustang was already smoking when the other machine-gun quit as well. Jammed!

I heard *Oberfähnrich* Esser's voice: "Let me have a go, *Herr Hauptmann*, I'm right behind you!" I pulled up and Esser closed in and fired. A moment later I heard a voice shout "*Abschuss*!" and saw the burning Mustang crash into a wood from a height of 600 meters. The pilot bailed out shortly before the aircraft struck the ground.

I continued to be plagued by problems with my weapons. My log book contains numerous entries such as: air combat with Il-2s and LaGG-5s, 1 LaGG damaged. It was the same on March 17, initially only one machine-gun would work. My *Schwarm* and I encountered a large number of unescorted Il-2s over the northern end of Lake Balaton. I fired at one bomber after another, but none went down. When my only weapon had expended all its ammunition I climbed up to direct the attacks by the other pilots. At the same time I watched to see that no one approached my brood. My men shot badly, however. I saw many Il-2s staggering along trailing smoke or with one undercarriage leg hanging down, but none of them would oblige us by going down. My three companions had certainly fleeced them badly (CK). I was furious, but more at my bad luck than at my pilots.

"I'm west of you at *Hanni* 1,500, come up!" The Il-2s had flown away and my comrades climbed slowly toward me. In the lead was my wingman, Lt. Müller. He had just about reached me when suddenly I saw an aircraft directly above me. It was turning and twisting and pulled ahead of me slowly. The LaGG-5 was perhaps 500 meters above me. When I had satisfied myself that the Russian was alone I climbed gingerly toward him. The Ivan appeared to be looking for something, as he soon began swaying to the left and right. I was now about ten meters behind and one meter below him, but he didn't see me.

I had decided to close in from behind and saw off his tail, but I wavered when I was caught in his slipstream. For sure he would fall into Lake Balaton, but it seemed quite likely that I would follow him, and there was no need of that.

I once again cocked my weapons and shook my Me about, praying that my guns might at least fire a single shot. Meanwhile the Russian continued to fly a few meters above me, swinging gently from side to side. Perhaps he couldn't make up his mind! He was almost over the north side of the lake, so I decided to risk a final attempt. The cannon fired two rounds, and that was all it took. The fuselage of the LaGG-5 exploded and broke apart. The enemy pilot nevertheless succeeded in bailing out. I circled round him at a distance until he landed in the water. Then I saw the Russian pilot free himself from his parachute and begin to swim. Apparently his bad luck had so infuriated him that he took the wrong direction and was swimming toward the German shore, where they appeared to be waiting for him.

What a favor I would have done my Russian opponents had I crashed while buzzing the airfield on March 20. Naturally alcohol was to blame. A war correspondent had turned up that day. By then I had 189 kills and the Oak Leaves, but no one had ever written a line or spoken a word about me.

Now I had never been a speaker, but this man from the propaganda service begged and pressed me so long that after two bottles of wine I finally agreed. Once I got going I was able to speak for more than ten minutes.

Finally I was supposed to climb into my aircraft, as tipsy as I was, and go get my 190th kill. Well alright! I took off with a *Schwarm.* As haze was reducing visibility from above I stayed low and flew along the front to Varpalota, where the ground station was reporting enemy activity. Not far from Varpalota I saw heavy anti-aircraft fire. Disregarding my position and the escorting fighters, I flew right under a formation of Il-2s and pulled up onto the tail of the last machine. I hit him so well that he sheared away from the rest of the formation without firing a shot, went down in a shallow dive and struck the ground.

In the meantime the other Il-2s had altered course to the left and were now seeking safety in flight as their fighter escort was still peacefully basking in the sun at 3,000 meters. I headed them off and again approached the close-support aircraft. As I did so a lone aircraft came from the right and passed right in front of my guns. I made a minor course correction, allowed a little deflection and fired all weapons. The Il-2 flew right into my burst of fire and blew up.

By now I had attracted the attention of the escort. Looking back I saw several coming down toward me. I turned toward them and spiraled upward, coming under fire from several Russian fighters in the process. They missed me, however, as I was constantly in motion. I looked around for my *Schwarm* and realized that none of my pilots were in the vicinity. Instead I saw a new wave of Il-2s approaching.

Without the effects of the alcohol I would never have risked another attack in this situation. But in my condition I had no fear and so I dove through the enemy fighters again. On this pass I fired at one of the three leading Il-2s. Even though there were enemy fighters behind me during the action and their tracer flashed unmistakably past my cockpit, I nevertheless opened the radiator flaps and reduced speed. Applying left and right rudder, I made it difficult for my pursuers to aim accurately while I couldn't miss the Il-2 in front of me.

By the time I had approached to within a few meters its wings and fuselage were already ablaze. I therefore left the Il-2 and began to turn for my life with the pursuing fighters. I intentionally dropped down to ground level, as I didn't stand a chance above. There was a whole enemy armada up there. Somehow I managed to escape the Russian fighters through the German flak and the falling bombs of the Il-2s, but I wasn't out of the woods yet.

On returning to the airfield I received another nod from fate. I flew toward the command post from an altitude of about 500 meters in order to indicate my three kills by waggling my wings. When I pulled up for the first time for some unexplained reason I pulled back the throttle, made a gentle turn and dove back down toward the command post. The aircraft picked up very little speed in the process. At about 100 meters I pulled back on the stick to pull out.

The Messerschmitt reacted, but so sluggishly that it sagged noticeably. Luckily it recovered at treetop height. Never before had I gambled with my life so carelessly. Afterward my knees were shaking and there was a strange taste in my mouth. The subsequent landing was relatively normal, but I was through flying for the day.

I made one more kill flying from Vesprem. Finally it was time for us to move again. This time we settled in at Papa for a few days. Nothing out of the ordinary took place during our stay. One day *General* Deichmann paid us a visit at the dispersal just as the Russians were beginning another low-level attack.

The general almost didn't survive the attack. He fell into a water-filled ditch and probably wouldn't have got back to dry land had I not come to his rescue.

Even by night the Russians gave us no rest, although our quarters were several kilometers away from the airfield. Within three days of our arrival Russian tanks were closing in. Although we had reported this fact to corps late in the morning they took their time as always. Orders to transfer to another base did not arrive until late in the afternoon. We pilots were visibly annoyed at this, because it was a damned uncomfortable thing to have to fly into a new and unfamiliar airfield in the evening.

Again there was confusion on departure. Each wanted to be first so as to arrive at the new field before darkness fell. Four aircraft collided on takeoff. I set course as soon as I was airborne. When I arrived at the new airfield the air was swarming with Messerschmitts. On the field itself were three crashed aircraft, precisely in the best part of the airfield for landing. When I lined up on final for the first time a 109 came down in front of me so that I nearly sawed off his tail. I had no choice but to pull up and go around. I was furious. My second approach also failed to result in a landing. This time a 109 came at me from the side and forced me to overshoot.

It had meanwhile become darker and I was determined to land somewhere. I swept in toward the extreme right side of the airfield and touched down smoothly. I rolled about 100 meters after landing and then noticed that the tail of my Me was rising slowly. Cutting the throttle and pulling back on the stick had no effect. I quickly switched off the ignition and pulled my straps tight. Then came the expected crash and I was hanging upside down in my crate. As I had flipped over quite near the dispersal the technical personnel were on the scene quickly and raised the Me. This time I waited until the canopy was opened before releasing my straps, then I let myself fall and was caught by several mechanics. Several pilots had already gathered at the command post. We watched the other aircraft land and commented on the crashes: there had now been seven. Sachsenberg and Ewald agreed that my somersault had been the prettiest crash on the airfield. One could clearly see how the aircraft had touched down. The tracks left by the wheels ran straight to the point where the machine – without changing direction – had flipped onto its back.

While the *Gruppe* moved to Parndorf, close to Vienna, the next day, I./JG 53 and I once again transferred to Pistian. Our old Oblt. Könnecke greeted us joyfully. At this time we were paid a visit by another high-ranking offer. *Generaloberst* Dessloch wanted to inspect I./JG 53. Unfortunately I could only tell him that there was little sense in committing this *Gruppe* to action and asked him to disband the unit. This happened some time later and I was forced to realize that the war was lost.

Flying from Novy-Dvor, to where we had moved in the meantime, I scored two more kills, raising my total to 199. But then I simply couldn't seem to get my 200th victory.

Together with Uffz. Neumann, I took off on my 680th combat sortie at 0905 on April 2. It was a *freie Jagd* mission. There wasn't much going on in the air. The ground station had no reports of enemy aircraft. We flew down to the mouth of the Marsch and from there headed in the direction of Pressburg (Bratislava), climbing steadily. Then Neumann reported a large number of flak bursts far ahead of us at a higher altitude. We increased power and climbed steeply, hanging on our propellers. At 4,000 meters I spotted a lone aircraft flying west at an altitude of 7,000 meters. It had to be an enemy reconnaissance machine. "Now I'll get my 200th!" I thought.

Unfortunately in my excitement I misjudged my approach and ended up 300 meters directly beneath the Russian. He must have spotted me at that moment. When I tried to turn away to the side and climb he turned with me. No matter what I did he kept me directly below him. I was desperate and at my wits' end. Neumann, however, was drawing ever nearer the Russian Pe-2.

Then the *Unteroffizier* was behind the enemy machine. I called him: "Neumann, that would be my 200th . . . but attack and shoot him down!" Neumann's attack inflicted no damage but it did force the Russian to turn. I was thus free to climb. Meanwhile my wingman made a second attack. His speed was too great, however, and he scored only a few hits. Finally it was my turn. The enemy reconnaissance aircraft used every trick in its defense and made accurate shooting difficult. But when I pulled away after closing to point-blank range the dorsal gunner's machine-gun was pointing straight up and the left engine was ablaze.

Neumann now attacked again and gave the Russian what for. In the midst of his attack I heard him call: "Damn it all! I can't see him any more, my windscreen is completely oiled up!"

"The Russian is right in front of you, I'll finish him off," I said. This time I approached carefully and held my fire until I couldn't miss. A few rounds were enough to cause the machine in front of me to blow apart. I noticed three parachutes among the burning pieces. Two of them opened, but one immediately caught fire and burned. The third parachute swung down toward Pressburg.

Neumann and I had become separated. When I arrived over our base I saw him taxying in. I landed and taxied to the dispersal. But what now? Who should get credit for the kill? It would have been my 200th. The command post was amazed that neither of us had waggled our wings, because they had followed the battle by radio. Then Neumann came in. His entire face was beaming. When I saw this joy-filled, enthusiastic face before me, I extended my hand: "I congratulate you on your victory, Neumann!"

We moved again. Included among our bases was Deutsch Wagram, a few kilometers from Vienna. Subsequently the *Gruppe* came to Fels am Wagram. I flew several missions from there, but there was little contact with the enemy and I made no kills. Each time I returned from a combat sortie there were flowers and champagne at the dispersal. But I simply couldn't get my 200th. Finally it all became too much and I banned these perpetual preparations to celebrate the "anniversary kill."

Then it was time to move again. I was to lead I./JG 53 to Brünn where it was to be disbanded for good. I was already sitting in my aircraft – enemy aircraft had been reported in the area – and the mechanic was turning the hand crank as the machine refused to start. The others took off. The mechanic tried again to get my mill started. When the third attempt failed I had the certain feeling that I wasn't meant to take off this time. I climbed out and drove to Brünn with my adjutant and friend Theo Handschug.

No combat missions were supposed to be flown from there, but as there was still some fuel left and since some of the aircraft were armed, I called *General* Deichmann and described my situation to him. He was completely sympathetic and authorized me to fly until their was no fuel or ammunition left.

I took off on one of the last combat missions on April 8, 1945, and led a *Schwarm* down the Marsch to the Danube. I firmly believed things would work out this time. We flew around the area for more than thirty minutes and were at an altitude of 4,000 meters when I saw a LaGG-5. He was below us and heading northwest at a leisurely pace. I was calm like seldom before as I gave my people their assignments: "You, Neumann, come down with me. If I should miss the Ivan you are to shoot him down. You other two stay up here, cover us and observe the kill!"

It was a masterful example of a perfect kill. I dove beneath the Russian, approached from below, matched his speed and was in an ideal position. I opened fire just as the unsuspecting enemy pilot began a gentle left turn. The LaGG immediately went down in flames. Congratulations poured in over the radio. After landing I was almost crushed by the well-wishers. 683 combat missions, 200 kills! The base commander, an *Oberstleutnant*, hugged me repeatedly, almost squeezing the breath out of me. I had never seen this *Oberstleutnant* Handrik before but in an instant we had become good friends. A very respectable party developed.

The *Gruppe* was disbanded. I achieved three more easy kills, so that on April 16, 1945 my total stood at 203. When I took off on my last sortie from Brünn I was once again tremendously lucky. My aircraft had picked up speed and was racing across the airfield when I realized that my elevator was jammed. And this while doing 150 kph! There was only one thing to do: throttle back and let the aircraft roll to a stop. I brought the machine to a stop a few meters before a slope far beyond the airfield perimeter. It turned out that a mechanic's wrench was wedged between the seating and the elevator. We were unable to determine whether it was a case of sabotage or just an oversight.

At the command post I learned that I had been summoned by *General* Deichmann. I took the *Storch* and flew to see him.

*General* Deichmann informed me in no uncertain terms that the war was definitely and hopelessly lost . . .

At Wels, not far from Linz, I met Ewald and Düttmann. They had been awarded the Knight's Cross. The Oak Leaves were waiting for me. I received the decoration from the hand of *General* Deichmann on April 17, 1945.

What was the sense? Three weeks later the war came to an end. After five-and-a-half years full of enthusiasm and sacrifice, full of triumph and deprivation, after the heroic deaths of so many comrades, we survivors not stood at the zero point.

We were tired but unbroken, and ready to begin our lives all over again. *Horridoh*!

# Lipfert's Aerial Victories

| Victory | Date | Location | Time | Type | Mission |
|---|---|---|---|---|---|
| 1. | 30.1.43 | Malaya-Balabinka | 12.47 | LaGG-5 | 17. |
| 2. | 25.2.43 | Fedorovskaya | 14.58 | Il-5 | 40. |
| 3. | 28.2.43 | Novorossisk | 13.15 | LaGG-3 | 44. |
| 4. | 7.3.43 | Popovichevskaya | 8.20 | R-5 | 51. |
| 5. | 7.3.43 | Ivanovskaya | 8.23 | R-5 | 51. |
| 6. | 14.3.43 | Novorossisk | 6.56 | Il-2 | 62. |
| 7. | 30.3.43 | Slavyanskaya | 6.25 | LaGG-3 | 83. |
| 8. | 30.3.43 | Anastasyevskaya | 15.15 | LaGG-3 | 84. |
| 9. | 20.4.43 | Abinskaya | 6.30 | Mig-1 | 106. |
| 10. | 25.6.43 | Anastasyevskaya | 16.13 | LaGG-3 | 130. |
| 11. | 25.6.43 | Deschi | 16.23 | LaGG-3 | 130. |
| 12. | 16.7.43 | Krimskaya | 5.45 | Yak-1 | 148. |
| 13. | 19.7.43 | Bakanskaya | 13.55 | Yak-1 | 157. |
| 14. | 21.7.43 | Anastasyevskaya | 9.37 | Yak-1 | 159. |
| 15. | 21.7.43 | Ustrikh | 16.43 | Yak-1 | 160. |
| 16. | 23.7.43 | Kievskoye | 5.54 | P-39 Airacobra | 165. |
| 17. | 23.7.43 | Krimskaya | 17.33 | Il-S | 167. |
| 18. | 3.9.43 | Kolontayev | 10.41 | LaGG-5 | 181. |
| 19. | 4.9.43 | Yurevka | 17.17 | Il-2 | 184. |
| 20. | 5.9.43 | Taranovka | 11.30 | Yak-1 | 186. |
| 21. | 21.9.43 | Koselets | 7.16 | Yak-1 | 219. |
| 22. | 24.9.43 | Yerkovtsik | 13.55 | Curtiss P-40 | 225. |
| 23. | 24.9.43 | Yerkovtsik | 16.40 | LaGG-5 | 226. |
| 24. | 25.9.43 | Pereyaslav | 17.35 | Il-2 | 228. |
| 25. | 28.9.43 | Pereyaslav | 17.35 | R-5 | 233. |
| 26. | 1.10.43 | Barbasta | 16.13 | Yak-9 | 235. |
| 27. | 7.10.43 | Annovka | 6.57 | LaGG-5 | 246. |
| 28. | 7.10.43 | Orlik | 11.07 | LaGG-5 | 247. |
| 29. | 7.10.43 | Orlik | 11.28 | Yak-9 | 247. |
| 30. | 8.10.43 | Akhtanisovskaya | 7.05 | Il-2 | 248. |
| 31. | 8.10.43 | Ilich | 8.23 | LaGG-3 | 249. |
| 32. | 8.10.43 | Fischerei | 8.35 | Yak-1 | 249. |
| 33. | 8.10.43 | Taman | 15.33 | Yak-9 | 251. |
| 34. | 8.10.43 | Achtanisowskaja | 15.42 | Yak-9 | 251. |
| 35. | 10.10.43 | Mishorin-Rog | 13.05 | Yak-1 | 252. |

| Victory | Date | Location | Time | Type | Mission |
|---|---|---|---|---|---|
| 36. | 10.10.43 | Borodayevka | 13.15 | Yak-1 | 252. |
| 37. | 20.10.43 | Popelnastoye | 7.30 | Yak-1 | 264. |
| 38. | 21.10.43 | Pyatikhatki | 5.55 | Yak-1 | 266. |
| 39. | 21.10.43 | Verkhnednyeprovsk | 6.08 | Yak-1 | 266. |
| 40 | 21.10.43 | Pyatikhatki | 12.30 | LaGG-5 | 268. |
| 41. | 26.10.43 | State Farm | 7.15 | Yak-1 | 275. |
| 42. | 26.10.43 | Melitopol | 7.17 | Yak-1 | 275. |
| 43. | 29.10.43 | Agaiman | 7.00 | Yak-1 | 279. |
| 44. | 2.11.43 | Chaplinka | 9.25 | Yak-1 | 287. |
| 45. | 5.11.43 | Kerch | 10.20 | Yak-1 | 291. |
| 46. | 6.11.43 | Eltigen | 11.55 | Yak-7 | 294. |
| 47. | 11.11.43 | Katerles | 13.45 | Il-2 | 301. |
| 48. | 11.11.43 | Bagerovo | 13.50 | Yak-1 | 301. |
| 49. | 12.11.43 | Kerch | 8.51 | Yak-1 | 302. |
| 50. | 12.11.43 | Basky | 10.47 | Il-2 | 303. |
| 51. | 13.11.43 | Bulganak | 5.43 | Yak-1 | 305. |
| 52. | 13.11.43 | Mayak | 5.47 | Yak-1 | 305. |
| 53. | 14.11.43 | Eltigen | 9.15 | Yak-1 | 307. |
| 54. | 14.11.43 | Katerles | 13.50 | Il-2 | 308. |
| 55. | 15.11.43 | Kolonka | 6.15 | Yak-9 | 309. |
| 56. | 19.11.43 | Taman | 6.30 | Yak-1 | 313. |
| 57. | 20.11.43 | Ilich | 6.40 | Yak-9 | 316. |
| 58. | 21.11.43 | Eltigen | 7.00 | Il-2 | 317. |
| 59. | 21.11.43 | Taman | 7.05 | Yak-1 | 317. |
| 60. | 27.11.43 | Gromovka | 9.48 | P-39 Airacobra | 329. |
| 61. | 27.11.43 | Eltigen | 14.40 | Yak-9 | 330. |
| 62. | 29.11.43 | Eltigen | 14.21 | Yak-1 | 331. |
| 63. | 30.11.43 | KayTakyl | 6.10 | Yak-1 | 332. |
| 64. | 30.11.43 | Eltigen | 13.45 | Yak-1 | 334. |
| 65. | 1.12.43 | Taman | 11.47 | Yak-1 | 336. |
| 66. | 2.12.43 | Kay Takyl | 6.39 | Yak-1 | 338. |
| 67. | 2.12.43 | Feodosia | 6.48 | LaGG-3 | 338. |
| 68. | 2.12.43 | Kay Takyl | 6.55 | LaGG-3 | 338. |
| 69. | 5.12.43 | Kossa Tusla | 7.25 | Yak-7 | 346. |
| 70. | 5.12.43 | Taman | 7.32 | Yak-1 | 346. |
| 71. | 5.12.43 | Kossa Tusla | 10.23 | P-39 Airacobra | 347. |
| 72. | 5.12.43 | Kossa Tusla | 13.55 | Il-2 | 348. |
| 73. | 9.12.43 | Katerles | 7.58 | Il-2 | 352. |
| 74. | 9.12.43 | Taman | 11.15 | Yak-1 | 356. |
| 75. | 11.12.43 | Mayak | 11.37 | Yak-7 | 362. |

| Victory | Date | Location | Time | Type | Mission |
|---|---|---|---|---|---|
| 76. | 17.12.43 | Starotitarovskaya | 6.43 | Pe-2 | 371. |
| 77. | 27.12.43 | Mayak | 12.08 | P-39 Airacobra | 381. |
| 78. | 28.12.43 | Mayak | 7.16 | R-5 | 382. |
| 79. | 29.12.43 | Melikut | 7.12 | Yak-1 | 384. |
| 80. | 29.12.43 | Mayak | 10.05 | Douglas Boston | 385. |
| 81. | 11.1.44 | Kay Tarchan | 11.27 | P-39 Airacobra | 401. |
| 82. | 17.1.44 | Bulganek | 6.46 | LaGG-3 | 411. |
| 83. | 21.1.44 | Churubech | 11.53 | Il-2 | 419. |
| 84. | 23.1.44 | Kerch | 7.08 | Yak-7 | 422. |
| 85. | 23.1.44 | Kerch | 12.08 | Yak-7 | 424. |
| 86. | 24.1.44 | Kerch | 6.30 | P-39 Airacobra | 426. |
| 87. | 25.1.44 | Bulganek | 12.27 | Yak-1 | 429. |
| 88. | 25.1.44 | Kossa Tusla | 12.40 | Douglas Boston | 429. |
| 89. | 1.4.44 | Feodosia | 9.25 | LaGG-3 | 435. |
| 90. | 1.4.44 | Feodosia | 9.33 | LaGG-3 | 435. |
| 91. | 7.4.44 | Taganah | 7.19 | Yak-7 | 442. |
| 92. | 7.4.44 | Chumak | 7.27 | Yak-7 | 442. |
| 93. | 8.4.44 | Chigari | 14.22 | Il-2 | 444. |
| 94. | 8.4.44 | Ivanovka | 14.32 | R-5 | 444. |
| 95. | 9.4.44 | Tomashevka | 14.40 | Yak-7 | 447. |
| 96. | 9.4.44 | Grammatikovo | 15.58 | Pe-2 | 448. |
| 97. | 10.4.44 | Tomashevka | 8.16 | Yak-7 | 449. |
| 98. | 10.4.44 | Megazinka | 12.22 | Il-2 | 450 |
| 99. | 11.4.44 | Dzhenkoi | 7.02 | Yak-7 | 452. |
| 100. | 11.4.44 | Dzhenkoi | 9.25 | Il-2 | 453. |
| 101. | 15.4.44 | Sevastopol | 10.47 | Il-2 | 460. |
| 102. | 17.4.44 | Duvankoi | 15.49 | Yak-7 | 462. |
| 103. | 19.4.44 | Sevastopol | 14.21 | Curtiss P-40 | 464. |
| 104. | 19.4.44 | Sevastopol | 17.05 | Il-2 | 465. |
| 105. | 22.4.44 | Sevastopol | 9.40 | Douglas Boston | 468. |
| 106. | 27.4.44 | Kodikovka | 10.50 | Yak-7 | 473. |
| 107. | 3.5.44 | Belobek | 18.35 | Yak-7 | 476. |
| 108. | 4.5.44 | Soki | 6.44 | Yak-7 | 477. |
| 109. | 4.5.44 | Belobek | 9.10 | Yak-7 | 478. |
| 110. | 5.5.44 | Balaklava | 10.38 | Yak-7 | 481. |
| 111. | 5.5.44 | Laspi Bay | 10.50 | Yak-7 | 482. |
| 112. | 5.5.44 | Belobek | 14.05 | Il-2 | 483. |
| 113. | 6.5.44 | Belobek | 7.30 | Yak-1 | 483. |
| 114. | 6.5.44 | Belobek | 7.40 | U-2 | 483. |
| 115. | 7.5.44 | Balaklava | 9.40 | Yak-1 | 488. |

| Victory | Date | Location | Time | Type | Mission |
|---|---|---|---|---|---|
| 116. | 7.5.44 | Sevastopol | 9.45 | Yak-1 | 488. |
| 117. | 7.5.44 | Balaklava | 9.49 | Yak-1 | 488. |
| 118. | 30.5.44 | Jassy | 16.01 | Yak-1 | 497 |
| 119. | 30.5.44 | Jassy | 16.04 | Yak-1 | 497 |
| 120. | 31.5.44 | Busila | 8.04 | Pe-2 | 499. |
| 121. | 31.5.44 | Jassy | 14.32 | Il-2 | 500. |
| 122. | 4.6.44 | Sulani | 18.56 | Yak-1 | 509. |
| 123. | 5.6.44 | Zahorna | 7.58 | P-39 Airacobra | 510. |
| 124. | 5.6.44 | Zahorna | 8.01 | Yak-7 | 510. |
| 125. | 5.6.44 | Carpiti | 11.35 | Yak-7 | 511. |
| 126. | 5.6.44 | Romanesti | 11.45 | Douglas Boston | 511. |
| 127. | 11.6.44 | Tateroi | 9.45 | B-17 | 516. |
| 128. | 24.6.44 | Stefanesti | 9.42 | B-24 | 519. |
| 129. | 27.6.44 | Jassy | 10.34 | Il-2 | 521. |
| 130. | 14.7.44 | Sezurowica | 7.55 | P-39 Airacobra | 527. |
| 131. | 15.7.44 | Horochow | 15.20 | Yak-7 | 531. |
| 132. | 16.7.44 | Plowa | 13.23 | Il-2 | 534. |
| 133. | 16.7.44 | Stojanow | 13.27 | Yak-7 | 534. |
| 134. | 18.7.44 | Zwezernesce | 15.12 | LaGG-5 | 535. |
| 135. | 18.7.44 | Turze | 18.12 | Yak-7 | 536. |
| 136. | 19.7.44 | Luboml | 16.40 | P-39 Airacobra | 537. |
| 137. | 19.7.44 | Luboml | 16.41 | P-39 Airacobra | 537. |
| 138. | 19.7.44 | Luboml | 16.45 | Il-2 | 537. |
| 139. | 20.7.44 | Luboml | 11.10 | Yak-9 | 539. |
| 140. | 21.7.44 | Busk | 6.25 | Yak-7 | 540. |
| 141. | 24.7.44 | Tuszna | 18.41 | Yak-9 | 545. |
| 142. | 14.8.44 | Sobotka | 17.14 | P-39 Airacobra | 555. |
| 143. | 16.8.44 | Opatow | 16.35 | Yak-1 | 558. |
| 144. | 23.8.44 | Geidar | 17.25 | Yak-7 | 564. |
| 145. | 31.8.44 | Löwes | 10.20 | P-51 Mustang | 569. |
| 146. | 17.10.44 | Hosszu-Palyj | 10.38 | Yak-11 | 575. |
| 147. | 21.10.44 | Öcföd | 10.52 | LaGG-5 | 581. |
| 148. | 23.10.44 | Solnok | 15.31 | Il-2 | 583. |
| 149. | 23.10.44 | Solnok | 15.32 | Il-2 | 583. |
| 150. | 24.10.44 | Feherto | 9.22 | Yak-7 | 584. |
| 151. | 27.10.44 | Büd Sz.Mihaly | 12.17 | Il-2 | 588. |
| 152. | 27.10.44 | Büd Sz.Mihaly | 12.21 | Yak-7 | 588. |
| 153. | 13.11.44 | Jaszbereny | 12.45 | Yak-9 | 589. |
| 154. | 16.11.44 | Tura | 12.39 | Yak-11 | 593. |
| 155. | 17.11.44 | Jaszbereny | 11.05 | Il-2 | 594. |

| Victory | Date | Location | Time | Type | Mission |
|---|---|---|---|---|---|
| 156. | 17.11.44 | Jaszbereny | 11.10 | Il-2 | 594. |
| 157. | 17.11.44 | Hort | 13.20 | Yak-7 | 595. |
| 158. | 23.11.44 | Atkar | 10.40 | Yak-9 | 597. |
| 159. | 5.12.44 | Hatran | 10.30 | Yak-9 | 599. |
| 160. | 9.12.44 | Csajag | 15.05 | Il-2 | 600. |
| 161. | 11.12.44 | Balatonkenese | 14.53 | Pe-2 | 602. |
| 162. | 22.12.44 | Stuhlweißenburg | 9.37 | Il-2 | 606. |
| 163. | 23.12.44 | Enying | 10.48 | Yak-9 | 607. |
| 164. | 24.12.44 | Seregelyes | 14.25 | Il-2 | 610. |
| 165. | 25.12.44 | Stuhlweißenburg | 12.08 | Yak-9 | 612. |
| 166. | 25.12.44 | Mor | 12.15 | Yak-9 | 612. |
| 167. | 2.1.45 | Bodmer | 11.15 | LaGG-5 | 614. |
| 168. | 2.1.45 | Vereb | 11.45 | Yak-9 | 614. |
| 169. | 4.1.45 | Tarjan | 8.26 | Il-2 | 616. |
| 170. | 4.1.45 | Tarjan | 8.28 | Il-2 | 616. |
| 171. | 4.1.45 | Bieske | 10.41 | Yak-9 | 617. |
| 172. | 4.1.45 | Tardos | 11.12 | LaGG-5 | 617. |
| 173. | 8.1.45 | Stuhlweißenburg | 14.13 | Douglas Boston | 621. |
| 174. | 8.1.45 | Stuhlweißenburg | 14.18 | Douglas Boston | 621. |
| 175. | 14.1.45 | Muzsla | 12.11 | Yak-3 | 622. |
| 176. | 14.1.45 | Muzsla | 14.36 | Yak-3 | 623. |
| 177. | 16.1.45 | Budaörs | 12.17 | LaGG-5 | 624. |
| 178. | 22.1.45 | Stuhlweißenburg | 13.24 | LaGG-5 | 628. |
| 179. | 27.1.45 | Adorzy | 14.45 | Il-2 | 630. |
| 180. | 22.2.45 | Bart | 14.00 | LaGG-5 | 643. |
| 181. | 22.2.45 | Bina | 16.25 | Yak-3 | 644. |
| 182. | 25.2.45 | Altsohl | 10.53 | Yak-9 | 645. |
| 183. | 8.3.45 | Sapolce | 14.10 | Il-2 | 650. |
| 184. | 11.3.45 | Suborgarol | 10.35 | Yak-3 | 653. |
| 185. | 11.3.45 | Siofok | 14.05 | Yak-3 | 654. |
| 186. | 13.3.45 | Pakozol | 10.13 | Yak-7 | 655. |
| 187. | 14.3.45 | Stuhlweißenburg | 12.07 | LaGG-5 | 657. |
| 188. | 14.3.45 | Pakozol | 12.11 | Il-2 | 657. |
| 189. | 17.3.45 | Lake Velencze | 16.15 | Il-2 | 662. |
| 190. | 20.3.45 | Stuhlweißenburg | 15.33 | Il-2 | 668. |
| 191. | 20.3.45 | Varpalota | 15.41 | Il-2 | 668. |
| 192. | 21.3.45 | East end of Lake Balaton | 11.58 | La-5 | 669. |
| 193. | 21.3.45 | Felstgalla | 15.30 | Yak-5 | 670. |
| 194. | 27.3.45 | Neutra | 14.15 | Yak-9 | 674. |

| Victory | Date | Location | Time | Type | Mission |
|---|---|---|---|---|---|
| 195. | 27.3.45 | Neutra | 14.18 | Il-2 | 674. |
| 196. | 27.3.45 | Neutra | 16.55 | Yak-9 | 675. |
| 197. | 28.3.45 | Neutra | 17.12 | Yak-3 | 676. |
| 198. | 1.4.45 | Dioszeg | 16.05 | La-7 | 679. |
| 199. | 5.4.45 | Gairing | 9.45 | La-7 | 682. |
| 200. | 8.4.45 | Hainburg | 15.54 | La-7 | 683. |
| 201. | 9.4.45 | Lundenburg | 17.20 | La-7 | 684. |
| 202. | 14.4.45 | Stokerau | 15.00 | Yak-9 | 686. |
| 203. | 16.4.45 | Göding | 11.20 | Yak-9 | 687. |

*Also from the publisher*

# SIX MONTHS TO OBLIVION

**The Defeat of the Luftwaffe Fighter Force Over the Western Front 1944/1945**

Werner Girbig

Size: 6" x 9"  236 pp.  hard cover
ISBN: 0-88740-348-4  $29.95

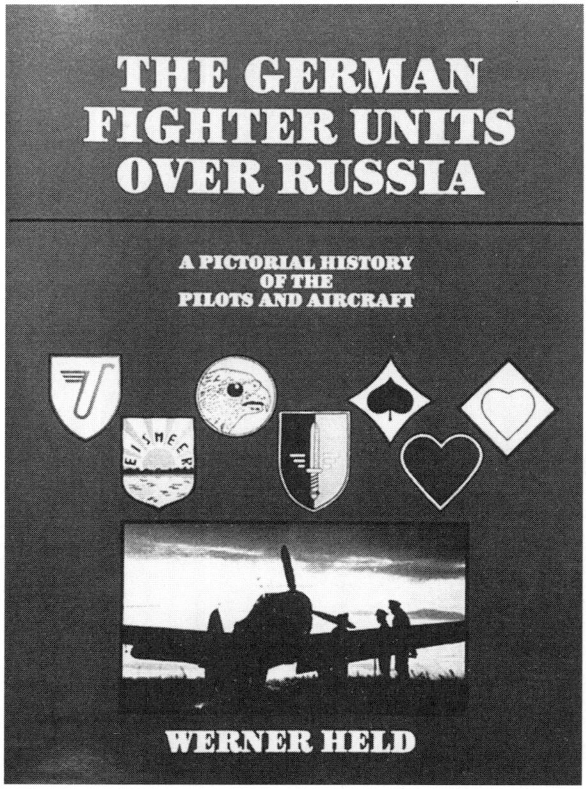


# THE GERMAN FIGHTER UNITS OVER RUSSIA

**A Pictorial History of the Pilots & Aircraft**

Werner Held

Size: 7 3/4" x 10 1/2"  192 pp.  hard cover
ISBN: 0-88740-246-1  $24.95

# THE LEGION CONDOR

**A History of the Luftwaffe**
**in the Spanish Civil War 1936-1939**

Karl Ries/Hans Ring

Size: 8 ½" x 11" • 288 pp. • hard cover
ISBN: 978-0-88740-339-2 • $49.95

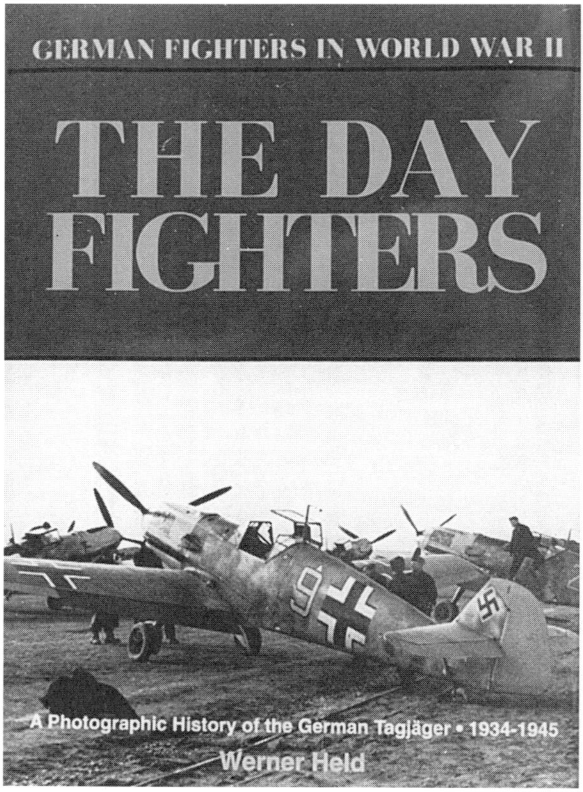


# German Fighters in WWII
# THE DAY FIGHTERS

**A Photographic History of the German Tagjäger 1934-1945**

Werner Held

Size: 7 3/4" x 10 1/2"    224 pp.    hard cover
ISBN: 0-88740-355-7    $29.95

# German Fighters in WWII THE NIGHT FIGHTERS

**A Photographic History of the German Nachtjäger 1940-1945**

Werner Held/Holger Nauroth

Size: 7 3/4" x 10 1/2" 232 pp. hard cover
ISBN: 0-88740-356-5 $29.95

# German Fighter Ace
# ERICH HARTMANN

### The Life Story of the World's Highest Scoring Ace

Ursula Hartmann/Manfred Jäger

Size: 8 ½" x 11" • 296 pp. • hard cover
ISBN: 978-0-88740-396-5 • $59.99

# Stuka Pilot
# HANS-ULRICH RUDEL

**His Life Story in Words & Photographs**

Günther Just

Size: 8 ½" x 11" • 288 pp. • hard cover
ISBN: 978-0-88740-252-4 • $59.99

# THE LUFTWAFFE IN THE NORTH AFRICA CAMPAIGN

**A Photo Chronicle • 1941-1943**

Werner Held/Ernst Obermaier

Size: 7 3/4" x 10 1/2"  238 pp.  hard cover
ISBN: 0-88740-343-3  $29.95